THIS BOOK *is presented to your library* by the National Federation of Temple Sisterhoods, a women's religious organization, whose program is devoted to Jewish and humanitarian causes. The Federation includes more than 400 units throughout the United States and in cities of five other countries of the United Nations.

It is our hope that the history recited in *Experiment E* will be read by the peoples of the United Nations, for it is the tragedy not of one man but of millions of men, women and children, particularly of the Jewish faith. If mankind is to unite to make impossible a repetition of the brutality of recent years, individuals must accept those disciplines of mind and spirit which make the degradation of one human being the degradation of all, the advancement of one people the advancement of all.

National Federation of Temple Sisterhoods

*Merchants Building*
*Cincinnati 2, Ohio, U. S. of America*

# EXPERIMENT "E"

*A Report from an Extermination Laboratory*

by LEON SZALET

DIDIER, Publishers
NEW YORK

*To the Memory of the
Unknown Martyrs of the Second World War*

Translated by
CATHARINE BLAND WILLIAMS

COPYRIGHT, 1945, BY DIDIER, *Publishers*

All rights reserved.

No part of this book may be reproduced in any form without permission of the publishers.

Printed in the United States of America

# *Foreword*

Long before I became acquainted with a German concentration camp—at the time Germany launched her attack on Poland—I had heard much about the horrors of these German torture chambers. Almost everyone who lived in Germany, native or foreigner, knew of someone who had once been in a concentration camp. Everyone had a vague idea of the punishment cells, whippings, starvation rations. But just how the mechanism of a concentration camp functioned, how a prisoner's day was spent, how he worked, what he ate, what and how he suffered—these things were known only to those who had once been cogs in such a mechanism.

And these did not speak. They did not speak because the fear of the Gestapo haunted them night and day; because on their release from the camp they were made to sign a statement that they would not make public the things they had seen and experienced; because the Gestapo sent those who broke this pledge back to the camp for "atrocity propaganda"; and because those sent back would soon come out again, this time in a crudely built wooden coffin.

Nor did those speak who had the good fortune to escape to freedom abroad. Many of them simply lacked a sufficient sense of responsibility toward their former comrades in suffering; many felt no impulse to spread the truth. Others were so broken in spirit that they could not bear to relive past horrors by describing them. Others, again, still had the fear of the Gestapo in their blood.

It was a long while before I felt strong enough to describe what I had seen and experienced. That I have been able to put it on paper at all, I owe to my daughter, whose untiring energy and resourcefulness not only accomplished my rescue but has also been an invaluable help in preparing the manuscript.

I.B.31.

# ALIENS ORDER, 1920.

*To the Alien.*

Leave to land has been refused in the case of the alien { passenger ~~Ship's Officer~~ ~~member of crew~~ }

na SZALET, Chasim Leib,

a subject of Poland

brought to the Port of Croydon

in the ~~ship~~ aeroplane PH-815

from the Port of Amsterdam

Grounds of refusal

art. 1.(1)
& 1.3(h)

His dependents who have also been refused leave to land are

Signature of Immigration Officer

Immigration Officer's Stamp

Facsimile of expulsion order, whereby Szalet was forced to return to Berlin, after his escape to England (see page 7).

## Part One

*1*

August, 1939.

The shadow of war lay over Berlin. Under cover of darkness, trucks packed with troops rumbled through the streets. Every stationer's shop displayed blackout materials for sale. Germany's press and radio were outclamoring each other in a rabid propaganda campaign against Poland. The Propaganda Ministry was fabricating stories about the mistreatment of German nationals in Poland, to blacken the character of the Polish people in the eyes of Germans and the rest of the world.

This campaign had reached its height in the last days of August. Angry crowds jammed the sidewalks around the newspaper kiosks and discussed the latest "Polish atrocities." Insults and stories directed against the "Polaks" and their government were heard on every side. Goebbels had keyed up the German people to the required pitch of fury. "The masses" demanded reprisals.

There were many, it is true, who saw through these maneuvers, drew parallels between them and the events leading up to Hitler's seizure of Austria and the Sudetenland; but their voices were only whispers, heard by none but their closest and most trusted friends.

The majority of the Polish residents of Berlin had left the city in the last week of August. Only the optimists had stayed behind, counting on the fact that England and France had renewed their pledges to stand behind the Polish government; the Pope and the King of the Belgians had offered to mediate between Germany and Poland; President Roosevelt had sent a peace message to Hitler—these were the straws to which the optimists clung.

On the morning of Saturday, August 26, I went to the Polish Consulate General on the Kurfuerstenstrasse. An anxious crowd was gathered in the waiting room. The same fear and the same question

1

haunted every pair of eyes. Would Hitler even yet give up his demand for the Polish Corridor, or would Germany for the second time in the twentieth century set the world ablaze?

In the consular building there was feverish activity. Doors were flung violently open and left to slam shut. Officials with grave, haggard faces hurried from room to room. None of them paid any attention to us until, at last, someone remembered the silent, waiting crowd. A minor official entered the waiting room and said haltingly, as if each word cost him an effort: "Everyone must act according to his own judgment. The situation is very grave. That is all I can say."

Silently we left the waiting room.

In front of the Consulate two policemen were pacing up and down. A group of idle onlookers stood around. Some uniformed members of the Hitler Youth amused themselves by deciphering the Polish inscription on the brass tablet. They accompanied their efforts at pronunciation with croaking, sneezing, hissing and spitting, to imitate the sound of Polish words. "That is the Polish cuckoo," said one man to his neighbor, pointing to the Polish eagle which spread its wings above the iron gate. Approving laughter rewarded this attempt at wit.

So our optimism was only a rainbow-colored soap bubble.

In wartime every man belongs in his home. My home was Poland. So I hurried back to my apartment to make the necessary preparations with my daughter Gucia. We settled the most pressing business and packed the most essential articles of clothing; then we went to the Bahnhof Zoologischer Garten to buy tickets for the evening train to Warsaw.

A train from East Prussia was just coming into the station. Feverishly excited passengers got out of the packed coaches and were instantly bombarded with questions. From their answers it appeared that there was already serious disorder on the frontier, and that this was the last train from the east.

Had we hesitated too long?

"Will the evening train for Warsaw leave according to schedule?" I asked the station master, when the crowd had dispersed.

"As far as we know at present, yes."

"Do you think the train will cross the frontier?"

"My dear sir, I am a station master, not a prophet. But if you want my opinion, things look bad, very."

Gucia looked at me questioningly. Should we risk taking that train? Which was preferable—to be caught at the frontier at the mercy of the infuriated local inhabitants or to face it out in Berlin and be interned?

"Let us go to Siemion and consult him," said Gucia. "We can always get the tickets later." Siemion had been our friend for years. His family had returned to Poland only a few weeks before, and he was to follow as soon as he had wound up some business affairs.

At his doorstep we ran into Siemion, carrying a suitcase. A taxi was waiting in front.

"Get in with me, quick," he said, "or I'll miss the six-o'clock plane for London."

Once in the taxi, Siemion told us that during the last two hours he had almost worn out our telephone wires trying to reach us. For we had to leave at once. No, not for Poland—travel across the border was already uncertain. We must fly to London, as he was doing.

Fly to London? That was impossible! We had no English visas. And the British Consulate had been closed to the public for several days.

But Siemion would not listen. "Don't you two know that yesterday Poland and England concluded a defensive alliance? Haven't you Polish passports? Do you think that England will turn away Poles cut off from their own country?"

That sounded logical. Of course, we would have difficulties on landing, but they would soon be cleared up. Besides, I was no newcomer to England. During the last few years, when negotiating with the British Steelwork Association about the patents for my prefabricated steel house, I had traveled back and forth to London several times a year. Luckily, the one-year visas were stamped in my passport. I could also take with me for identification purposes my correspondence with various people in English public life. And then there was my London lawyer, who had already been trying to get permanent-residence permits for Gucia and myself. Siemion was right. There was still a way out.

"See you in London," we called to each other, as we waved farewell at the Tempelhof Airport.

"Sorry, all seats sold out through Monday," said the man at the ticket window when we asked for two plane tickets. "Would you like to make reservations for Tuesday?"

"Tuesday? That is too late," said Gucia. "Is there no chance of getting places before then?"

The man was annoyed. "That's what I've been asked hundreds of times in the last twelve hours. I'm sick and tired of hearing it. Do you think I can pull seats out of my hat?"

"Won't you at least put down our names, in case vacancies occur at the last moment?" asked Gucia.

"That is a pipe-dream, lady, but have it your own way. May I see your visas?"

"Unfortunately, we have no visas," said I. "We decided only today to make this trip and, as you know, the British Consulate has been closed for several days."

"Why didn't you tell me that before?" said the man angrily. "No visas, no seats. Next, please!"

"Listen," I made another effort, "we will get it straightened out at Croydon."

"You're holding people up; next, please!" And we were pushed aside.

At that our last faint hope melted away. What was to be done now? Should we take the evening train to Warsaw after all? Could we risk it?

Our taxi drove through South Berlin. In the streets agitated preparations were going forward. Men in blue overalls were painting white demarcation lines on roadways and sidewalks. At important street intersections guiding lights were being mounted on lamp posts. Berlin was making ready for war.

At the Hallesches Tor I had a sudden inspiration. "Driver, take me to Unter den Linden."

A talk with the porter of a well-known hotel, a royal tip, and the trick was done. A ticket for the Sunday-evening plane to London would be at my disposal tomorrow. Then suddenly I realized that the porter had said *one* ticket. And that ended the whole London project for me.

But Gucia became obstinate. "We must take this ticket anyway. This is the finger of fate. You know very well that in Germany men are always more in danger than women. I shall be all right. And I'll certainly follow you, somehow, by way of Switzerland or Holland or Sweden! But you mustn't lose any time."

We sat up all night arguing the pros and cons. Early Sunday, when the newspaper headlines announced the issuing of ration cards, and when any "backing down" seemed out of the question, Gucia would give me no more peace. She packed two handbags and made me promise to leave at once, alone.

At the airport everything was unexpectedly easy. The ten Reichsmarks, which every traveler was allowed to take with him, were unhesitatingly changed into shillings for me; the baggage investigation went off without a hitch. The passport and baggage officials were not at all disturbed because I had neither the required tax-clearance certificate nor an English entrance visa. The exit date was stamped in my passport and I was allowed to pass. They appeared only too glad to be rid of one more Pole.

A few minutes later I was sitting in the Dutch plane which provided regular passenger service between Berlin and London.

On Sunday, August 27, at 6 P.M. I flew from Berlin. On Monday, August 28, at 2:30 P.M., in the same plane, I landed at Tempelhof Airport again. In spite of all my arguments, the immigration officer at Croydon refused me entry and, without consulting the Home Office, had ordered me sent back to Germany.

When I landed at Croydon I had ready in my hand all the papers I wanted to show the authorities.

"Where is your English visa?" the control official asked, when my turn came.

"It was no longer possible to obtain an English visa," I answered. "But I speak English very badly. If I could talk with someone who knows Polish or Russian or German, I would explain the situation." Since the immigration officer himself happened to speak German, we went into the matter then and there.

I explained that I was a Polish citizen with my passport in order. I handed him my letter of recommendation from the American director of the Friends' Service Committee. I told him of the one-year visas in my passport and offered him the correspondence I had with me. My lawyer, I pointed out, would represent me at the Home Office. In conclusion, I emphasized that I would continue my journey to Poland by way of Scandinavia should the Home Office refuse me permission to stay.

The immigration officer briefly consulted a colleague, then turned to me. "We will submit the case to the Home Office early tomorrow.

Probably a decision will be reached by noon. Until then you must stay here."

I was taken to the detention room at the airport. From a distance I caught sight of Siemion and some other friends. (I had, of course, arranged with Gucia that she should notify Siemion by long-distance telephone of my arrival and had promised to call her as soon as the formalities were over.)

The room in which I now found myself was very small. The only furniture consisted of a threadbare sofa without pillows or coverings; a dirty toilet completed the arrangements. The windows were barred.

After a while Siemion and my other friends appeared outside the window, for they were not allowed to come in. They too had been informed that my case would be submitted to the Home Office early the next morning and had been asked to return Monday at about ten o'clock.

I spent the night trying to think of the quickest way to get Gucia out of Germany. I could hear a policeman pacing up and down before the door. So I was a real prisoner. But the policeman had forgotten that even a prisoner has physical needs. I had eaten nothing since that morning and drunk nothing since the afternoon.

When morning finally came, I knocked on the door and asked if they would order coffee for me from the airport hotel. The coffee worked wonders, and when, about 8:30, two long-legged Tommies appeared to conduct me to the airport office, I followed them, refreshed and full of confidence.

And then, when I reached the office, the immigration officer informed me that I was to be sent back to Berlin in the same plane that had brought me to Croydon!

I could not believe my ears. "You cannot possibly do that," I said. "I have no German re-entry visa and I am Polish. You know what that means under the present circumstances. Do you realize what is in store for me in Berlin?"

The immigration officer paid absolutely no heed. He gave the Tommies a wink and instantly both my arms were seized in an iron grip.

I was desperate and at my wits' end. "You cannot do that!" I cried, wholly beside myself. "I am a Polish citizen. I insist that you communicate with my Consulate before you send me back. You must let me speak with my solicitor. I am a Pole!" I cried in a loud voice. "Do you hear? I am a Pole!"

The immigration officer was completely unmoved. The Tommies took a firmer grip on me, pointed to the runway where the plane was waiting to take off, dragged me to the plane and put me into it by force. The door was slammed quickly, as if I had been a criminal.

I was dazed. What had happened to me was monstrous. So that was chivalrous, humane England, the nation which prided itself on the words "gentleman" and "fair play"!

But was *that* really England, I asked myself, when I had grown a little calmer. Could I hold England responsible for the pig-headedness of one official? And I tried to look at the situation with calm, unprejudiced eyes.

Then suddenly another picture rose before me. I saw a scene in the British Consulate in the Tiergartenstrasse; a long line of hunted, desperate, hopeless people who had been waiting for hours to apply for permission to enter one of the British territories. I saw a British official enter the waiting room, heard him say: "Non-Aryans step over here, please," and then I saw him attend to the German Aryans first. And while the non-Aryans waited day after day in a separate line, German women traveled unhindered to England, disguised as domestic help, to act as spies for Germany.

My expulsion had suddenly taken on another aspect. For I was not only a Pole. I was also a Jew. The English expulsion order in my passport had become a symbol of English "tolerance" under the Chamberlain government. I opened my passport to look at it. And I could not believe my eyes. From the official stamp it was clear that the immigration officer had issued the order for my return on the evening of my arrival. My case had not been submitted to the Home Office at all. When the officer had told my friends to come back at ten o'clock Monday morning, he had been making fools of them. He knew that by that time I would already be on the other side of Holland.

"Here's an interesting bird that has flown in," said the passport controller at Tempelhof, as he handed my passport to the Gestapo official.

The Gestapo man looked at the German exit stamp of August 27 and the English expulsion stamp of the same date. Then he shook his head several times and clicked his tongue.

"Must be a very queer customer," he said finally, "if his own friends throw him out before he's had a chance to say 'how do you do.' We must look him over *very* carefully indeed." Then, turning to me, he continued glibly: "You have crossed the German border without a visa. That is violation of the frontier. Do you know what that means today? And you're a Pole besides. We must have a little talk at once, you and I."

He beckoned to a baggage official, pointed to my handbags, which the English police had thoughtfully put aboard the plane, and called out: "This baggage must be very carefully searched. Every seam examined. Understand?"

"Good God!" the thought flashed through my mind. "Do they take me for a spy?" But there was no time to think. I had to explain my round-trip flight.

"Well, I must say you've explained it away beautifully," said the Gestapo official, when I had finished. "So you're just an innocent civilian who wanted to save his precious life, and your friends the English only sent you back because you had no English visa." Suddenly he roared like a madman: "Are you trying to make a fool of me?"

Then began a cross-examination in which every possible means was tried to trap me. After that came hours of waiting in another airport detention room. It was evening when the door opened at last. Then came further humiliations and questionings.

First I was taken to the Alien Police in the Burgstrasse, then to the prison on the Hackescher Markt and finally to the prison of the Berlin Police Headquarters on the Alexander Platz. At about 9 P.M. I landed in Station 3A, many feet underground, among about sixty assorted criminals: thieves, pimps, blackmailers, homosexuals and some famous figures of the Berlin underworld. A legion of bugs, undaunted by the electric lights, completed the company, promenading everywhere on the walls and bunks. Thus, within twenty-four hours, I made the acquaintance of five different prisons.

On Tuesday morning at eight o'clock I was summoned for questioning to Section II of the Alien Division of Police Headquarters. There I saw Gucia waiting outside the door. All at once the whole situation looked less grim. It was good to learn that Gucia knew where I was; I had not expected that. True, I had phoned her from Tempelhof shortly after my arrival and asked her to come at once to the airport to pay for my return ticket and to take charge of the handbags. But that was all the two Gestapo officials standing over me had let me say.

Later I learned from Gucia that our unexpected meeting outside the Alien Division had occurred by pure chance. When she had asked at Tempelhof where I was, the officials at the control office had professed to know nothing. So she had made the rounds of all the police stations and, when Monday passed without results, had renewed the search on Tuesday morning.

The examining officials in Section II seemed to have had a great deal of experience with aliens. Apparently they had thoroughly studied my police dossier and had convinced themselves of my blameless record. They accepted my statements and finally called in Gucia, reassured her and allowed us to talk to each other.

Wednesday morning I was once more taken from the cellar. Gucia had somehow managed to obtain permission for an interview. In the visitor's room we faced each other across a grating, I in a row of prison "regulars" and Gucia in a row of their respective wives and girl friends. Two policemen sat near by.

Neither of us could utter a word. Several valuable minutes of the ten allotted to us passed. Gucia was the first to recover. Calmly, as if this were the most natural situation in the world, she told me she had learned that I was to be taken before the Schnellgericht on Thursday. But there was no cause for uneasiness. My case was clear. She had even decided not to engage a lawyer.

The next morning I was taken before the Schnellgericht, a summary court which officiates without jurors, consisting of the public prosecutor and the judge. The judge has plenary power, and there is no appeal.

The trial began with the reading of the charge: "Unauthorized crossing of German territory." Then I was called upon to describe everything that had happened from the time I left the Berlin airport until my return to Tempelhof. When I had finished the account of my experiences at Croydon, the judge pounded his desk.

"So you see," he remarked, "those are your allies!"

The audience laughed gleefully at this remark, and the irony of the situation struck me like a blow.

Then the public prosecutor summed up. "The case calls for

leniency," he said. "The accused did not cross the German frontier as a free agent but was compelled to by the English."

"Besides," added the judge, "it might be pleaded that he did not cross the frontier at all, but merely flew over it."

I listened incredulously. Here the roles were reversed. My friends, the English, had not listened to me at all; my enemies, the Nazis, showed more understanding than I had expected. The sentence was very mild: a fine of ten Reichsmarks, which the judge declared had been served out by my three-day imprisonment.

I was free again. Gucia, who, of course, was among the spectators, signaled that she would wait for me. It was about 11 A.M. when I was taken back to my cell. I waited impatiently. But hour after hour passed and nothing happened. It was not until 3:15 P.M. that I was released.

Gucia afterwards told me that I had only by a hair's breadth escaped being carried off to one of the Berlin Gestapo dungeons. After the trial she had waited for me before the entrance to the prison. As the hours passed she became uneasy. Finally, she knocked at the prison gate and after much persuasion talked the guard into finding out what had become of me. "Acquitted by the civil judge but detained at the disposal of the Alien Police and the Gestapo," was his report.

But Gucia would not give up. She took a taxi to the Alien Police Headquarters in the Burgstrasse, arrived a few minutes before the office closed, asked to see the head of the Alien Police and actually succeeded. Ten minutes later, he telephoned the prison personally in her presence and ordered me released at once.

On Thursday, August 31, at 4 P.M. I was released from prison. In the gray dawn of September 1, Hitler's armies attacked Poland. Gucia and I had become enemy aliens.

Of course, we realized that sooner or later all enemy aliens would be interned. Astonishingly, we were left in peace at first. But on September 13, at 5:30 A.M., the doorbell rang long and shrilly. I knew then that the time had come.

I opened the door myself. A policeman entered.

"Are you the Polish Jew Szalet?" he asked.

"Yes, I am."

"Then dress and come with me. But hurry. I'll give you five minutes."

I had so often pictured this scene to myself that I remained completely calm, especially since the policeman, thank God, had said nothing about Gucia.

"What is the reason for my arrest?" I asked.

"You'll find out at the police station. Now hurry up. I can't waste the whole morning on you."

Might I shave, wash?

"Out of the question," said the policeman. "Don't you understand German? I said *hurry*."

"Officer," I heard Gucia ask, "may I give my father a few things to take with him—underwear, money, something to eat?"

"Don't ask questions!" said the policeman.

I finished my dressing in the greatest haste, emptied all my pockets, took my hat and coat and went into the hall. Gucia was standing there with the policeman. We clasped hands in silence. There was no time for more.

The street was still asleep. Only a milkman and a "newspaper girl" came around the corner, chattering. Opposite my house stood a policeman holding a man by the arm. I knew the man by sight; he was a Pole too. The neighborhood of the police station to which we were both brought was unusually animated. From all directions similar groups approached and vanished through the open doors of the building.

The interior was full of policemen. They had the straps of their helmets buckled under the chin and carried rifles in addition to the customary pistols. A state of emergency, evidently.

My countryman and I were pushed into a room which was already crammed with people. Men of all ages stood around the walls. A few cripples and a deaf-mute were among them. With alarm everyone observed the group of policemen who sat around a table in the middle of the room and took down the particulars about each new arrival. No one spoke a word. Only the deaf-mute from time to time emitted strange gobbling sounds. Some of the new arrivals, when they stepped forward to register, asked the reason for their arrest. "Shut your mouth!" was the invariable answer.

While each of us was being questioned by the policemen, a loudspeaker was blaring full blast. The police radio was broadcasting news for policemen. With satanic glee the announcer described how the "Polish sub-men in Bromberg," had murdered German "Volksgenossen" and mutilated their bodies. The radio prophesied a terrible revenge: "Blood will flow in double and triple measure." From time to time one of the busily writing policemen would pause, listen awhile to the broadcast and nod in a pleased and knowing way.

Terror seized me. The radio accusations fell like the blows of a sledge hammer, and the policemen's manner made me suspect some connection between the alleged Polish atrocities and our arrest.

Suddenly the radio stopped. Only the scratching of the policemen's pens broke the oppressive silence.

At 7:30 the registration was finished. A heavily armed police detachment escorted us out. In front of the building stood a police truck in which about fifteen anxious men were already standing. We were ordered to climb in. The floor of the truck was very high and many of us were no longer young and active, but the policemen assisted us with truncheons and rifle butts, and at last even the oldest and most infirm were loaded aboard.

Around the truck, in a semicircle, held back by the police, stood a curious crowd—women with milk bottles, workingmen with lunch boxes and a flock of children from a nearby school. In the front row stood Gucia. When she caught sight of me in the truck, she dodged around the policemen and ran up close to the car.

"Head high, Papa!" she cried in a loud voice.

The truck began to move. As we drove down the street I heard her voice again, calling loudly: "Head high, Papa! Do you hear me? Head high!"

The truck went very fast and jolted violently. We were hurled from side to side, stumbled and fell. But by the time we had completed our round of the various police stations, we were jammed so close together that it was impossible to fall, or even to move.

At the Bluecher Barracks in Southeast Berlin we made our first long stop. This was one of several collecting stations into which the Poles of Greater Berlin were being rounded up. We were ordered out of the truck, counted and then taken to a room where we were registered again. Then we were conducted to the large barracks yard, where about 150 men were already assembled. There, for the first time, we came out of the paralysis which had held us. We looked around for familiar faces, began to talk to each other and exchanged speculations as to our probable fate.

Our ordeal began when at about noon the whole human mass was loaded into a number of trucks and the cavalcade moved off in the direction of North Berlin—apparently toward the Stettiner Bahnhof. That boded ill. The Stettiner Bahnhof was the point of departure for Oranienburg, where the Sachsenhausen Concentration Camp was located.

But could they put us into a concentration camp? I reflected. We were not Germans: we were enemy aliens. Germany would not dare such a breach of international law. The Swedish government, which had taken over the representation of Polish interests, would not tolerate it. I remembered suddenly that I had heard some time ago about new barracks which were being built near the city of Stettin. Surely we were to be interned there and that was why we were being taken to the Stettin train.

When we turned the corner into the Invalidenstrasse, my house of cards collapsed. The vicinity of the Stettiner Bahnhof was black with people, obviously in a state of great excitement.

"Down with the Bromberg murderers!" "Kill them!" "Vengeance!" they shouted, as the trucks slowed down and passed as if on parade through the throngs lining the way.

"Bromberg murderers?" I repeated to myself. "Bromberg murderers? What does that mean?"

Suddenly the significance of the whole affair dawned upon me. Goebbels had thought of a brilliant stunt to impress the people of Berlin—we were to pose as the alleged "Bromberg murderers." All of us had been residents of Berlin for years; some of the younger ones had been born in Germany and had never seen Poland at all; some had even lost their Polish citizenship. But mere facts never stood in Goebbels' way.

The crowd screamed in ever-mounting fury. The curious mass frenzy peculiar to Germans had seized them. With self-hypnotizing regularity they now shouted in chorus:

"Vengeance! Blood! Vengeance! Blood!"

Had it not been for the policemen with fixed bayonets guarding each car, the crowd would have stormed the trucks.

The cars stopped in front of the station. "Get out!" thundered the command. "Leave everything you've brought with you behind!"

As we climbed down, further orders came: "Cross your hands behind your heads! Advance at the double to the train! Forward march! At the first sign of disobedience you'll be shot."

We threw everything away, crossed our hands behind our necks and ran. The crowd was so near that they could easily spit in our faces. Policemen drove us forward with truncheons and rifle butts, laying about them indiscriminately. There was none of us who did not get several heavy blows. Blood trickled down many faces. It was like rounding up game.

At the sight of blood the crowd went crazy with joy. Were not the Germans an efficient people? The war with Poland had lasted only thirteen days, and already the long arm of German justice had overtaken the perpetrators of crimes against the German folk. Adolf Hitler was a wonderful leader; he kept his promises. . . . And Joseph Goebbels was a very successful stage manager.

In the station a special train was waiting. Several hundred prisoners were already in the coaches, yet somehow places were found for us too. But the train still waited for more. Finally the shipments of prisoners from all over Berlin were packed inside. Some eight hundred people were penned together like cattle destined for slaughter, and the terror of the slaughterhouse came over us.

From the time we left the Stettiner Bahnhof, we were in the custody of the Gestapo. To look out of the window was "verboten," to talk was "verboten," to move from one's place was "verboten." A group of SS men strode through the train, leaving behind them in every coach a mass of physically and spiritually battered human beings.

When the train began to move, our self-control and our powers of resistance collapsed. Men began to sob like children. The wounded whimpered with pain. Hopelessness, fear and despair seized the whole train.

Gestapo officials guarded every coach and enforced "order." We had to hand over everything we had with us, except money or papers. Many men had brought photographs of their wives and children. These the Gestapo men pounced upon with glee, tore to pieces and, with comments too filthy to be repeated, scattered on the floor.

My neighbor, a pious old man with white hair and beard, held a small Bible in his trembling hands. A Gestapo man snatched it from him and gave the old man a shove that made him collapse on the bench. Then, with practiced fingers, he pulled out the pages, tore them into shreds and, with the words, "This is your last anointment, Jew," sprinkled the pieces over the aged head.

All the life had drained out of the old man's face. With closed eyes and blue lips he sat where he had fallen, his hair and beard strewn with words from the Holy Scriptures. When we were herded out of the train at Oranienburg, he did not stir. He was dead.

"All present!" announced a troop leader at the Oranienburg station, when we had been driven out of the train, ordered to form fours and counted. Then a double row of storm troopers flanked us on either side, and the march from the station began.

From the station platform a small raised passageway and a flight of steps led out to the street. Each one of us, as he walked or was pushed along this passageway, was held up to view like an actor on a stage. Tens of thousands had traveled that road since 1933, but the inhabitants of Oranienburg had not yet wearied of the spectacle.

An avid crowd of both sexes was standing at the foot of the steps, even mothers with children were among them. The scene at the Stettiner Bahnhof was repeated. Old and young, men and women, joined their voices in a dreadful, bloodthirsty chorus:

"Kill the Bromberg murderers!"
"Vengeance for our brothers in Poland!"
"*Blut fuer Blut!*"

But they did not stop at shrieks and howls. Stones, chunks of wood, nails and street filth were flung at us. Men were struck in the face, in the eyes. Many were blinded and fell down. But we were not allowed to help the fallen, not allowed to look around us; we had to keep running. Forward!

The road to the concentration camp was about two miles long. We left a two-mile trail of dead and injured behind us. Anyone who fell lay prostrate until the boots of the SS men had gotten him to his feet or he was dead. Several patrol cars drove slowly along the road behind us to pick up the victims: dead or alive, the total number of prisoners consigned to the camp had to be delivered. In Germany, order prevails.

The road to the camp led through a residential section in process of construction and past various imposing administration buildings. Part of the SS staff assigned to the camp lived there with their families. Little by little the whole SS apparatus of the Province of Brandenburg was to be transferred here. Everywhere prisoners were at work.

At the camp gate a deputation of storm troopers whose strength was still fresh took over. More cuffs, more blows rained down on our heads. We were driven inside—at the double. Running was the only pace allowed. We ran across an open square, past numerous wooden barracks to the Kommandantur building. There we had to run through a long tunnel, ending at another gate, the entrance to the camp proper. As the shadow of the tunnel closed over us, familiar words flashed into my mind: "Abandon hope all ye who enter here."

Beyond, in a huge open square, we were ordered to halt. Another counting began. The bodies piled up in the patrol cars were pitched out like bundles of hay. While we were being counted, a number of prisoners ran up, carrying tables, benches and typewriters. Once more we were registered and had to answer a questionnaire four pages long. When it was finished, the Gestapo had an exhaustive knowledge not only of our personal histories but of our financial standing as well.

At this ceremony the Kommandant appeared with his SS staff, paced along our lines several times and took a good look at each of us. If any one of us had some characteristic that made him stand out from the mass, if he was particularly short or tall, fat or thin, if he had a bald spot, a big nose, an unusual shade of hair, he was pulled out of the line and made to stand apart. Then the horde fell upon him and he was beaten to the ground with well-directed blows. When he no longer moved, they poured a few bucketsful of water over him and, if that did not revive him, he was simply thrown onto the previously unloaded heap of dead.

Then the Kommandant ordered us searched. This offered an occasion for further brutalities. Some of the strictly orthodox believers had disobeyed the order to hand over everything except money and papers. They had kept their phylacteries; and the search brought them to light.

This disobedience had a religious motive. The fact that we had been arrested on the eve of the Jewish New Year feast had impressed the orthodox as a judgment of God. Convinced that their last hour was at hand, they would not part with their tefillim, which contained the sacred "Hear, O Israel" prayer.

The discovery of the phylacteries put the blockfuehrers (men in charge of the barrack blocks) into a mood not only of rage, but of hellishly gleeful anticipation. First they pulled the capsules off the straps, tore out the written prayers and made them the object of insult and mockery. Then they took the offenders out of the line, tied them together in couples with the leather straps and ordered them to dance. Photographers took pictures of the whole scene.

It was heartrending to see the pious men in their orthodox dress, with their long, fluttering beards, hopping about awkwardly, executing comic spins and continually tripping over each other. But the blockfuehrers held their sides with laughter. "Just look at the he-goats hopping!" shouted one. And another took up the jest: "Mmmmah, mmmmmah, mmmmmah!"

Suddenly the Kommandant indicated he had had enough. The dance was broken off and the merry-making ended with the slaughter of the dancers. The assembly square rang with the shrieks of the tortured men. The rest of us, who had had the good fortune to be submerged in the crowd, were forced to look on in silence.

Then the Kommandant and his guard retired and we went through the rest of the "reception" prepared for us. We were directed across the courtyard into a huge room, which was divided into two parts. In the front stood tables and benches; in the back was a shower room. The benches were used for undressing. Several SS men sat at the tables and took charge of each prisoner's money and papers. We had to guess to which SS man we were to give the money and to which the papers. Woe to him who guessed wrong! I guessed wrong—a well-aimed blow in the stomach corrected my mistake. I fell on a bench. At this moment a blockfuehrer entered the room and when he saw that a prisoner was being beaten, he wanted to join the fun. He too beat me until I lay swooning on the floor.

The undressing, like all the activities in the camp, had to proceed at lightning speed. Eight hundred men had to be cleaned and dressed in the prescribed concentration-camp garb. So they divided us into groups. While one group undressed, another had their heads clean-shaven and a third was bathed.

We stood in a long line in front of the shower room. Urged on from behind by feet and fists, we pushed against each other and stumbled rather than walked into the room. But the floor of the shower room was slippery and one after another of us lost his footing.

My head throbbed as if someone were beating it with hammers, when I struck the stone floor. But I pulled myself together and immediately got to my feet. Now the SS men on duty in the shower room also wanted to have a bit of fun with the Polish assassins. Suddenly a jet of water as thick as my arm struck me in the stomach. The impact of the water was terrific. It was as if my whole stomach was burning. I screamed with pain and crumpled up. Another jet struck me in the eyes. When I put up my hand to protect them, it was aimed at the lumbar region. Suddenly it was no longer one jet, but three, traveling over my whole body, which burned like an open wound. Three SS men, armed with fire hose, stood in front of me and laughed, laughed!

I struggled desperately to keep my balance. But the pressure of the water was too strong; my limbs grew weaker and weaker. I fell once more.

"Aha!" said one of the hose heroes. "He's afraid of water. You can see the Polish swine hasn't bathed for at least a year. Just wait, my lad; we'll soon teach you German cleanliness."

After this speech I was finally allowed to go to the shower. The water was ice cold and unspeakably refreshing. But the shower was controlled from the boiler house. Suddenly the SS man on duty in the boiler house also had a clever idea, and boiling-hot water poured down upon us.

When the inspector had pronounced us clean, we were driven out of the shower room to make way for others. As we went out, a prisoner handed each of us a bundle of clothes. It contained an undershirt, underdrawers, socks, shoes, pants, a cap and a jacket without buttons. The articles of clothing—a hodge-podge of old police, military, prison and penitentiary uniforms—looked like the contents of a rag bag. My shirt had about twenty patches of different colors. The jacket and trousers did not match each other either in material or in size. The clothes fitted only in rare instances and had to be swapped, and, of course, the worst problem was the shoes. And since there was very little time to dress, we were driven out of the barrack half clad, to finish our toilet in the open air.

The picture that presented itself was indescribably comic. We were all bruised, our heads were completely shaven and we looked quite unlike our former selves. Many wore only underdrawers and had caps on their heads; others had on boots and jackets. By the time the rest of the clothes had been haggled over and exchanged, the whole thing looked like an unsuccessful masquerade.

Then several SS men appeared before the barrack. "Down, Jews, the whole pack of you," they ordered. "Snouts to the ground." This was meant as a new humiliation. Actually it gave us a pause for breath, which might have refreshed us if we had not heard every moment the agonized screams of those still being "bathed" in the shower room; but at last, when the whole "Polish rabble" was clean and dressed, we were taken to our quarters.

The prisoners' barracks, or blocks, were all built on the same plan. Each barrack was divided into five sections. In the middle there was a washroom and a toilet room. In the washroom were two basins of about $1\frac{1}{4}$ yards in diameter, equipped with running water, of course cold. These basins had to be used by eight or ten prisoners at once. The toilet room was equipped with six water closets.

Adjoining were Wings A and B of each barrack, which constituted the living quarters. Each wing was divided into two rooms. First came the day room: it was about 90–100 square yards in area, furnished with cupboards, five tables and benches. Each cupboard was supposed to be used by four men; in it the prisoners kept their eating bowls, towels, and—if they were fortunate enough to have them—their soap and toothbrushes.

Then there was a dormitory of about 110–120 yards in area, which provided room for sixty to seventy persons. There were, however, about 150 of us crowded into this space. When the German troops occupied Warsaw and great masses of Poles were sent to German concentration camps, the number in each wing increased to about 165. In a cemetery, thirty graves occupied the space which in Sachsenhausen was assigned to 165 living men.

Each barrack in Sachsenhausen was under the command of a block-fuehrer, who was, of course, an SS man. He was the absolute master of the inmates of his block and could do with them as he saw fit. In addition there was a room senior, with an assistant to help him. The room senior was a prisoner, and his position usually differed little from that of the other inmates. However, the room seniors appointed by the camp authorities for the three Polish blocks were prisoners of a special kind. They were chosen from the hardened criminals who, after serving a term in the penitentiary, had undergone a "period of education" in the camp.

The room senior allotted to my block, No. 38, had a penitentiary term of fifteen years behind him. He was a lanky fellow, with excessively long arms and excessively large hands. He had protruding ears and protruding eyes rimmed with red, stubbly lashes. His name was Paul.

Paul had no glimmer of native intelligence and he was barely able to write his name. But he had made a reputation for himself as a first-class brute. When Paul walked, his long arms swung at his sides as if they were feelers, eager to encounter an obstacle on which they might exercise themselves. If anyone stood in his way, he would beat that person until he could beat no more—but not because he hated us as individuals. Paul had nothing against Poles or Jews. He beat us because beating was a delight to him. And being in command of a Polish block, he could gratify his passion to his heart's content without anyone's raising an objection.

Only two things worried Paul. He could not give both wings of the barrack the attention he felt they required, and the assistant, to whom he had entrusted Wing B, proved slack. Four days later, Paul got him replaced by one of the Danzig criminals who had a particularly evil reputation in the camp.

From the moment of our installation in the barracks, we were separated from our fellow sufferers in the other blocks. We saw each other only from a distance when we assembled in front of the barracks for roll call. But the bloodcurdling shrieks which daily and nightly reached our ears told us that our separation was only physical. We all shared the same dreadful fate.

When we had been taken to the barracks it was 6:30 P.M. The evening roll call was imminent. Paul hastily gave us temporary instructions about answering the roll call and led us back to the assembly square. During the first six months of our stay in Sachsenhausen, this was the only time that we took part in a general roll call, for the next day the "Bromberg murderers" were declared isolated, and this altered the camp routine for us.

To be "isolated" meant that we were cut off from the rest of the camp. Our roll call was therefore held in front of our own blocks. The blockfuehrers could "educate" us to their hearts' content without the rest of the camp knowing anything about it. To be isolated also meant a long list of hardships to which the other prisoners were not subjected. We had to sleep on damp, dirty sacks of straw. Except for the assembly period, we spent the whole day in the overcrowded dormitory. We could not buy anything in the canteen, possess books, read newspapers. We had to spoon up our tea or coffee out of our eating bowls (the others had mugs). We were not allowed to use the toilets except at fixed times. During the first part of our stay we were even forbidden to talk to each other.

The daily routine of the average prisoner in Sachsenhausen was strictly regulated by a camp schedule. The day began at 5:30. The room seniors of each block were responsible for seeing that the prisoners got up at the right time, washed and received their morning ration, which was distributed at 6:15. In the interim, the dormitory as well as the day room had to be put in order. Then the prisoners marched to the assembly place.

The roll call began with a general signal at seven o'clock. In winter, when it was still dark at this time, the assembly place was lighted by searchlights. The roll call consisted of the usual counting off and generally lasted about fifteen minutes. Then working squads were assembled and ordered to the various work places inside or outside the camp. The rest of the prisoners were marched back to the barracks, where they had to hold themselves ready in case of need or take some kind of "exercise."

For those who remained in the camp, a roll call was held at noon. After that, the midday ration, usually turnip soup, was distributed in the day room. The food was never salted, only flavored with soda. The noon recess lasted about an hour. Then the indoor squad had to wash the dishes, and the morning labor was resumed until it was time for the evening roll call.

For this roll call all the prisoners had to return to camp. It was always held by daylight, consequently the time changed every few months. After roll call the evening ration was distributed. Like the morning ration, it consisted of bread and a liter of fluid. Sometimes the fluid looked like tea, sometimes like coffee, but it never tasted like either. The morning and evening supply of bread, totaling one-half pound per person, was usually brought to the barracks in the afternoon. So the morning bread ration was nearly always hard and stale.

After the evening roll call, the prisoner's day was over. He could, according to the time of year and the mood of the room senior, stay up for about an hour, remain in the day room and talk with his fellows or read newspapers.

In the Polish blocks an entirely different regime prevailed. The only determining point of our schedule was that, three times a day, we had to leave our barracks for roll call. The manner in which we spent our days was left entirely to the caprice of the blockfuehrers, the room senior and any other individual in camp who wore a uniform. Paul, for example, gave orders on his own authority that we must get up at 4:45 A.M. He had decided that while the waking was going on, the indoor squad—there were about fifteen to each wing—should wash first. The others, stripped to the waist and towel in hand, had to wait at the door of the washroom until their turns came. This was merely a symbolical act, for Paul allowed only half an hour for the three hundred men in the two wings to use the washroom.

While we were washing, a special dormitory squad put the dormitory in order. All the straw sacks were collected and piled up against the windowless wall; the blankets had to be stacked against the opposite wall. In the meantime Paul went to the office to receive whatever commands might be forthcoming for the day.

Our roll calls usually lasted longer than fifteen minutes and were accompanied by various torments. Our rations were arbitrarily reduced or withdrawn altogether. In the months when we were not sent to labor in the Klinkerworks, our time between roll calls was filled with every possible kind of "exercising." When the day's schedule was over, we had to go to bed immediately. Until December we were not allowed any light, and as the evening roll call in winter took place between 3:30 and 4:30, our nights began at five o'clock.

Our first roll call in the concentration camp passed without incident. We returned to the barracks completely exhausted, and were glad when Paul ordered us to bed. The straw sacks were already laid out in four rows: sixteen to each row along the sides of the room by the windows, and fifteen in each of the two adjoining rows in the middle of the room. The middle rows had to be shorter to allow a clear space for the door to open. This arrangement left a long narrow passageway between the middle rows and the window rows on either side for anyone who wanted to inspect us. The number of sacks had, of course, been calculated in accordance with the normal capacity of the room, and, as this had been more than doubled, two and often three men had to share one straw sack.

It was good to be able to stretch out at last. But my body and mind were keyed up to a state of high tension. The thought of Gucia took away what was left of my powers of resistance. Had she also been arrested, was she going through the same tortures? The uncertainty was horrible.

The events of the past twelve hours passed before my eyes. I tried to grasp their meaning, but in vain. What was going to happen now? I kept asking myself. Would the Swedish Minister, upon learning of it, protest against this incredible breach of international law? Was this only a one-day revenge of the National Socialist "supermen," and would we, after tomorrow, be treated in accordance with our status as enemy aliens? Or would the crimes committed against us, like so many others, be buried in the obscurity of the Berlin Gestapo headquarters and never come to light?

I did not think of myself as a hero. There was nothing heroic in having to let oneself be trodden on like a worm, without any possibility of defense. What were we, then—hostages? martyrs?

From all the pallets came sounds of suffering, choking sobs and groans of pain. No one could escape from these thoughts and only a few found sleep.

It must have been about nine o'clock at night when the door was suddenly flung open. Paul stood in the opening and shouted with all his might, "Achtung!" We jumped up in terror and stood on our straw sacks. During the few hours of our stay in the camp we had already learned that we had to be on the alert every moment if we valued our lives.

When Paul had instructed us in the elementary rules of the camp, before the evening roll call, he had emphasized that at the command, "Achtung!" all the prisoners must jump up and stand at attention, no matter what they were doing. One of my barrack mates, a short, slight man of about fifty-five, had thereupon asked timidly: "But, Herr Room Senior, what are we to do at night, when we're asleep? Suppose we don't hear the command?"

Paul ordered the questioner to step forward and answered in his racy Berlin dialect: "There's no 'Herr' here, see? I'm a prisoner like you. And don't ask questions—not on your life. And never sleep.

Here you've got to keep on your toes, or else you're a corpse on leave." Then he raised his giant fist and brought it down on the prisoner's head with such force that the man crumpled together like an accordion.

This scene was firmly fixed in our memories, and that is why we sprang up like lightning when Paul shouted his command. Unfortunately, some of the men were in a deep, drugged sleep and had not heard the order. Even their sack mates' hurried and furtive efforts did not succeed in rousing them. When a group of blockfuehrers entered the dormitory and turned their flashlights on us, the sight of the sleeping men filled them with monstrous fury.

"All into the corner!" shouted one of them, pointing with outstretched arm.

We began to run across the straw sacks, jostling each other. The sleeping men, who still lay motionless on their sacks, were in our way. At first we stepped over them. But the blockfuehrers were at our heels, urging us on with their truncheons, so we no longer heeded where we were stepping and ran across the bodies of the sleepers as if they were the straw itself. Then at last they awoke and yelled with pain and terror. Their cries roused the blockfuehrers to still greater fury.

"Just wait, you trash; we'll quiet you quick enough!" shouted one of them and gave Paul a wink.

Paul disappeared into the day room. In an instant he was back, his arms loaded with steel rods, broomsticks and boards, which he handed out to the blockfuehrers. Armed with these instruments, some of them began to belabor the prostrate men; others made for the human mass squeezed up in the corner.

Of course, the men in front got most of the blows. The blockfuehrers apparently considered this an injustice, for suddenly they ordered us to run into the opposite corner. We were hounded diagonally across the room, and again we trampled on the prostrate bodies. But this time the men who were stepped on did not cry out. The blockfuehrers had seen to it that they would be silent forever.

A few minutes after the blockfuehrers had left us, Paul stuck his head in at the door and called to the questioner to whom he had given such an impressive lesson before the roll call: "Well, shrimp, didn't I tell you to keep on your toes?"

During the night death made further inroads in our ranks. Among the dead was the "shrimp."

The whole thing was like a monstrous witches' Sabbath, an evil dream. Confusion filled my brain. I was no longer sure whether I was waking or sleeping. Suddenly a dreadful thought struck me: I had only imagined all this; my mind was unhinged. "Dear God, don't let my mind give way," I prayed. "Only give me strength to endure patiently whatever burden you may lay upon me." The prayer worked like a miracle. I fell asleep.

The next morning, when the straw sacks were removed and we started to dress, we found that our clothes were hopelessly mixed. Piles of clothing were scattered everywhere and we burrowed into them frantically. Men began to quarrel over articles of clothing, insulted each other, and finally a free-for-all fight developed.

This might have ended in a catastrophe, for disturbance of the peace was considered mutiny and liable to the most severe punishment. But Paul, though in a somewhat drastic manner, saved the situation by throwing a bucketful of water over the heads of the contenders. This calmed them down. It also soaked the piles of clothes, but we had already learned not to be particular.

Most of us, however, found ourselves minus a right or left shoe, a cap, jacket or shirt. Finally someone suggested searching the straw sacks, and, sure enough, all the missing articles came to light. During the man hunt of the previous night, they had been caught in the openings of the sacks and had been dragged away during the morning routine.

We had hardly finished dressing when Paul drove us out in front of the barrack for the roll call and ordered us to line up in ten rows according to height. After the experience of the previous night, however, everyone was afraid to stand in the front line. Besides, there were many of us who had no conception of formal drill and wandered like lost sheep from one row to another. But the claws of the concentration camp went into action. A group of blockfuehrers, who had stolen up on us unnoticed from a side path, was suddenly in our midst, raining blows on us. After they had beaten us up to their satisfaction, one of them ordered: "Now form an orderly front, or else the whole Polish-Jewish pack will take a roll for half an hour." With that they marched off.

Paul and his assistant now took over the command. Presently we were standing in rank and file, an irreproachable graded square of ten rows. Then Paul gave us further instruction in the camp rules. First he demonstrated what the blockfuehrer had meant by "take a roll." He took a man out of the first row and ordered him to throw himself on the ground.

"So," said Paul. "And now spin round your axis, first to the left, then to the right. Fur-ther, fur-ther, al-ways further, al-ways further." In this way he made the man roll twenty-five yards across the ground, while he himself followed behind. At last the man could not move any more. "Further!" roared Paul, giving the man such a push that he spun around twice. Then Paul left him and turned back to us, without any comment on the performance.

We had to practice the prescribed manner of greeting a superior: a superior, of course, was anyone who wore a uniform. Paul ordered: "Cap off, eyes left, cap on. Cap off, eyes right, cap on."

When we had completely mastered the greeting, Paul suddenly came up close to us, leaned over confidentially, jerked his thumb in the direction of the blockfuehrers, who were approaching us again, and said softly: "And if anyone asks you how that happened"—he pointed with his other hand to the bleeding face of one of the men—"the answer goes, 'I fell, Herr Blockfuehrer'!"

"Well, now we'll just see if the pack of Jews can practice proper military discipline," said one of the blockfuehrers, when the group had reached us. Of course, "the pack of Jewish swine" had not the foggiest notion of military discipline. So the blockfuehrers took charge of operations themselves. They corrected the order of heights, distributed kicks and stomach blows. Then they made us count off according to rows for about fifteen minutes. With that the roll call ended, and we were driven back into the barracks.

The counting off, which was repeated at every roll call, was to prove a constant source of trouble. Each of us had been assigned a certain place in the formation, which he had to take every time we assembled. So each man had a certain number, which he knew by heart and shouted out automatically when his turn came. But as a result of the continual murders our number became smaller every day. The formation had to be rearranged and the numbering changed accordingly. Among the three hundred-odd men in the block there were always a few who could never remember that they had to allow for these changes. They made mistakes in counting off, which resulted in the withdrawal or reduction of the daily ration for the entire block.

When we returned to the barrack, the first ration of the day was given out: about half a pound of sticky black bread, which looked so revolting that we could not bring ourselves to eat it and hid it away in our pockets. According to the rules we should have received something to drink. But the distribution of drinks required labor squads, which had not yet been appointed in the Polish blocks. So Paul at once set about selecting an indoor squad. He made us step forward, and with the eye of a connoisseur picked out thirty men from the two wings—the largest and most brutal-looking among us.

This duty involved responsibility. The indoor squad must see to it that the rations were distributed three times a day and consumed as quickly as possible and the bowls then polished till they shone. On the other hand, the duty brought the thirty men invaluable advantages. Like the room senior, they enjoyed the privilege of sleeping in the day room where the air was better. They could reserve for themselves as many blankets as they wanted. In dividing the rations they had an opportunity to give themselves a larger portion than the others. Finally, the men of the indoor squad were allowed to spend their working hours in the day room, where they could rest and escape most of the tortures that went on in the dormitory.

Paul had scarcely finished selecting the indoor squad and instructing its members in their tasks, when a detail of prisoners from the office came into our barrack. They had brought typewriters and questionnaires. For the fourth time in twenty-four hours we were registered.

After that, it was time for the noon roll call. At this not only the blockfuehrers but high officers of the SS detachments stationed in the vicinity appeared. Of course, all official Oranienburg wanted to look at the "Polish assassins." Our one-day stay in Sachsenhausen must have been an unusual "success," for they walked around us several times, commenting approvingly on our bloody faces. Then the highest-ranking officer whispered something to a blockfuehrer, who, grinning with pleasure, walked up to the group and said: "Jewish spawn, where did you get those bruised faces? Have you been hitting each other, maybe?"

"From falling, Herr Blockfuehrer," we answered in chorus.

Our examiners seemed amazed that we had acclimated ourselves so quickly. Paul smirked with pride.

The blockfuehrer carried the joke further.

"Aha, from falling! While running, I suppose? In Berlin you didn't fall so often. You could run better there, couldn't you, you sons of bitches? Here it's a little too uncomfortable for your sensitive bones, eh? Just wait; we'll teach you swine to run!" Suddenly his voice went shrill and cracked altogether. "You are responsible for the Bromberg murders and we don't trifle with murderers. Remember that!"

Our limbs were paralyzed with terror. The threat, issued in the presence of high SS functionaries, had taken on the character of an official decree. The shock was so great that many fell into a deathlike swoon when we returned to the barrack.

While we were looking after the unconscious men, the kettles with the daily ration arrived. They were brought by prisoners who belonged to the elite, so to speak, of the prison population. They were members of the SA, SS or other National Socialist formations, who had committed some offense and had to undergo an "education" period, which might be shortened or lengthened at discretion.

Among them were persons of high standing; consequently, they enjoyed a special position in the camp. They were billeted only sixty to a block, slept in comfortable beds, wore special uniforms and stood apart from the others at roll call. They were, it is true, subjected to rigorous military drill and also served in the fire brigade. Otherwise they performed no work, except that several of the rank-and-file had the job of carrying rations to the "isolation districts," which comprised the Polish blocks, the barracks of the equally "dangerous" Bible students and the "punishment squads."

The membership of the elite block changed from time to time, but the brutality of the occupants was always the same. All of them regarded the Polish prisoners as free game. When they considered themselves slighted, they vented their anger on us. They came alone or in groups whenever the notion struck them. More than once the whole block raided us. Often they surpassed the blockfuehrers in their excesses.

But, apart from their own invasions, the elite block was a constant source of trouble, because their barracks were visited several times a day by blockfuehrers or other Party members. The path to the elite barracks led past the Polish blocks and we too received brief but disastrous visits. So we were overjoyed when the Party block was sent to the front in the spring of 1940 and no more "elite prisoners" came to Sachsenhausen.

The threat of the blockfuehrer at the assembly place had had such a crushing effect on us that no one felt equal to eating his soup. The general loss of appetite nearly proved fatal. We could not simply pour the soup back into the kettles. They had to be returned empty and clean. We could not leave it in the bowls either; Paul would have killed several men for that. But we could not conceal soup in our pockets, as we had done with the bread that morning. It was still more unthinkable to pour it into the toilets. That would be construed as sabotage. So many of the prisoners forced themselves to eat. But their stomachs rebelled and the soup came straight up again.

Then we had a piece of luck. Paul was unexpectedly summoned to the office. No sooner had he left the barrack than we dashed into the toilet room and tipped up the bowls into the water closets. A few minutes later all the bowls were washed and back in the cupboards.

In the meantime the swooning men had recovered consciousness. There was only one who could not be revived, despite all our efforts. When Paul returned we informed him and he went off again to report the case to the office. He came back with a message of evil omen. The camp authorities had decreed that from now on every prisoner must carry in his right pants pocket a slip of paper on which his personal data was recorded.

The order filled us with terror. We all knew that soldiers have to wear identification disks so that the bodies may be recognized. If the same thing was demanded of us, it could only mean that we were already regarded as potential corpses. Thus we were assured that the blockfuehrer's threat had been meant seriously and not merely for the sadistic pleasure of frightening us. It was plain that we were to die; the only question was *when*. Would they kill us off quickly or drag out the process?

September 14 was the first day of our New Year holiday, and the sacred words of the prayer which forms the culminating point of the New Year ritual came to my mind: "On New Year's Day the decree is inscribed and on the Day of Atonement it is sealed how many shall pass away and how many shall be born; who shall live and who shall die; who shall attain the measure of man's days and who shall not attain it. . . ." And I prayed fervently to God that He would have pity on us and that if He had destined us for death He would let us die quickly.

That same evening, when Paul drove us out to roll call, he did not fail to inquire if everyone had his identification slip in his pants pocket. Full of forebodings, we formed our ten-line square. The room senior and his assistant were in a remarkable state of excitement. They ran around us, continually improving the formation, and Paul kept repeating: "If you don't stand to attention smartly, I'll make you do knee bending for a whole hour."

"Knee bending," like "taking a roll," was a form of exercise and one of the favorite punishments, especially for the old and weak. Paul had given us a practical demonstration of it. The subject was an old man, accused of spilling water in the washroom and failing to wipe it up. Paul assigned him fifty knee bends as a punishment and beat time with his foot while the old man, with outstretched arms, sank to his knees and rose again, up and down, up and down. After a few minutes of this, the victim could hold out no longer. He sank to the ground, gasping and red in the face. We were afraid he was having a heart attack. At that, Paul stopped the exercise, ordered the old man deluged with water and promised glumly: "Tomorrow we'll take this fellow in hand again."

We knew that Paul always took care to make good his threats. So now, when the blockfuehrers arrived and he called, "Achtung!" we summoned up all our strength: our deportment was perfect. The blockfuehrers inspected each individual as critically as if we had been an elite regiment on parade. But they found nothing to take exception to and had to content themselves with obscene insults.

We breathed freely again. It looked as if, against all expectation, the roll call would pass without incidents. But we had underestimated the sadistic mania of the SS. Suddenly the leader of the blockfuehrers came up close to us and asked: "Which of you is a rabbi?"

No one answered.

"What?" said he. "Is there no rabbi among you?"

Again no one answered.

The blockfuehrer turned to Paul: "Which of these swine is a rabbi?"

Paul could not answer the question, and the blockfuehrer's anger increased.

"All right, then, there's no rabbi here," he said. "But if I find out that you've lied, we'll make short work of you."

Then he tried another tack: "Which of you has ever been in prison?"

Two men reported themselves.

"Step forward," ordered the blockfuehrer, and when they had both done so, "Speak up and tell the reason."

"Embezzlement," said one.

"An automobile accident," answered the other.

But the blockfuehrer was not yet in the right mood. He suddenly turned his back on us and started toward his companions. Halfway there, he halted, reflected a moment and came back. There was a diabolical grin on his face.

"Of course you know that all Poles are criminals, don't you?" he asked.

We held our breath. Our throats went dry with fear. The stillness was uncanny.

The blockfuehrer waited motionless. Suddenly he raised both fists threateningly and his curses rattled down on us like hail. "What! You won't answer, you Polish swine, you Jew dogs, you Jewish bastards, Polish assassins, Polish scum . . . *verdammte Judenbrut!* . . ."

In each of us pride struggled with the instinct of self-preservation. In a few minutes they would leap upon us like beasts and trample us beneath their boots.

Suddenly a voice was heard: "Jawohl!"

The tension was broken. But the SS man was not satisfied. "All of you must answer," he shouted.

Again there was a moment of silence. The inner struggle continued. Suddenly, as if an invisible baton had given the signal, we all cried in chorus: "Jawohl!"

It was a bloodcurdling cry. We ourselves trembled from the force of it. But it did us good. All the shame and torture that had been inflicted on us, all our misery, all our anguish, found release in that cry.

The bellowing "Jawohl" intoxicated the blockfuehrer. Like a drunkard craving one more drink, he demanded: "Now all of you repeat three times in chorus: 'All Poles are criminals.' Loud, mind you."

But there is a limit to everything, even to self-abasement. The other blockfuehrers, who had been watching the scene from a distance, now joined their comrade, waiting to see how we would react, poised to spring. What if we did not answer?

Our comrades from Blocks 37 and 38 were still lined up in front of their barracks—the law of the concentration camp was "all for one." If we did not answer, the punishment would fall on all three blocks, some eight hundred human beings! And as if each of us had arrived at the same conclusion, the cry rang through the camp:

"All Poles are criminals!"

"All Poles are criminals!"

"All Poles are criminals!"

The bodies of the blockfuehrers relaxed. They had won.

We had weathered the crisis. But our spirits were completely shattered. The mental struggle had taken away the last remnant of our strength.

On the main assembly place the rest of the camp was still drawn up. The number of prisoners did not check with the roll. In such a case the whole camp had to remain standing until the mistake was cleared up or the missing men were found. Whether this took one hour or many, whether it was snowing or blowing, hot or cold, day or night, made no difference. Sometimes we stood for eight hours, sometimes for twelve hours, and once, so I was told, the whole camp had to stand for two days.

When at last the dismissal signal sounded from the main building and we were hounded back into the barrack, it was pitch dark. Hastily the sacks were laid out—it was too late for bread and tea. Everyone groped his way to his own place.

The air in the barrack was close and oppressive, the heat of an unusually warm September day had collected in the room. Soon we began to sweat. The room was so crowded that we had to lie on our sides. But, even so, our bodies pressed against each other. Sweat, breath and all kinds of bodily effluvia mingled together. In a very short time the air was used up.

But all the windows and doors had to remain tightly shut. We could have opened the trap door in the roof, but Paul ordered us to keep it closed. He gloated over our struggle for breath.

And yet in this confinement, in this poisoned air, I felt well. Well-being is a relative thing. To a thirsty man a drink of water, to a starving man a piece of dry bread, is the most precious thing in the world. For me that evening the strip of sack on which I could stretch out was the sum total of all desire. Most of us were too tired to moan or weep. There was a blessed stillness in the room. I was thankful for the darkness and the chance to be alone with my thoughts.

When a man sees no future before him, he takes refuge in the past. I reviewed my whole life. My parents appeared before my eyes, and the little town where I played as a child. I thought of my marriage and my wife's early death. Once more I watched my daughter growing up, lived through her school and university days, my anxieties and hopes for her. Then I cast up accounts with myself, and when I had made a reckoning of my good and bad deeds, a great peace came over me. If only I could fall asleep now and never wake up! The world would go on just the same, the war would be fought just the same. No one would feel the difference.

No one? Suddenly a white, terrified face came toward me out of the darkness, nearer and nearer. It was the face of my daughter. I heard her voice quite plainly: "Head high, Papa. Do you hear me? Head high!"

It was the voice of life, of my will-to-live. Helplessness, passivity, fell from me like a weight. The thought of my daughter had come to my aid when I needed it most. I had to live and I *would* live. The despair, the resignation, of the past two days disappeared. Nothing was in vain. Everything in life had its meaning and its purpose.

Even our sufferings seemed all at once to have meaning. We suffered in order that those who came after us might be spared such anguish. Some day we would come out of this hell; if not all of us, then a few, perhaps only one. This one would go out into the world, where there would be many who had suffered like him. They would join forces in a common task, and that task would be to speak, to relate, if necessary to shout, until the conscience of the world was awakened from its lethargy, until the peoples of the earth had vowed to see to it that *one* nation should never again attempt to enslave the world.

Now I was able to look at our situation with the eye of a strategist. What was the enemy's purpose, what methods would he use to attain it and how could we combat them?

In the first place, the Nazis did not want our lives alone; they wanted to break our morale. To prevent that, we must protect not only our bodies but our spirits.

From my experiences of the first two days in camp, I could already draw another conclusion. The first law of defense was to bury oneself in the mass, not to stand out in any way. With this in mind, I began to analyze my own appearance. The only striking feature I could find was my eyes, which were at that time very large. I determined to keep them narrowed, and that narrowing has remained a habit with me to this day.

Suddenly my reflections were interrupted. Restlessness took possession of the room. After the first exhaustion had worn off, desperate weeping began. From one corner came sobs that pierced my heart. I sat up. Everywhere I saw the raised silhouettes of men shaken by weeping. My recovered confidence protested against such senseless squandering of our reserves of strength. This was the very thing the Nazis were hoping for. If they had only sought our lives, they would have stood us against a wall and shot us, as they had done to so many. What they wanted was the pleasure of torturing us to death, of gloating over our pain, of watching our spirits break. We must not play into their hands.

I jumped up on my straw sack. It was dangerous; it was "streng verboten." But that did not matter. I had to tell my comrades what I had just realized so clearly.

"Stop that crying!" I shouted. "Don't be martyrs. Don't let them break your spirit."

Suddenly a flood lamp lighted up the windows, making the landscape as bright as day. I hurled myself to the ground a split second before the door was flung open by a horde of blockfuehrers, who flashed their pocket torches into every corner of the room. Behind the blockfuehrers Paul's uneasy face could be seen. He had slept too soundly and had not been aware of their arrival until they were inside the barrack. There was fear in his voice as he cried, "Achtung!"

We jumped up instantly and stood at attention on our sacks, a comical battalion of half-dressed, pitiable figures. But our room senior looked still funnier. Because of the unusual heat, he had slept in his shirt, and when the blockfuehrers startled him out of his sleep, he had had no time to put on his pants; the shirt reached only to his thighs, and his long, unbelievably crooked legs were revealed.

Against the farthest wall of the barrack lay several dying men. They made a desperate attempt to pull themselves up at the word of command, but their strength failed them and they sank heavily back on the straw. The probing fingers of light came to rest on them. The high boots went into action. In a few brief minutes the dying had become the dead.

Then one of the blockfuehrers turned to the room senior, who still seemed not fully awake and shouted: "And you, jump into your pants double quick!" Paul vanished like a frightened mouse, and the blockfuehrers turned their undivided attention back to us.

"Get behind the straw sacks, the whole pack of you!" shouted one.

That was a strange and baffling order. What did "behind the straw sacks" mean? Weren't the sacks lying flat on the ground?

Some crawled under the sacks, others lifted them above their heads, others stood the sacks on end and got behind them; often there was a silent and surreptitious struggle between men who shared the same pallet. For every two or three bedfellows there were two or three different interpretations of the order. And since each man believed himself in the right, they tugged the straw sacks to and fro. The whole thing looked like a scene in a madhouse.

The blockfuehrers watched this spectacle for quite a while and literally shook with laughter. Suddenly their laughter stopped and they got down to business.

The straw sack nearest the door belonged to three men. They had stood it on end; one man had placed himself behind it and was holding it up with his hands; the other two flanked him on the right and left, standing smartly at attention. The blockfuehrers approached the group and silently observed the three men. Then one of them put his fists on his hips and turned to his companions.

"Look at that! The Ikeys look pretty funny, don't they?" And he roared to the men, "Lie down!"

The two men flanking the straw sack instantly threw themselves to the ground. The man who was holding up the sack hesitated a moment. Then he turned around, let go of the sack and threw himself down like the others, expecting it to fall on top of him. But it slipped out of his hand and tipped over into the group of blockfuehrers.

Then all the devils of hell were let loose.

"Lie down," roared the blockfuehrers in a confused chorus. "Snouts to the ground! Lie down!"

Frantically we threw ourselves to the ground and pulled a piece of sack over our heads to shield them as best we could. Like a horde of savages running amuck, the blockfuehrers pounced upon us, beat and trampled everywhere, screamed like wild beasts. The room rang with our shrieks of pain. This only incensed the blockfuehrers still more.

"Absolute silence," ordered one of them. "Anyone who screams will be shot!"

We saw them draw their revolvers. Instantly we stifled our screams with our hands.

The first fury wore itself out. "Stand up!" came the next order. We had already grown used to the tempo of the concentration camp. In a few seconds we were on our feet. Only a few, who could no longer move, still lay on the floor.

"Stand up, *all* of you," roared a hoarse voice. "Damn you, hurry!"

But the prostrate men did not move. Paul, who in the meantime had jumped into his pants, ran up officiously and with a few powerful kicks summoned each man to rise. When they did not respond even to this, Paul turned them over on their backs with his foot and after a moment announced: "Dead."

"Dead, eh?" said a blockfuehrer. "That's as it should be; the whole *Judenpack* will croak soon."

Then the game began again. This time the command went: "All under the straw sacks, so that not a bit of you can be seen." We threw ourselves down and pulled the sacks over us. Scarcely had we lain down when the order came, "Stand up!" and then again, "Lie down!" and again, "Stand up!"

At last the blockfuehrers had had their fill. "Now keep as quiet as mice or we'll be back," one of them promised. With that they left our dormitory. From the pitiful screams which reached our ears we knew that they were torturing the other two blocks in the same way.

Paul, who was still uneasy over his own carelessness and did not want another visit from the blockfuehrers at any price, opened the door for a good-night message. "I warn you, don't make any blah-blah and don't bawl, or else the blockfuehrers will come again."

The blockfuehrers kept their word. About an hour later they appeared at the windows and turned their torches on us. But as utter stillness reigned in the dormitory, they vanished again. We were safe for the rest of the night.

Looking back today on those first forty-eight hours in the hell of Sachsenhausen, comparing them with the later torments, which were much crueler and more severe, it still seems to me that the first two days were the hardest of all. It was the suddenness, the ceaselessness of the horror, which made it so hard to bear. Later—strange as it may seem—we had grown accustomed to terror and to the tempo of the camp.

That night the air in the barrack was particularly stifling. There were some asthma sufferers among us; these began to cough, in paroxysms that shook their weakened bodies. Then an odd thing happened. The coughing spread to the other prisoners. First one and then another caught the contagion, until the whole barrack was coughing.

This must have waked Paul. Suddenly he threw open the door in a towering rage.

"This is rioting, do you hear?" he bawled. "I'll report you to the office tomorrow. Do you want the patrols in here? If you don't pipe down this instant, I'll fix you so you won't ever cough again."

With a supreme effort, we pulled ourselves together. Little by little the coughing ceased. Only the asthmatics went on gasping in helpless agony.

When Paul's alarm clock went off at 4:44 the next morning, we could scarcely move. Nevertheless, we tried to keep all our wits about us so as not to anger him, for he was in an unusually bad mood that morning. Although our clothing was again scattered about in confusion, we took care to keep order. But Paul, who had not forgiven us the interruption of his sleep, tormented us worse than the previous morning. Like a slave driver, he stood in the small corridor that connected the two wings, through which we all had to pass to reach the washroom and toilet room. He beat us mercilessly, hounded us into the room and out again, and forbade us to use the toilets.

When we went out to roll call, Paul had thought up a devilish idea. The casualty list of the nocturnal attack in the two wings was five dead. Paul had the bodies brought out in front of the barrack and, partly to wound us and partly to win the favor of the blockfuehrers, he had them stacked up staircase fashion, so that each head projected beyond the one above.

We were like men turned to stone. Paul was gratified—he had avenged himself for his broken slumbers.

"You scoundrels," he shouted, "I'll soon show you how we'll finish you off."

We had to stand there unprotesting and allow our very dead to be made the object of insult and mockery. Suddenly a voice cried out: "That is desecration of the dead!"

Paul jumped as if he had been stung by a tarantula. That we should dare to criticize him!

"Step forward!" he screamed. "Step forward, Jew!"

We did not move. For a minute we thought that Paul would have an epileptic fit. Foam flecked his lips. At that critical moment the room senior of Block 37 came up to him and whispered in his ear. Terror-stricken, our eyes followed the newcomer's outstretched arm. In front of Block 37 lay more dead men. They too were piled up step fashion. (The room seniors of the Polish blocks always tried to outdo each other in good ideas and followed each other's lead. This time Paul's idea set the fashion. The tribute put him into a good humor and he forgot his anger.)

The blockfuehrers accepted very graciously the diversion Paul had prepared for them. They gazed with pleasure at the array of dead and exchanged comments.

"The Jewish swine are croaking too slowly."

"The Polish dogs are only taking bread out of German mouths. We must round up the whole brood and shoot them."

"No, shooting won't do. Waste of good German powder. We must hang the filth, or poison them."

So saying, they gave the bodies a few well-aimed kicks, which scattered them in all directions. Then, with minds at ease, they began our roll call, under a deep-blue sky with a rising sun.

Scarcely had we returned to the barrack, when about one hundred workers with nails and carpentering tools appeared in front of our block. They fastened the windows inside, then nailed them to the window frames from outside. The hammering rang through the whole place. The same work was going on at the two other Polish blocks. We watched this activity uneasily. No one understood what it could mean.

When the windows were nailed fast, the foreman of the working squad shook them to make sure that they would not give way. Then he came inside the barrack, closed the trap door in the roof, which could be opened and shut by means of a rope, climbed high up against the wall, drove in a staple and wound the rope tightly around it.

At last the foreman finished his work and started out of the room. In the doorway he turned, looked at us pityingly and said under his breath: "I can't help it. They're cooking up something new."

By this time the whole camp was already at work; only the Poles had not yet been assigned to their tasks. But we too must be kept busy. So a horde of blockfuehrers paid us a morning call.

"Can you sing?" asked one of them.

"Jawohl," we answered in chorus.

"Hold up your hands, turn around in a circle and sing," he ordered.

We threw up our arms and began to revolve. Since he had not said what we were to sing, every man struck up whatever tune occurred to him at the moment. It was ear-splitting.

The blockfuehrers listened to this abominable noise for several minutes. Then one of them interrupted in a thundering voice, "This isn't a synagogue," and they began to beat us without pity.

Among us there was a professor of music, Rosebery D'Arguto, who had made a great name for himself in Germany as a singing instructor and director of workers' choruses. He stepped forward, stood at attention, and called out: "I am a professor of music; may I lead the prisoners in a song?"

"So, a professor? Not a doctor?" asked a blockfuehrer, and hit him on the head. The professor dropped to the ground like a felled tree. Blood trickled from one of his temples.

"Stand up!" roared the pack of brutes.

The professor scrambled up.

"Come forward," ordered a blockfuehrer, "and show us your degenerate art."

The professor was deathly pale. The only color in his face was the thread of blood which ran from his temple. He staggered, wiped away the blood with the back of his hand and tried to pull himself together.

"We will sing 'Das Roeslein auf der Heiden'!" he said in a trembling voice. Apparently it was the only song he could think of.

We began to sing:

> "Sah ein Knab' ein Roeslein stehen,
> Roeslein auf der Heiden. . . ."

What a mockery it was—the sweet melody and lovely words of this German song in that place! The representative of the "nation of poets and thinkers" fidgeted uneasily, then grew angry.

"Stop!" the order thundered out. "Professor, step forward."

The professor staggered forward.

"You Jewish dung!" screamed the blockfuehrer into his face. "First you said you were a professor and now you act as if you were the governess of these scoundrels and sing nursery songs." And he rained blows on the professor till his victim lay motionless on the ground.

That ended the singing. Another blockfuehrer now took us in hand.

"You bastards are better at screaming than singing. Now shout as loud as you can, 'We are Polish Jewish criminals,' and at the same time throw up your arms and keep turning around!"

We shouted with all the strength that was in us and turned round and round, in the same direction, for five minutes, ten minutes. Suddenly the whole building began to reel around us. Dizziness seized one man after another; we stumbled, bumped into each other, staggered like drunken men. A few minutes longer and the whole group would have fallen as one man.

Then came the releasing order: "Lie down. Hands behind your backs. Snouts to the ground. And don't move."

Relieved, we flung ourselves on the ground. It made no difference how, so long as we could just lie.

Our relief was short-lived, for the blockfuehrers surged over our bodies like stampeding cattle. Their iron-studded boots cut into our flesh. The pain was excruciating, yet no one dared to scream.

When they vanished into the day room, we breathed again. We hoped we could relax at last. But Paul appeared on the threshold and said in a malicious, cutting voice: "You'll lie where you are and not budge an inch, or I'll give you birds a little exercise."

With that he disappeared again, unable to endure the foul air. But every few minutes he would stick his head in the door to see if we were obeying his orders.

Our position became more and more unbearable. Our limbs ached from the unaccustomed and totally unnatural posture. Since the straw sacks and blankets were piled up against the wall, the room was even narrower than at night. We lay pressed together like sardines. Sweat poured from us in streams; it ran into our eyes and stung. Our eyes began to water and the tears mingled with the sweat and flowed down our faces. Our throats were bone-dry, and we eagerly licked up the salty drops.

Hour after hour passed in this way. No release came. I suffered more from thirst and want of air than from all the blows I had received. I longed for the once dreaded roll call. If it were only time! I kept thinking. If only we could get out into the air and breathe, breathe!

Suddenly screams of pain, the most dreadful we had yet heard, rang out from the day room. The blood stopped in our veins. What could be happening? The shrieks sounded insane. In fear for my comrades, I forgot my own anguish.

At last the door opened. A dozen men bolted into the dormitory as if the devil himself were on their track. They ran pell-mell over our bodies, their faces crazed with horror. Seeing us lying prone, they threw themselves down also, but their dazed minds did not grasp the fact that our position was an unusual one, so their bodies stood out from the others.

The blockfuehrers had counted on that. They followed upon the men's heels and stood in the doorway to see how their victims would meet the situation. When the men failed to assume the prescribed posture, they were ordered to stand up.

The blockfuehrers took them into the day room in relays and made them exercise there. First they had to stand on tiptoe and hop, with their arms stretched out in front of them. But the tortures they had already undergone had drained their strength; they kept falling. This enraged the blockfuehrers still more and they imposed even more strenuous exercise. They gave each man a stool to hold and ordered him to do a hundred knee bendings with the stool in his hand. Of course, no one was equal to this task; one after another collapsed after the first few knee bends. The result was murderous beating. Finally, the men were thrown back into the dormitory half dead.

From that moment a horrible stink of excrement spread through the dormitory. At first we did not know where it came from, but after a while we traced it to the men who had just been thrown back. After the roll call we learned the whole story.

While the carpenter squad was nailing up the windows of our barrack, these comrades had secretly slipped into the toilet. Their return had been cut off by the blockfuehrers who visited our block soon afterwards. Terrified, they had remained in the toilet, with the faint hope that they might thus escape the beatings in the dormitory. At first no one had noticed their absence. But then another group of blockfuehrers happened to look into the toilet and discovered the men hiding there.

A series of special tortures followed. First these men, like the prisoners in the dormitory, had to sing, turn around in circles and insult their own countrymen. Next they were pitilessly beaten and rolled about on the urine-covered floor. Then the perverted criminals ordered them to drink out of the toilet bowls. The men could not bring themselves to obey this devilish order; they only pretended to drink. But the blockfuehrers had reckoned with that; they forced the men's heads deep into the bowls until their faces were covered with excrement. At that the victims almost went out of their minds—that was why their screams had sounded so demented.

After the blockfuehrers had sufficiently vented their spite, they ordered the men to wash. But the urine, filth and excrement had soaked into their clothes and could not be removed; this was the source of the horrible stench that had pervaded our dormitory.

It was becoming ever more clear that what was inflicted on us was not the product of the individual blockfuehrer's diseased imagination, but part of a prepared plan of demoralization and annihilation. If that was how matters stood, then there was no hope of escaping the tortures, not even if we learned the most faultless military discipline. The punishments and tortures had been determined on in advance; the blockfuehrers would always find some pretext—and they were always right. We had seen an example of it. The evening before, the same blockfuehrers had beaten a man in my block almost to death because they claimed that he had torn the pocket off his coat. "That is sabotage," one of them had roared. "I'll teach you swine to show more respect for the property of the German Reich."

When at last it was time to go out to the midday roll call, we noticed that some of our comrades did not stir. They were dead. But we were so terrified that we dared not even give them a glance.

Numbly, as if we were dead to all compassion, we walked out. The air refreshed us, but we were too full of fear to recover fully.

This time, however, the blockfuehrers would not have anything to do with us. When they came to the roll call they wrinkled up their noses.

"The pack of Jews stinks to high heaven. What is the matter with them?" one of them asked Paul.

Paul whispered the explanation. Thereupon we were counted with the utmost haste and the blockfuehrers disappeared in a twinkling.

Paul had shortened our noon recess that day on his own authority. And since we were allowed to use the toilets only during the meal period, not many were able to relieve their needs. Stick in hand, Paul stood in the doorway of the toilet and beat unmercifully anyone who dared to approach it. Then he herded us back into the dormitory, and again we had to lie on our bellies and cross our hands behind our backs. In the meantime the heat had become wholly unbearable. The sun had passed the zenith and streamed in on us with full force through the windows on the other side of the room, pursuing its course through the heavens, indifferent to our parched throats and burning bodies. It seemed as if man and nature had joined forces against us. True, the frightful stench had ceased, for the men who caused it had changed their clothes. But the heat was unspeakable. Our bodies steamed as if in a Turkish bath. When Paul opened the door to inspect us, a cloud of vapor billowed toward him.

A few men were near suffocation, others were literally dying of thirst. We knew that they were dying and that a breath of air, a drink of water, could have saved them. Sick at heart, we had to look on impotently while they gasped their lives away. At last, a comrade who lay near the door could bear it no longer. He knocked on the door with his foot, called to Paul and begged him to bring a few drops of water for the dying. Paul took no notice whatsoever.

He must have thought better of it, though, for presently he opened the door and asked who wanted water. We turned our heads toward him unbelievingly. There was a devilish grin on his face and something in his voice warned us not to answer. But one man succumbed to the tempter. Paul promptly ordered him into the day room—a few moments later he was thrown back into the dormitory with a broken rib. He was one of our strongest comrades. We had not heard him scream, but now his pitiful groans, which filled the barrack, told us of what he had gone through.

It was plain that Paul meant us to die of thirst. To die of thirst in a desert is horrible, certainly. But to die of thirst, knowing that only a few yards away fresh, clear water is flowing abundantly, that only the brutal strength of a human being stands between life and death—can there be an end more agonizing than that?

A few minutes passed, then Paul opened the door again; he had a bucket in his hand. "Who wants water?" he asked.

But this time no one answered: we had seen what it had cost our comrade. Surely it was only a trick to pick out one of us and beat him up.

"What?" said Paul. "All of a sudden nobody's thirsty, eh?" His loathsome face was laughing and angry at the same time. Suddenly he put on a sulky expression and said with a well-acted air of injury: "I can't help it. I wanted to treat you to water, but the noble company don't want it any more. Well, I'm on to you now."

With a mighty swing of his arm he threw the precious contents of the bucket into the room. A few men were completely drenched. They reveled in the water which ran over them and greedily licked up all the drops that had fallen on their arms or clothes. When Paul noticed that he had, after all, treated some of us to water against his will, he ran out and slammed the door. We heard him cursing and raging in the day room and we knew that he would make us pay for his unintentional generosity.

That afternoon would not come to an end. We were completely stiff. Every cell in our bodies hurt. Several blockfuehrers appeared before the windows from time to time and when they thought that we were not lying as we had been ordered, they beat on the windowpane and heaped the vilest insults upon us. In terror lest they should come in, we lay as rigid as mummies, scarcely daring to move.

Paul had not let us use the toilet during the noon recess, and we had all gone for nine hours without relieving ourselves. In the barrack there were many who suffered from bladder trouble and now began to groan with pain. They called up all their strength to resist the impulse. But nature was stronger than their self-control. And as time went on, many of those who were not so afflicted could hold back no longer.

The sight and smell of urine nauseated the men lying near the others and made them vomit. The urine and vomit steamed in the heat; the mingled fumes stung our eyes and made us gag with nausea. For anyone who, only two days before, had been accustomed to bathe night and morning, this was almost beyond endurance. But there was only one alternative before us: either to keep our civilized sensibilities and lose our minds, or to sink into bestial indifference. This was the very purpose for which the Gestapo had established the concentration camp.

Suddenly we heard the order "Achtung!" shouted in the day room. Our hearts turned over. So they were back. We lay tense, ready to jump, but nothing happened. We knew that they were in the day room listening to see if we were keeping still. Suddenly the door was thrown open. Several blockfuehrers entered. No one shouted "Achtung!" but we instinctively jumped up. At that they all roared together: "Down, you swine, down! Who gave you polecats leave to stand up?" Terrified, we threw outselves on the floor again. Then they made merry at our expense. "Lying is a little uncomfortable; you get rather bored with it after a while, eh?"

"Let's bring a little life into the premises," suggested one of them and ordered, "Stand up—lie down, stand up—lie down." The commands came so quickly that it was impossible to obey. Some men were getting up while others were still lying down, and this disorder was the signal for the beating to begin. After we had all had our share of blows, the blockfuehrers took fifteen men into the day room and beat them unconscious.

It was horrible to hear the screams and to know that it was only a question of time until it would be one's own turn. There was no escape; even when a man was not being beaten himself, he suffered the torments of his neighbors. Even if he did not see them, he had to hear them, and the shrieks and blows went through him until he believed himself near madness. The worst thing was knowing that these horrors were not taking place only in our wing or in our barrack, but in all three Polish blocks of Sachsenhausen and among countless numbers of our countrymen in Weimar and Dachau and wherever German power prevailed.

Thinking of this, we grew more and more apathetic. Soon we no longer moved at all and the sighing ceased too. Only the gasps for breath continued and reminded us that death was in our midst. When at last it was time for the roll call and we could stand up once more, we moved as if in a daze. Many could no longer walk and we had to support them. The fresh air was overpowering, and everything whirled before our eyes.

When the blockfuehrers arrived, Paul reported, according to the regulations: "Block 38 present for roll call; 223 men, seven dead."

"Seven dead? That's too few," said a blockfuehrer in a hectoring tone. He walked up to the front line and looked with a pleased smirk at our disfigured faces. "A little hot today, eh?" he asked cynically. "But that's nothing. In the winter you'll make up for it by freezing." Then he went off, although the dismissal signal from the central tower had not yet sounded.

Paul was now running up and down in front of us. But he vouchsafed neither word nor look. I tried to read his inscrutable face: had he, after all, some qualms of conscience about the seven suffocated men whom he could so easily have saved? Or was he taking the indirect reproach of the blockfuehrer to heart and pondering how he could increase the toll of dead?

We could have wished that the roll call would last forever, so great was our horror of the stifling barrack. But just as we began to revive, the assembly ended and we had to go back. Bread was quickly distributed. Only a few took any, but we pounced upon the bowls of tea and drank it greedily. There was plenty of tea left in the kettle and we begged for a second helping. But Paul poured out the contents. Our hopes were now centered on the few moments when we would be allowed to go to the toilet room, where there was a water faucet. But Paul had taken care of that. "There's no time to waste in drinking," he explained spitefully. He had ordered the strongest man from the indoor squad to stand guard over the faucet. But this man could not bring himself to keep guard over the water when his comrades were nearly dead of thirst. He offered only a sham resistance, and a few men actually succeeded in getting a drink. But Paul soon noticed it and drove us out with a wooden truncheon; and he beat the guard insensible.

Then began a terrible night. Fear that the blockfuehrers would take us by surprise kept most of us awake. So the next morning we were dead from lack of sleep, although the SS men had not come. Our appearance had altered still more during the night. Most of our faces were covered with scabs and our heads with swellings. This sight threw us into a panic fear, and finally one man asked Paul if anything could be done about it. Paul grinned all over his face and said smugly: "There's nothing to be done. The Kommandant doesn't mind those potato heads one bit. Besides, what difference does it make? You're going to feed the worms anyhow."

As we came out for the morning roll call, a fresh breeze was blowing; our shaven heads felt a distinct sensation of coolness, and our hearts rose: the barrack would not be so hot as on the previous day. But our hopes were soon dashed. When the blockfuehrers arrived and Paul made his report, they did not remain as usual to count us but went inside the barrack and beckoned Paul to follow. This was a departure from routine and we knew at once that something was wrong.

While the blockfuehrers were storming about inside, throwing open cupboard doors and slamming them again, we tried to guess what new deviltry they were up to, so that we might be prepared. In a few minutes they were back. One of them had some pieces of bread in his hand and screamed in a voice hoarse with rage: "Whose bread is this?"

We all began to tremble. The men who had thoughtlessly left the bread in the cupboard that morning were dumb with fear.

"What?" shouted the blockfuehrer still louder. "You damned saboteurs won't answer? You dare to waste German bread? You turn up your noses at it? Just wait, you scum. I'll teach you to value it better. Then turning to Paul, he added: "No bread for forty-eight hours and the liquid ration is to be cut in half."

"And now do knee bending," he ordered.

It was the first time that our whole block had had to do knee bending and consequently the men did not keep time. "Aha!" snarled the blockfuehrers. "The pack of Jews won't do it. That's mutiny." And hell broke loose. When at last we were dismissed, we could barely drag ourselves back to the barrack.

A few days later we learned that the room senior of Block 37 was to blame for the withdrawal and reduction of our rations and the terrible beatings. Several of the prisoners in Block 37 had hidden their bread in the cupboards for the night and had not removed it quickly enough the next morning. Their room senior had noticed it and, to get into favor, had gone immediately to the office and denounced his block. The result was a search in all three blocks.

It was shortly before the noon roll call, and we were once more lying on our faces with our hands crossed behind us when Paul entered the dormitory with an important expression. He carried sewing materials and a large bundle. "Which of you are tailors?" he asked. Instantly thirty men jumped up. They thought they were needed for a sewing job and could thus escape the terrible sweat cure. But Paul disappointed them. "You're crazy," he said. "I need four, five at the most. That's plenty," and he picked out five men; the others had to stretch out again.

Then he opened his bundle. It contained triangles of red and yellow material. In Sachsenhausen every prisoner had to wear not only his prison number but a triangular piece of colored cloth on the left side of his coat. The color of the triangle indicated the reason for imprisonment. A red triangle meant "political"; a brown, "antisocial"; a blue, "attempt to escape across the frontier"; a violet, "Bible student"; a rose, "homosexual"; a green, "dangerous criminal"; and a yellow, "Jew."

Prisoners accused of more than one offense wore several triangles side by side. All of the Jewish prisoners wore more than one triangle. Whether they were stigmatized as Communists, money smugglers or homosexuals, they must display the Jewish triangle as well. Furthermore, the Jews were not allowed to wear their insignia side by side but must stitch one above the other so that the two triangles formed a star of David. A Jewish prisoner accused of two offenses must also wear two yellow triangles: in this way each emblem of crime was completed with yellow angles to make a Jewish star. Thus, even in the camp itself, the Nazis' anti-Jewish propaganda did not stop.

Paul told the tailors how to attach the triangles to our coats and ordered them to finish in time for roll call. The tailors worked at lightning speed, and when we went out to the assembly place a brilliant red-and-yellow Star of David shone on our left breasts. I felt that our sacred symbol, which the Nazis were using as a brand of insult, was a badge of honor.

Our comrades from the other two blocks were decorated in the same way. In front of all three barracks, the room seniors and their assistants were running around excitedly to see if the stars were in the correct place. Paul was utterly dissatisfied with his tailors' work. He cursed till the air turned blue, and promised to make the tailors pay dearly.

As the blockfuehrers approached, they began to laugh and crack jokes about us. "Just look at those Bolsheviks!" they kept shouting. "So the dream of world domination is definitely out," said one, and another proposed, "Let's just see if these would-be world conquerors can hop at least. Get going! Hop!"

For twenty minutes we hopped without interruption, bathed with sweat from the strain. One after another of the old and weak fell to the ground. While we went on hopping, the blockfuehrers devoted their attention to the fallen. When at last we were allowed to stop, three men were dead.

Completely exhausted, we returned to the barrack. Our first reduced noon ration was distributed. And then a curious thing happened. Whether it was because of the first cool day or because our bodies had used up their reserves, most of us all at once felt ravenously hungry. But there were only half-rations in the kettles.

Of course, Paul kept his promise to the tailors. When we lay down again, he took the five men into the day room and beat them until they could scream no longer. Then he flung them back into the dormitory. A few minutes later he came in himself and made his first and only speech.

"Now see here, tailors," he said, "I tell you once and for all I won't put up with sloppiness. I told you plainly enough how to sew on those stars, but you scoundrels made a hash of it. I can't use such bunglers. Where's the other twenty-five tailors?"

Strange to say, only four men reported themselves this time. "What!" cried Paul, flying into a rage, "Where have the others gotten to all of a sudden? They can't all be dead. There were only three corpses today, weren't there?" But still the other tailors did not report themselves. Then Paul grew threatening. "Of course, I've got enough with this bunch of shrimps here," he said, "but I'd give a lot to know who's got the nerve to disobey me. If the others don't report in five minutes, I'll yank them out." He said "yank them out" in a voice which purred with anticipation. Before the five minutes were up, all twenty-five tailors were on their feet.

Paul took his chin in his great fist and scratched the back of his head with his other hand, as he always did when thinking. After a short pause, he said: "If I wanted to I might have some fun with you birds, but I'll put that off till later; I'm not quite in the mood right now. My punches have got to do some good, see? But I've sprained my right hand on those damned hoppers. Everybody's got to be lucky sometime, and you birds are plenty lucky now."

Then he ordered: "The tailors that reported themselves first can stand up; the rest of you lie down." The men who, thanks to Paul's sprained hand, still had sound limbs threw themselves down in a twinkling. The four chosen men stood rigid, especially one of them, a short, stout fellow, who might have been on parade. Paul did not care for such tokens of respect. "You, Patachon"—he turned to the short, stout man—"you needn't stand so stiff. I'm no blockfuehrer." Then he addressed all four tailors. "Just remember this: I won't stand for any nonsense. So, tomorrow you'll sew the prisoners' numbers on the coats and take off those that are sewed on wrong, and put them in the right place. And get the lousy workers to give you the sewing materials." With these words, he opened the door and disappeared. We could see that he was very pleased with himself.

This scene had brought a noticeable cheerfulness into our dormitory for the first time. Paul's self-conscious twaddle was so ridiculous. The name "Patachon," which he had applied to the short tailor, was so apt; instantly we thought of the film comedian Patachon. The amusing memory diverted our minds. Patachon, to whom, of course, this nickname clung thenceforward, and his three colleagues became the butts of general raillery. Some of the other tailors declared that the four were not tailors but pressers, and they plied the four men with technical questions. But since the four were no fools, their quick-witted rejoinders made us laugh, and for a while we forgot our unhappy situation. For the first time in two days there was laughter in our barrack, and we began to talk together in whispers.

But when the subject was exhausted, our cheerfulness visibly evaporated. We were once more aware of the heat, which had grown worse. The sun was shining remorselessly again, and the asthmatics suffered pitifully. We listened with anxiety to their gasping breath, and it wrung our hearts that we could do nothing to help them.

Fortunately, we had found a makeshift to help the men with bladder trouble. A comrade who usually lay beside one of the outer walls suddenly discovered that there was a hole in the floorboard close to the window. During the noon recess we had surreptitiously probed the opening with a broomstick. When the hole proved fairly deep, we decided that from then on all the bladder sufferers should lie near that window, so that they could crawl to the hole in case of need.

Crawling there was dangerous. We held our breaths for fear that just at that moment Paul might come in or the blockfuehrers peer through the window. But, after all, those were lesser evils. What mattered most was that this expedient gave the sufferers some relief. The spectacle of these unfortunates, shaking with fear as they crawled on hands and knees to the hole and relieved themselves lying down, is one of my most terrible memories of Sachsenhausen.

Late in the afternoon, Paul in great excitement snatched open the door and ordered us to form ranks in front of the barrack. Through the window I saw that in both other blocks all the men were on their feet and hurrying out. As I ran through the day room, I glanced at Paul's alarm clock. It was only 3:45, an unusual time to hold a roll call. Evidently something special was afoot.

When we were standing in rank and file, I noticed that a loud-speaker was set up on the roof of a neighboring block. I whispered it to my neighbor. The news spread along the rows like wildfire. Hundreds of frightened eyes turned toward the loud-speaker. Was the war over? Had Warsaw surrendered? Our excitement and suspense grew from moment to moment, but nothing happened to give us any clue. Strange to say, there was not a blockfuehrer in sight. At last—it must have been nearly six—a signal sounded from the main tower. Then we heard drumming, which seemed to come from a platoon of drums. Orders rang out in the distance. Then Paul, too, issued orders: "Stand still, eyes right." He himself and the room seniors of the other two blocks also stood rigid. Suddenly the loud-speaker began to roar. But it was out of order; we heard only gurglings and here and there disconnected words. Apparently a speech was being made. But about what?

We stood like that for about twenty minutes. Then a salvo of shots rang out. Fear overwhelmed us. Were prisoners being executed? And were we next in line?

When a group of blockfuehrers approached, we were convinced that our last hour had come. But they merely ordered Paul to make us sleep that night on the bare wooden floor. This increased our misgivings. When we were back in the barrack, black depression took hold of us. The strictly orthodox comrades withdrew into a corner and recited the prayers for the dead, preparing themselves for death.

From all sides came sobs and bitter lamentations, and everyone spoke only of dying.

"What difference does it make," asked my neighbor, "if we are shot tomorrow or the day after? And there are worse things than being shot."

"It isn't a question of the easiest way to die," said another. "My pride rebels at the thought that those perverted brutes should have the power to kill us whenever it pleases them. If I were not so old and weak, I'd take my own life. But you young ones will be cowards if you let those butchers decide when your lives shall end."

Strange! I could not feel as most of my comrades did. On the day of our arrival in the camp, I had sustained myself with the thought of suicide. I had furtively kept back my trouser belt when we had to give up our civilian clothes. During the first night, I had worked out a plan, and the next day I had looked at every beam in the barrack to see if it was capable of supporting a man. And even on the second night, after I had won back my confidence, there were moments when I could scarcely resist the temptation to end my life. But on the following morning, when I saw how Paul piled up the dead bodies like steps of stairs, how the blockfuehrers played football with them, I put from me all thought of suicide; then my horror of death in Sachsenhausen became even greater than my horror of life there. And my one prayer, which trembled on my lips every moment, was that I might come out of this den alive, even if it were only to die in cleanliness and freedom.

The same scenes of despair that took place in our wing were repeated, of course, in Wing B, where Paul's assistant was in charge. He observed the lamentations for a while and could not understand what had upset the prisoners so. At last he asked them and the comrades told him of their fears.

Now, Paul's assistant was a quite decent fellow and felt sympathy for the men. On condition that Paul should learn nothing about it, he told them what had happened on the assembly place. Two prisoners from the Bible students' block had been publicly executed because they had expressed the opinion that war was a crime and every soldier a murderer. Their room senior had overheard these remarks and reported them to the office. Thereupon the men were taken to the Bunker and horribly tortured. Their shooting, in the presence of the whole camp, was intended as an example.

After this account, our comrades' agitation subsided and their one thought was to pass on to us the reassuring news. Under cover of darkness, one of them slipped into our wing. The story was whispered from man to man, and we breathed freely again.

The floor, on which we now had to stretch out, was slimy with filth. Urine, sweat and other bodily exhalations saturated the planks and gave off a disgusting smell. It turned our stomachs to lie on that floor, but we had been so prostrated by fear and so exhausted by nervous tension that we could not long resist the need to lie down.

Now we understood why we had to lie on the bare boards that night: it was a punishment for the crime of the Bible students. To be sure, we had nothing to do with the Bible students, but we had already learned that we had to suffer for every offense that was committed anywhere in the camp.

That night the blockfuehrers visited us three times at short intervals. Again they left several dead men behind. Our numbers were so reduced that from then on it was no longer necessary for three men to share a straw sack.

How long were they going to torture us in this way? I pondered when the room was quiet again. Would not our official representatives interfere? In truth, the Swedes were chiefly to blame for our situation. If they had taken seriously their pledged word to uphold Polish interests, and had promptly demanded an assurance from the German government that Polish enemy aliens should be treated according to international law, we would never have come to Sachsenhausen, we would not have been arrested with the stain of the alleged "Bromberg murders" upon us—our murdered comrades would still be alive.

Naïve though it seems to me today, I still believed then that the Swedes would make up for their neglect. They must have learned by this time what was being done to us, for our families must have gone to the Swedish Legation in Berlin and reported our arrest. Surely the Swedish Legation had then asked the Foreign Ministry for full particulars. So our release could not be long delayed.

The next morning was our fifth day and our first Sunday in the concentration camp. When we went out to roll call, heavy clouds hung in the sky. This promised rain, and we rejoiced that the sun would not torment us that day.

Paul presented his report book as usual and announced the number of dead.

"What, so few?" said a blockfuehrer. "The vermin are too tough; they just won't die."

Then he mustered our ranks. Our faces were like death masks. The blockfuehrer looked at us cynically.

"What, wasn't it nice sleeping on the floor?" he asked. "You swine don't know how well off you are. The pigs in Poland haven't even a roof over their damned heads and here you are being fed—on good German bread."

Brutal and cynical speeches no longer made the same impression on us as at first. We knew that they were designed to break our spirits and we had grown indifferent to them.

Paul was in a particularly malicious mood that morning. He left his assistant to supervise our formation, while he himself stalked up and down with a devilish grin on his face. "To make up for last night, you get goulash with real Pilsener today," he said and laughed loudly at his own wit.

The assistant was remarkably excited and beat us severely, which he had never done before. Paul followed him with an angry look. We sensed that something was wrong between the two, and after the noon roll call we found out. Paul, who had learned in some mysterious way that the assistant had told us about the shooting of the Bible students, had accused his subordinate of laxness and sentimentality. The terrified assistant had beaten us that morning to clear himself of this accusation. But Paul was not to be bluffed. Immediately after the roll call he went to the office and demanded a more efficient helper.

Later in the morning, when we were lying on the floor as usual, Paul came to us with a list of prisoners and a bag full of numbers made of cloth, which had to be sewn on the prisoners' coats.

"Which of you can read and write properly?" he asked.

Each one of us reported himself.

"Oh, yes," said Paul, "I know the answer; you're all very educated. But I just need one man and he's got to be good. I can't read just any old scrawl. It's got to be like in the books." (By this he meant printing.)

Then he chose several men and made them write out samples of their penmanship. He criticized the samples as if he were a teacher of penmanship, and finally picked out one man, whom he ordered to copy the list of prisoners.

In the meantime Paul distributed the prisoners' numbers and ordered the tailors appointed on the previous day to sew them on. The work had to be ready by the noon roll call, and Paul warned the tailors in both wings to hurry, or he would put them "on the retired list." The tailors worked with flying needles, but nothing was right for Paul that morning. He cursed, abused them, ran from one wing to the other. In Wing B particularly he screamed, beat and threatened, "There'll soon be order here. I've seen to that."

We too, in our wing, were very uneasy. The day before, several comrades had contracted a strange inflammation of the eyes, which was growing worse and spreading to other prisoners. Although the lids were not closed up, the men found it difficult to see. We were afraid it was some very serious disease and that our comrades might lose their sight. Their appearance shocked us. Their blood-red eyes, which formed such a glaring contrast to their prevailing pallor, made their scratched and swollen faces still more repulsive. And we were afraid that the blockfuehrers, who were always looking for peculiarities in our appearance, would pick out these unfortunates and beat them to death.

Paul saw our uneasiness. We could see that he knew the cause, but he pretended not to notice. When one man asked what could be done for the sick, he gave no answer at all. Instead, he drove us out to roll call twenty minutes earlier than usual. It was pouring in torrents, and Paul could not deny himself the satisfaction of seeing us drenched through.

Of course, Paul's example was immediately followed by the room seniors of the two other blocks. At first we found the rain actually refreshing. After the stifling closeness of the barrack, we breathed eagerly the clean, rain-washed air. It was the first time since the day of our arrival that we had come in contact with so much water, and after all the filth we had been smeared with, this was a precious luxury.

But the streaming rain soon penetrated our thin cotton clothes, and the water ran down our bodies and into our shoes. The loose soil in front of the barrack had become mud, in which we stood ankle-deep. Several SS officers came out of the elite block wearing high waterproof boots and spick-and-span rain capes with hoods. "The

Polish pigs will at least be clean for once," they remarked as they passed us.

In the barrack, the floor was covered with puddles, which mingled with the filth and dust to form a nauseating mixture. It revolted us to lie down, drenched as we were, and soak up more filth into our clothes. But there was no help for it. We had to lie on our faces, cross our hands behind our backs, and sweat, sweat. Our clothes soon began to dry on our bodies. In the heat of the room the moisture evaporated quickly, but it remained in the air as a thick, penetrating fog.

Late in the afternoon we saw Paul's assistant leaving Wing B with a bundle under his arm. Soon afterwards his successor arrived—Rolly, the Danzig criminal.

The new assistant looked like an ogre out of a fairy tale. Not that he was especially large; but his body was like a pillar: strong, compact, massive. His head rested on his shoulders as if he had no neck. His walk was the walk of a gorilla; when he moved, everyone fell back before him to keep from being trampled down. In his iron grip, ribs snapped like matches, and the man whom he hit on the head never got up again.

Our comrades in Wing B told us later how Paul introduced the new assistant. "Your friend's gone for good," he had said. "Here's the substitute. But I can promise you this much: things are going to be very different from now on. Eh, Rolly?"

Rolly winked. "I sure won't make the mistake the other guy did," he answered. "I'd rather beat the whole bunch to death than let anybody call *me* sentimental." And to show Paul that he meant what he said, he ordered forthwith: "Stand up and then lie down slick as a whistle—and not a peep out of you, either—or I'll make short work of you."

When they were lying down again, he set about "correcting mistakes." At that Paul left Wing B quite satisfied. Rolly's correction was so thorough that several men were left dead.

When Paul thought that Rolly had had time enough to "make friends" with his charges, he summoned him to our wing. "These are my pupils," he said. "But when I'm not here—you know how much I've got on my shoulders—then you can run the show."

"You can count on me, Paul," said Rolly.

We shuddered at the sound of his voice. It was hoarse, deep, drunken and indescribably brutal.

From that day on a new regime began in our block. Paul and Rolly carried on a contest in beating, and we suffered as never before. But there were always more dead in Wing B than among us, for while Paul's passion was beating, Rolly's was murder.

We had rightly feared that the installation of the new assistant would bring down upon us a special visit from the blockfuehrers. About three o'clock in the afternoon a large number of them arrived. They made us stand up and lie down for fifteen minutes, and when we were completely out of breath they took us through the whole routine of exercises: hopping, knee bending, rolling, frog-hopping and "pumping." The pumping required unusual muscular strength, for the exercise consisted in lying face downward with bent elbows and then straightening the elbows and rising until we stood on the tips of our toes.

The exercises were accompanied by beating; then we were trodden upon. The treading had now become a system: the blockfuehrers aimed their footsteps where they would be most effective. When we lay on our backs they aimed at the liver. When we lay on our faces they aimed at the kidneys. Usually it required only a single footstep to "assist" a victim "into eternity."

When the blockfuehrers were finished with us, they went to Wing B, then to the other Polish blocks, for further celebrations of Rolly's appointment.

On the morning of September 18, our sixth day in camp, something unexpected happened. As we went out to the morning roll call a "runner" came up. He had a notice from the office, which he handed to Paul. The name of a man in my wing was called out, and before we realized what was happening the runner and our comrade, an engineer named Heller, were hurrying off together to the office.

We were completely at a loss. What did Heller's summons mean?

Back in the barrack, wild speculation began. Heller had been on the executive committee of the Federation of Polish Jews in Germany. Many of us suggested that because of this position he would be held accountable and shot. Others believed that Heller was merely wanted for questioning. Some extreme optimists thought that he would be released. The majority, however, would have nothing of this last hypothesis. Why should Heller be released first? This, of course, was unreasonable; somebody had to be first. But the anxious, broken men were no longer capable of logic.

Paul wrapped himself, as always, in an air of ignorance. During the whole morning he made no comment on what had happened. When we rose for the noon roll call, he remarked very casually: "Your buddy is now a head shorter. And your turn will come—all of you."

That morning Rolly had reveled in his job as assistant. But his field of operations in his own wing was too small for him. So he paid us a visit to bring order. Paul did not oppose this intrusion into his own domain. For he was beginning to be afraid of his assistant.

Rolly went to work at once. When we were all lying on our faces he walked over us, just as the blockfuehrers did. Rolly, however, weighed about 275 pounds. But Rolly had also carefully observed the blockfuehrers during their visit to his wing, and had learned from them where the kidneys were. It was not long before several of his victims were silenced forever.

Rolly also took over the supervision of our formation at noon roll call. So, when the SS men arrived, we were more dead than alive and could stay on our feet only with the greatest effort.

After roll call, while we were dragging ourselves back to the barrack, the mystery of Heller's departure was unexpectedly cleared up. One of the comrades from Block 37 contrived, at great danger to himself, to run past us and call out to the nearest man: "Heller's been released—there's no doubt of it." This message passed from mouth to mouth, and for a time our hearts beat in a new, hopeful rhythm. If Heller had been released, would he not immediately inform the Swedish Legation of conditions in Sachsenhausen? And if the Swedes had hitherto made no efforts on our behalf, would they not intervene now?

But the sceptics would not listen. Heller would be too frightened, they said, to report on conditions in the camp. Didn't every prisoner on his release have to sign a statement that he would say nothing? And how could we be sure that Heller had really been released? They would not allow themselves to hope. The only certainty before us, they maintained, was that we would either smother or be beaten to death. And with that they dismissed the "Heller affair."

But the comrade from Block 37 had really told the truth, and we later found out why Block 37 had been sure about Heller's release. That morning a room senior of a neighboring block had visited the room senior of Block 37, and the indoor squad had heard the visitor say angrily: "Can you beat it? I've seen all sorts of funny things, but I never would have dreamed that one of the Bromberg murderers would be released."

The day after Heller's release Rolly took the reins into his own hands. He behaved as if he were the room senior and Paul his assistant. Paul boiled with suppressed rage, but he dared not put Rolly in his place. He could not lay the ghost he had conjured up.

Rolly now paid us regular visits. Once he appeared a little later than usual. "You thought I'd forgotten you, I guess," he said. "Fat chance!" Then he fell to work on us like a man who has to perform his daily stint, but suddenly he stopped beating us and asked abruptly: "Which of you are criminals?"

None of us were—and this lowered us in Rolly's estimation. "You're a bunch of sissies," he said scornfully. Then he returned to his beating.

From that day on, Rolly took it upon himself to see that the "sweat cure" was carried out according to orders. He used to open the door when we least expected it, and woe to anyone who was caught moving at such a moment. Rolly also took care that the door between the day room and the dormitory should remain closed, even while we were at roll call. Thus the stifling air was no longer renewed at all.

But as the danger of suffocation became worse, one of our comrades had a saving thought. We must try to open the trap door in the roof, at least during the night. It was not nailed up, merely made fast to a hook high on the wall. To open it, all we had to do was to unwind the rope from the hook. The plan meant risking the lives of the whole wing, perhaps of the whole barrack. Nevertheless we all voted for it because it was our only chance of surviving the next few days, which might perhaps bring some change in our lot.

Several of the younger men volunteered to make the attempt. When we lay down at night, they arranged to lie near each other. They waited until the camp was entirely dark and silent. Then one climbed on another's shoulders until the topmost man could reach the hook on the wall. The rest of us, in desperate suspense, held what little breath remained in our lungs.

The rope was unwound, the trap door opened. For the first time in days, fresh air poured into the room. We slept very little that night for fear that we might oversleep and fail to close the trap door before Paul awoke in the morning.

When this attempt succeeded, we decided to keep the trap door open each night thereafter. At first we opened it only a crack, but soon we left it wide open. During the remainder of the attempt to suffocate us, which lasted until September 29, the cool night air coming in saved the lives of those who had any resistance left.

Often there were dangerous moments. One night it began to rain heavily. Before we could close the trap door, the straw sacks beneath it were soaked through. Upon collecting the sacks the next morning we succeeded in hiding the wet ones between the others. Another time, the rope caught on the trap door, and all our efforts could not untangle it. We had only a few moments before the alarm clock went off. Again one of our comrades had an inspiration: he folded his blanket into a tight roll and with the whole weight of his body hurled it against the trap door—the rope slipped free.

On September 20, two days after Heller's release, another comrade, a man named Leitner, in Block 37, was summoned to the office by a runner. I was then convinced that the two releases had some connection, and I firmly believed that they meant a decisive turn in our fortunes. There would now be two witnesses to inform the Swedes of our fate.

My confidence proved illusory. Swedish representation of Polish interests was a shameless farce. After my release Gucia told me how indifferent the Swedes had been to all appeals for help. Leitner and Heller had indeed reported all the cruelties to which we had been subjected. Polish women, individually and in groups, had appealed to the Swedes for intervention. Gucia, believing that facts are stronger than words, had compiled a list of all the casualties in the camp and submitted it. But the Swedes did not lift a finger. Obviously they did not want to risk, for our sakes, their friendly political and trade relations with Germany. Thus the Swedes bear part of the responsibility for the lives snuffed out in Sachsenhausen.

The day after Leitner's release, instead of an improvement, a new wave of terror set in. I could not understand it. Only later, when we came in contact with other prisoners who had access to newspapers, and I learned what had been happening both in the camp and in the outside world, did I realize what determined the time-table of SS terror.

The SS staff of the concentration camp recorded, with the sensitivity of a seismograph, every event connected with the campaign in the east. Our bodies were the roll of paper on which the seismograph traced its record; our blood was used instead of ink. Our wounds and our casualties plotted the graph of German difficulties. When the handful of Polish heroes so bitterly defended the Westernplatte, when the heroic city of Warsaw refused to surrender, the curve of our sufferings automatically rose.

There was no anti-German manifestation anywhere abroad which did not affect the three Polish blocks. Every public speech sympathetic to Poland was repaid by the SS with the extinction of several Polish lives. The more plainly the conscience of the world expressed itself, the more our blood flowed.

During the night of September 20–21, it rained heavily. When we went out to roll call that morning, the ground was soaked. That gave the blockfuehrers a good idea: they made us lie face downward in the mud, crawl on our bellies toward the barracks and drink out of the puddles which had formed in the hole-pitted ground. When the comrades had dragged themselves to the holes, Rolly stood ready to pounce on anyone who only pretended to obey the order, and to force him to drink.

After this performance, we were dismissed. Scarcely had we returned to the barrack when another devilish act began. Armed with a heavy cudgel, Rolly ordered the comrades in Wing B to run into our dormitory. Then Paul appeared and announced that we had all been ordered to lie in the same room.

"Of course, it will be a little cramped," he said, "but don't worry; we'll manage all right." With these words, he went off and left the field to Rolly.

Rolly planted himself in front of the door, swung his cudgel with relish and took care to leave us in no doubt of what his presence meant.

"I'm staying here," said he, "and any saboteur that opens his trap will be hauled off in a hurry."

We looked around us. How could we all lie down together when there was barely room to stand? But orders must be obeyed. We made ourselves as small as possible and squeezed up together as best we could. Many had to lie on top of each other, but the impossible was accomplished somehow.

Rolly, however, had planned matters otherwise. We had to lie on our bellies, as on the preceding days. When his criminal eye ascertained that this was physically impossible, he ordered: "A thin man on top of a fat," and immediately proceeded to put this arrangement into effect. With each hand he pulled out a thin man and tossed him into the air, while his legs forcibly disentangled the human knot, until he had rolled two fat men together, then he threw the two thin men down on top of them. Like Gulliver amid the Lilliputians, he moved among our bodies, threw us around as if we were wood, seized us by the neck, the leg, the arm, wherever he could get a grip.

For a few breathless minutes we suffered it. Then came the unexpected. As if at a signal, we all began to scream deafeningly. Rolly's grip relaxed for a moment; he let fall the two men he had just picked up and looked around him with a baffled expression. Then his face grew fiery red, his eyes glared with the lust to kill. But our screaming did not stop. Suddenly it became too much for Rolly; he ran out of the room.

It was not long before he was back. Apparently he had hurt his hand during the beating, for he was rubbing it as he returned. We knew the hurt hand would not lessen his power to beat; it had only goaded him to worse fury. His eyes were savage, and his body crouched like that of a beast of prey, ready to spring. The look of him made us shudder, for we knew it spelled death for many.

But Rolly's purpose was frustrated. Suddenly the dormitory door was opened from without, and several blockfuehrers, accompanied by camp guards, stood on the threshold. Apparently the guards had heard our screams and reported them to their superiors. Rolly looked very pale and so did Paul, who had not shown himself until now. Neither of them had reckoned on the appearance of the guards and the blockfuehrers.

When Paul shouted "Achtung!" we were slow in getting to our feet because of the crowd. Strangely enough, the SS men made no objection. "What are the Polaks yelling bloody murder for?" one of them asked. Paul answered that we had stubbornly refused to lie on our stomachs.

"Hm," said the blockfuehrer doubtfully. That the "Bromberg murderers" had refused to carry out an order sounded incredible to him.

"Lie down," he ordered suddenly. Somehow he seemed a little less callous than the others.

"Hm," he muttered, after we had taken a long time to squeeze together. Then, followed by his escort, he went into the day room without another word and beckoned Paul and Rolly to follow him. As the indoor squad told us later, he gave them no praise, but decreed that the Polaks should be left as they were. Although the sole purpose of putting the two wings together was to double the congestion and hasten the process of suffocation, the SS man had been generous enough to grant that at least we might suffocate in a more agreeable manner.

Our instinctive cooperation had gained us a victory. For a while we rejoiced in this mournful triumph over the two dehumanized criminals, although we knew that we should eventually pay for it. Rolly had planned the "thin on fat" arrangement—just as Paul had planned the staircase arrangement of the corpses a few days earlier—for the special diversion of the blockfuehrers. He would not forgive us for spoiling his joke and robbing him of the expected recognition.

With twice as many men in the room, the air was becoming perceptibly fouler and our bodies more evil-smelling. The discharges from our wounds stank. The moisture which steamed from our mud-soaked clothes gave off an odor like that of marshy soil. Again we were confronted with the needs of the bladder sufferers, who did not dare to disengage themselves from the solid human mass and crawl to the hole. They wet their clothes and filled the air with the reek of urine and ammonia fumes. Many wet their neighbors as well, and this led to outbursts of resentment.

In this inferno-like atmosphere some comrades breathed their last, squeezed up in the solid human block. Their dead bodies remained pressed against their comrades and so grew stiff. It was a fearful death, and yet our anguish of soul was so great that for a while we envied the suffocated men their sordid end. We felt so lost and abandoned, so shamed and degraded, that we found the thought of living unbearable. Many began to lament their powers of resistance, which prolonged their lives only to expose them to greater shame.

In those terrible hours, in which so many of my comrades sweated out their lives, in which the only certainty before the survivors was death in a stinking mass grave, I envied the soldiers at the front their death in battle. How sweet to die defending one's country, fighting for an ideal; how bitter to die shamed, degraded, with only the animal functions left!

After the First World War a stricken world had built a monument to the memory of the Unknown Soldier. After the Second World War a purified world must build a monument to the memory of the Unknown Martyr. An Eternal Light must burn for the nameless millions who have languished and perished in the cities, villages, ghettos and concentration camps of this tormented world.

The news that the two Polish wings had been put into one soon spread through the camp. From time to time new groups of blockfuehrers came to our windows to watch the Polish Jews suffocate. One group opened our door, stationed themselves outside it and diverted each other with remarks about stinking "Jewish vermin." Several of them even ventured into the sweat-box, holding their noses. But they could not stand it and retreated as quickly as they had come.

That day more men died than ever before, and we knew that the night would claim still more lives. We dreaded the coming of darkness, which fell quickly. When the evening ration—only a few of us could touch it—had been distributed, and the last possible moment for laying out the straw sacks had come, Paul at last condescended to give us an explanation. Reluctantly he informed us that we were to be separated for the night and might even sleep on the straw sacks. This was deliverance. In our relief many of us began to sob aloud. Others began to laugh. Still others collapsed weakly, without uttering a sound, while the more materialistic pulled their bread out of their pockets and hastily began to eat.

Then, at about eight o'clock in the evening, when everyone was asleep, the loud-speaker on the roof of our barrack suddenly went into action. A chime of bells played the opening notes of the old familiar folksong which the Germans consider an expression of their national character:

> Be true and honest all thy days,
> Up to the hour of death;
> And err not from God's holy ways
> Even by a finger's breadth.

> *"Ueb' immer Treu und Redlichkeit*
> *Bis an dein kuehles Grab,*
> *Und weiche keinen Finger breit*
> *Von Gottes Wegen ab."*

It was the customary interim signal of the German radio station "Koenigswusterhausen."

A few moments later the announcer's voice was heard introducing a broadcast of the "Strength through Joy" organization. A Party member began to speak and, in the usual Nazi cant, described how a German family should spend its leisure time. Then music flowed from the loud-speaker, rippling and surging, swelling and exulting. They were playing Bach's *Toccata in D Minor*. The organ notes, falling like pearls, filled me with sorrowful joy. I forgot where I was, I forgot all suffering; I thought only what I always used to think when I heard this toccata—such harmonies must the ancients have had in mind when they spoke of the music of the spheres.

The music stopped. My joy vanished and in its place was an unrest which filled my heart to bursting. All at once I realized what sadism had prompted the sending of such a broadcast to a concentration camp. What had the prisoners in Sachsenhausen to do with leisure? Why did the Nazis dangle before the eyes of men hopelessly enslaved this picture of happy family life? It was the most cunning form of spiritual torture.

In those few terrible days I had forgotten that there was such a thing as freedom. This voice from the outer world awoke in me a longing I had believed extinct. For a time I lost control of myself altogether. So fierce a hunger for freedom burned in me that I felt I could not endure another day in this prison: I *must* make an effort to escape. I sat up. With frantic haste I put on pants, jacket, boots. But when I started to get up, it was as if a hand had been laid on my feet, pinning them to the floor. A voice spoke in my ear: "Fool! What are you doing? You are going, not to freedom, but to certain death. And your comrades will suffer for your folly. Have you forgotten? 'All for one' is the law of the camp!"

The frenzy left me. I was calm again, and I felt ashamed of my weakness, which might have sent not only me but my innocent comrades to destruction. As quietly as I could, I undressed again. As I was putting my boots under the head of the mattress, where we had to keep them, my neighbor awoke. "What are you doing?" he asked.

"I had a terrible dream," I stammered in embarrassment. But my neighbor did not even hear; he was much too tired. He turned over and went back to sleep at once. And I was thankful to escape further questioning, for I would not for the world have admitted my weakness.

But I could find no more peace that night. The radio broadcast had thrown me entirely off balance. The blood pounded through my veins as if racing for a wager. Later, when we went out to work and I was able to speak with other prisoners, I heard that the periodic radio broadcasts had the same shattering effect on all of them. No one could resist it, although everyone knew very well that such broadcasts were designed to harrow us and to break our spiritual resistance.

That same night as I tossed sleeplessly from side to side, I suddenly noticed that the window of Block 37 was lighted up—this meant that the blockfuehrers were there. I woke my sackmates. We listened, holding our breath. In a few minutes terrible shrieks reached our ears. So they were beating again, and we would be able to tell when they had finished with Block 37 and were on their way to us. Soon everyone was awake.

When the door actually did open and Paul cried "Achtung!" we were prepared. In a few seconds we were all on our feet. The blockfuehrers were taken aback. Incredulously they swung their torches over the room. What? Not a single "dreamer"? In spite of all their efforts, they could not find one. They merely told us to lie down again. It was the first time they had not beaten us. We owed this to the fact that we were not the first but the second block to be visited that night. In a concentration camp such trivial accidents were matters of life and death.

About ten o'clock the next morning our two tormentors reappeared. "Who's got some money in the camp deposit?" asked Paul.

The unexpected question puzzled us. Almost all of us had money with us when we arrived at the camp and had been required to give it up in the shower room. Had the camp treasurers now decided to give us receipts? Were we to be transferred to an internment camp and did the camp authorities want to find out which of us could pay for his own transportation? Or had the moment for which we had so long waited and hoped come at last?

Paul interrupted our meditations. "Damn you!" he yelled. "Are your mouths sewed up? Out with it; I'm waiting." Hastily everyone who had turned over money reported himself. But Paul gave us no inkling of what he was up to. "I want to know how much everybody handed over," he demanded. Each of us reported the sum in question. Then Paul condescended to give an explanation.

"I guess you saw the flowers around here when you were brought in. You can't pick 'em and put 'em in your buttonholes, but you can smell 'em all the same. That treat costs money and you Polaks needn't think you're getting such a luxury for nothing. Every Polish block has got to come across with 500 Reichsmarks to support those flowers, see?"

We had in fact noticed to our great astonishment when we arrived at the camp that there were beautiful flower beds scattered about the grounds. Even our barracks were surrounded with flowers. The camp authorities saw to it that these plots were kept up with the greatest care: every day numerous prisoners were busy working in the flower beds with seedlings, trowels, manure and water.

Through many sleepless nights I had been haunted by the tragic contrast between the beautiful beds of flowers and the crime-soaked atmosphere of the camp. Often when I reflected on the loving care which the Gestapo butchers lavished on these flower beds, I thought I would lose my mind. In this place where the most cold-blooded murderers studied and practiced the murder of human beings, flowers were cherished and kept alive with the greatest affection. Numerous prisoners had been bestially murdered between these lovingly tended borders, and the flowers planted with their own hands had been watered with their own blood. Truly the German soul is a phenomenon difficult to understand.

"How much is each man to contribute?" asked one of the prisoners. Paul had no answer ready. He looked questioningly at Rolly. Then one comrade proposed that the fifty prisoners who had the largest sums at their disposal should each contribute 10 Reichsmarks. Paul had no objection to this, and the clerk whom he had brought with him began to take down the names and numbers of the fifty men who instantly volunteered to pay.

Then Rolly took over and beckoned Paul to follow him into the day room. When the two reappeared, we saw at a glance that the matter had been decided otherwise. Rolly had suggested charging the whole amount to one man, who had had 600 Reichsmarks with him, and Paul had approved the plan. With a wide, oily grin on his face, he explained: "I've got a better idea. You won't all chip in. The Polak with the 600 Reichsmarks will treat the whole bunch. He's rolling in money, and it'll save me and the office a lot of paper work."

It was an order, mad to dispute, especially when Rolly capped Paul's speech with the remark: "It doesn't matter who gives the money; you've all got to croak anyway and you'll never see your money again." Paul went off with a satisfied expression to report his dictatorial decision to the office. He returned in an excellent humor. "All settled," he announced and turned to the involuntary "treater" with a mock-confidential air. "You've gotten to be a celebrity in this camp." And he began to laugh loudly.

But we did not laugh. The man who was "rolling" was really desperately poor: the 600 Reichsmarks represented his entire fortune and a ruined future. Just before the outbreak of war, he had decided to emigrate to South America, and friends had raised funds for his ticket. He had been so afraid of losing the sum that he always carried it on his person, and this was why he had had it with him when he was arrested.

That evening was the beginning of our Feast of Atonement, in Jewish tradition the holiest day in the year, a day for which men must prepare for ten days in prayer and penance. But in the camp praying was strictly forbidden and cruelly punished. Everywhere in the world, thieves, criminals, even murderers, enjoy the privilege of praying and attending divine services. To the prisoners in a concentration camp this right is denied. The Bible students, the German as well as the Polish clergy, were not allowed to pray. Of course, every man can carry God in his heart and pray silently alone, but for Jews bound to Jewry by religious or even merely traditional ties, it is inexpressibly painful not to recite the ritual prayers on the Day of Atonement. Our souls hungered for the comfort of the words with which we had grown up. Grief and depression laid hold of us with a force we had not felt before and plunged us into a deep lethargy. Only our gasps for breath showed that there was any life left in us.

That day my breathing was much more difficult than usual. It was as if I had expended the last remnants of my strength and my lungs would give up at any moment. But the weaker I became, the stronger grew my will to live. "God give us strength to survive this crisis," I repeated over and over, as if the words of the prayer were a shield which could defend me from death. "Strengthen our spirit and let us meet your holy day with clean souls, though our bodies and clothes be unclean." And, as always when I prayed, a strange peace came over me; I had no fear; I trusted in God and I wished fervently that I could impart to my comrades something of this peace.

"God is not on the side of the big battalions, as Prussian philosophy will have it," I whispered to my comrades. "He is with the righteous and the steadfast in spirit; and He will be on our side. We were the first victims of Hitler. Now we are no longer alone. Our blood, which has flowed in streams, has at last washed clear the eyes of the world. All the oppressed are now our allies and all the righteous are on our side. The floods of our wrath will sweep away the 'iniquity' and dash it to pieces against the Bar of Judgment."

Suppressed weeping answered my words, and I was content. That at least was a reaction; the deadly lethargy had not yet wholly destroyed the spirit of my comrades. I would have liked to speak without ceasing, to prolong their weeping. I felt that the tears lightened their hearts. But it cost me great effort to speak. With every word, more breath, more strength, went out of me, and suddenly everything went black before my eyes and I fell . . . and the abyss into which I fell had no end.

When I came to myself, many hours later, I was on the assembly place, where my comrades had dragged me. My stupor had been unusually deep, and I was so weakened that during roll call I could scarcely stay on my feet. But the others pressed close on either side and supported me with the weight of their bodies. After roll call, when we were again allowed to sleep in separate wings and I stretched out on my straw sack, I fell for the first time into a deep, dreamless sleep.

Suddenly I heard, as if from far away, a voice calling "Achtung!" My sackmate helped me to my feet. In the door of the barrack an unusually large group of blockfuehrers appeared. The SS knew, of course, that this was the beginning of our greatest holiday and had made up their minds to torment us especially on that occasion. They beat us more bestially than ever before, and when leaving to visit the other blocks, they promised to come back.

Pain and the fear that we might not hear those submen returning kept us awake. A cloudless sky, thickly set with glittering stars, looked in upon our grief-filled prison. The moon shone through the window. Its light was dazzling that night and gave the pale, wasted faces of the prisoners a ghostly appearance. It was as if all the life had ebbed out of them. I shuddered with dread, for it suddenly occurred to me that I was the only living man among corpses.

All at once the oppressive silence was broken by a mournful tune. It was the plaintive tones of the ancient "Kol Nidre" prayer. I raised myself up to see whence it came. There, close to the wall, the moonlight caught the uplifted face of an old man, who, in self-forgetful, pious absorption, was singing softly to himself the sorrowful melody with the familiar, deeply moving words.

In the liturgy of every religion there are certain prayers and hymns which have special power over the religious emotions of the believers, humbling them with the sense of their own insignificance. In the Jewish religion the "Kol Nidre" prayer, which forms part of the liturgy for the Day of Atonement, has this compelling power, which, through the tragic circumstances in which we spent that holiday, affected us even more overwhelmingly.

The man who prayed was an orthodox believer whom we revered for his unfaltering piety. The manner in which he accepted the misfortunes that had fallen upon us won our astonished admiration. We others might groan and weep with pain; he never complained, never murmured. He seldom spoke, but when he did, he exhorted us to show humility and submission to the will of God; and words of deep wisdom came from his lips. It was not strange, then, that by reciting aloud the "Kol Nidre" prayer he instantly recalled us to the mournful, devout mood that belongs to the Day of Atonement. His prayer brought the ghostly group of seemingly insensible human beings back to life. Little by little, they all roused themselves and all eyes were fixed on the moonlight-flooded face.

We sat up very quietly, so as not to disturb the old man, and he did not notice that we were listening. As if transported into another world, he chanted the prayer to the end, so softly that the words were scarcely distinguishable to those who did not know them by heart. His old, quavering voice held us in a spell. When at last he was silent, there was exaltation among us, an exaltation which men can experience only when they have fallen as low as we had fallen and then, through the mystic power of a deathless prayer, have awakened once more to the world of the spirit.

The blockfuehrers kept their word. Toward midnight, the wild horde broke in upon us and began another murderous assault, which we, exhausted by the storm of feeling we had just gone through, had little strength to withstand.

At the next morning roll call, a blockfuehrer asked: "What holiday do you swine keep today?"

"The Day of Atonement," we answered in chorus.

Then the blockfuehrer took a man out of the formation and questioned him further. "What does this Day of Atonement mean?"

Our comrade explained: On the Day of Atonement, Jewish people must end all their quarrels with others; they must fast, do penance and pray for the forgiveness of all the sins they have knowingly or unknowingly committed; they must resolve to be better than in the preceding year.

"So the hogs must fast!" shouted the blockfuehrer. "I'm all for that. Today you'll get no food, so you can celebrate properly."

That morning Rolly also was in an ominous mood. Even before the blockfuehrers had appeared, he had an animated conversation with the room senior of Block 37, and from their manner we could see that they were plotting some especially malicious trick.

Our fear that this holiday would be attended with special tortures was soon confirmed. About ten o'clock in the morning—we were lying herded together in our dormitory—Rolly appeared on the scene, made for the pile of blankets, threw them at us and ordered us to shroud ourselves in them completely, even our arms.

"That's so you won't catch cold on your most sacred holiday!" he cried with a devilish grin.

When the blockfuehrers came a little later, they were enchanted by the spectacle we presented. Our torment seemed to fascinate them so that, in spite of the evil-smelling air that streamed toward them, they remained on the threshold and unloosed an inexhaustible flood of curses and abuse. Like a beaten dog, which has at last succeeded in getting some recognition from its master, Rolly ran around us to make sure that everyone was properly shrouded.

Our misery was indescribable! Beneath the blankets, our bodies were on fire. It was as if the blood were boiling in our veins, as if our bodies would explode. The September heat had not yet abated. We sweated so freely that the water poured from us and the blankets were soon drenched. The sick among us, who up to then had kept themselves going by superhuman strength of will, were snuffed out all at once, like sparks in the wind. And even in the healthy men the instinct of self-preservation began to break down. All of us simply waited for the end.

When the longed-for noon roll call came, we could scarcely walk. Every one of us was so exhausted that we looked more like human ruins than men.

"Really it's not right that this reducing cure costs you nothing," one blockfuehrer mocked. "You swine used to go to the baths for it and pay fabulous sums."

But no one paid him any attention. We were too weak to care, and, however incredible it may sound, standing exhausted us to such a degree that our one overmastering thought was to get back into the barrack and be able to stretch out.

Since no food was distributed after the roll call, we had no noon recess and were compelled to shroud ourselves in the blankets at once. But our apathy was so great that we did not rebel, even in thought. Then, when our misery was at its worst, we had an unexpected bit of luck which saved the lives of many comrades. On that day, which was a Saturday, there was one of the meetings for the SS men that were held from time to time. So the evening roll call was set forward to three o'clock, and since we had to make ready for the night after evening roll call, no matter when it took place, we were released from the terrible sweating.

At roll call the camp director unexpectedly appeared and paced along our ranks. When the inspection was ended, we heard him tell the blockfuehrers that on Sunday morning clean underwear was to be distributed and some medical orderlies would have a look at us. We could not believe our ears. Clean underwear? We had almost forgotten that there was such a thing as cleanliness.

According to the camp rules, clean linen for all the barracks was given out on Saturday. But since we had arrived on a Wednesday, the camp authorities considered it an unnecessary luxury to change our linen after only half a week. So for eleven days, twenty-four hours a day, we had worn the same garments next our bodies, rolled them in filth indoors and out, wet them with urine and sweat, soaked them with pus, till at last we gave off an unbearably vile stench even in the open air. Now they had remembered us at last; we were once more to smell the odor of newly washed underwear. The prospect was so good that we could scarcely believe it.

When we returned to the barrack, we were not herded together but allowed to go into our own wings. This slight alleviation rekindled hope in our despairing hearts. It seemed a divine dispensation that we might spend the last hours of the Day of Atonement in peace.

From the depths of our crushed hearts thankful prayers ascended to heaven. Everyone murmured to himself fragments of the holiday service. God had sorely chastened us, but He had not abandoned us. What would not any one of us have given, a short time before, to spend at least one hour of this holiday in devotional exercises, to be able to say one prayer? Suddenly the most fervent wish of our hearts had been gratified, peace had come to us for a space, not only spiritual but bodily peace. For the blockfuehrers were too busy with their meeting to bother about us. The disfigured, bleeding, malodorous, bruised and battered forms crouching on the floor had become a devout congregation of worshipers, the most touching congregation in which I have ever prayed.

When at last we stretched out on our straw sacks for the night, all hearts were filled with thankfulness. And hope grew. How strange, I could not help thinking, is that spiritual force which men call hope. Twenty-four hours earlier, when all my physical strength had left me and the end seemed at hand, I had clung to Gucia's two words of hope, "Head high," and the mysterious power of those words had not failed me.

On Sunday morning clean underwear was distributed, as ordered. Paul and Rolly saw to it that this too should be an occasion for brutal beatings. The camp-director had commanded that we should wash and have showers before changing, but Rolly could not bear to let us enjoy the cleansing process, to which we were looking forward eagerly. Cudgel in hand, he drove us into the washroom in relays of fifty men each and ordered each group to finish in ten minutes.

Under such limitations of time and space, washing was out of the question for most of us, to say nothing of showering. We crowded around the basins and the only shower. Rolly's cudgel, fists and boots broke up the crowd. Everyone had his share of blows before he was driven out of the washroom, and if anyone succeeded in slipping past unbeaten, Rolly hauled him back and gave him a double portion.

After we passed through this barrage, we had to run out naked to the front of the barrack with the bundles of dirty clothes in our hands. Paul stood outside with several assistants from the indoor squad and decided whether each man was clean. Most of them, of course, were not. Paul sent them back, with curses and insults, to the washroom, where Rolly renewed his baiting. The procedure lasted about two hours, during which Rolly untiringly beat, screamed and blustered. It was inconceivable that a human being, even with the bull-like strength of a Rolly, could rage for two whole hours without cessation and not fall down exhausted.

When we had all changed our linen, several medical orderlies, accompanied by blockfuehrers, appeared in front of the barrack. A few benches and a table were provided. The medical orderlies stationed themselves at the table with a bottle of formalin solution, a bottle of sublimate solution, a bottle of tincture of iodine and rolls of cotton and bandages. Then it was announced that anyone who had suppurating wounds should come up for treatment.

Immediately a long line formed in front of the table: men with discharging wounds on their heads, necks, chests and every other possible part of their bodies. It was a hideous procession.

The treatment proceeded as follows:

"Step forward," the orderly would call.

The next man in the line stepped forward, his hands at his sides.

"What is the matter?" asked the medical orderly.

"Open discharging wound," answered the prisoner and pointed to the affected spot.

"Undress," growled the orderly.

After the prisoner had removed his jacket or pants, as the case might be, the medical orderly and the blockfuehrers took a look at the infected area. Then the blockfuehrers would decide who was to be treated and who was not; if they decided against treatment, the applicant was simply removed from the scene with a kick. If the blockfuehrers decided for treatment, the orderly picked up his lancet and cut into the inflamed, festering flesh till the pus spurted high and the blood began to run. The victim moaned with pain.

"Shut up!" ordered a blockfuehrer and gave the patient a blow to quiet him.

Then the orderly, who had meanwhile soaked a wad of cotton in formalin or sublimate solution, dabbed it into the gaping wound. The antiseptic stung fiercely. The victim screamed so loudly that the waiting men felt the gooseflesh rise.

"Damned swine! Shut up, I said," yelled a blockfuehrer and gave another blow.

Then the orderly dipped a wad of cotton into the iodine and painted the inflamed area; the blockfuehrer gave the man a third blow even before he began to scream with pain. With that, the treatment was usually at an end. In some cases where the bleeding did not stop, the orderly might feel called upon to put a compress in the wound and bind it up carelessly.

I had a large wound on my right shin bone which caused me much pain and anxiety. The inflammation spread from day to day; the whole leg was swollen, and I was afraid that sepsis was developing. So I had taken my place in the line. When I saw the kind of treatment administered, everything went black before my eyes. But it was too late to retreat.

When my turn came I pulled up my pants leg and showed the wound. The orderly told me to take off the pants. But the blockfuehrer was not of the opinion that my leg needed treatment.

"Not necessary," he snapped to the orderly. At the same moment his fist landed on my stomach.

After what seemed an eternity, I gathered up my aching bones from the ground and dragged myself out of the way, utterly spent.

Luckily it was nearly time for the noon roll call and the treatment farce was soon broken off. Those who thus escaped being manhandled were unspeakably thankful, though in many cases the condition of the wounds was critical. The medical orderlies returned no more.

Sunday afternoon passed without incident. We had to lie on our faces as usual, but we were not herded in together, and that seemed, in comparison with the last two days, a blessed relief. The late afternoon, however, brought an occurrence whose effects remained with me for months.

Unexpectedly the loud-speaker on our roof opened up with one of the numerous Sunday broadcasts. As if the program had been designed especially for us, the subject was: "Impressions of the battle for Warsaw." A more cunning and deadly blow to our morale could not have been devised.

The physical suffering, the fear and danger, with which we were beset had made me forget for a while the most important thing of all: the criminal assault upon Poland and the butchery of its defenseless civil population. The broadcast reminded me of the tragedy. Were the announcer's assertions that Warsaw, despite stubborn resistance, would fall at any moment boasting or truth? Was it true that the Polish Army had collapsed so quickly? Had Poland fought fiercely through a century and a half for its independence, only to lose it after twenty-one years? Was it only German propaganda or was it true that Poland had been left in the lurch, not only by her French and English allies but by her own government? Had the Polish cabinet ministers really fled to safety? Had the High Command of the Polish Army really deserted?

I pressed my hands to my ears. It was unendurable to listen to these charges, to be a prey to uncertainty. What if only a part of these accusations were true? What would be left to believe in?

I struggled with all my power to resist these defeatist thoughts. I clung to the words of the announcer, who had spoken of the dogged resistance of the population of Warsaw. Those people, whom the German announcer abused as "assassins" and "franc-tireurs," that mayor who had taken the defense of Warsaw into his own hands and refused to surrender the Polish capital to the German beasts of prey, were the proof that there were still heroes in Poland.

Poland was not yet lost! Even if the capital should be lost for a while, it would be won back. The Germans would be thrown out in the end, as they were in 1918.

The Warsaw of twenty-one years ago rose before me: the three November days which marked the birth of independent Poland: the streets black with people, the whole city celebrating in a frenzy of enthusiasm the return of Pilsudski from his imprisonment in the German fortress of Madgeburg. A handful of Polish legionnaires, driven by the hatred of the exploiters which had been mounting through three long years, had disarmed the German garrison. Civilians had torn the epaulettes from the shoulders of German officers, and the members of the master race had not defended themselves, but were glad to get off with their bare lives. And then the news had spread that the German governor general had asked Pilsudski for safe conduct for his troops and had himself escaped from Warsaw, under cover of dawn.

And now once more the enemy was at our gates, a more terrible, infinitely more cruel enemy than the enemy of 1914–1918, an enemy to whom we ourselves had tragically opened the way into our country.

It was no use refusing to call things by their names. Poland had much to answer for. She had been the first power to conclude a pact with Hitler Germany and thereby, in effect, had strengthened Hitler's hand against her own friends. But Poland had also been the first power with the courage to plant herself in the path of the juggernaut. Not the mighty British Empire, not the once-so-daring "Grande Nation," not sturdy Czechoslovakia, not old Austria, but Poland, first faced Nazi Germany in arms. Poland had shown the world that a nation may atone nobly for its mistakes and that honor is no empty word in the Polish dictionary.

These sins and this glory belong to Poland. The German announcer's accusations could not alter them one iota. I longed that I and my comrades might be spared to see how, out of the rubble of smashed dwellings, out of the ashes of burned houses, out of the sea of tears which flowed in Poland, a better, greater, stronger and wiser nation would arise.

The broadcast had repercussions which we felt immediately. When the blockfuehrers appeared at the evening roll call, we saw at once, from their sullen, bitter faces, that new tortures were in store. Without seeking any excuse in faulty exercising or incorrect behavior, they attacked us instantly. After they had beaten us horribly, they ordered us to lie down. Then we had to roll, and they pushed us with their boots as if we were empty barrels, to expedite our rolling. We gasped desperately for lack of breath. But there was no letup for us.

This time the beating was more than mere sadistic enjoyment of our pain; it was bloody vengeance, foaming fury, the craving to retaliate. After the radio broadcast of the afternoon, I knew what they were avenging: the losses of the German Army before the gates of Poland's capital, the impatience of the German Fuehrer, who was awaiting his entry into Warsaw. This assault upon us was another part of the battle for Warsaw, another kind of assault upon defenseless Poles.

When at last we had been hounded back into the barrack, the food was distributed and gulped down at lightning speed; at lightning speed we were forced to lay out the straw sacks, undress and lie down. That evening only a few could use the toilet. The results were again horrible.

Soon the dormitory stank like a sewer. The men who lay in their own filth moaned and wept with discomfort and disgust. Their moral wretchedness was crushing. The stink gave the blockfuehrers, who visited us several times that night, welcome occasion for new frenzied beatings. The next morning Paul and Rolly held a trial, sought out the guilty and punished them in their own efficient way.

If we had believed on the morning of the Day of Atonement that we had reached the summit of our sufferings, we learned that Monday morning that there is always a "beyond." The screw was constantly being tightened. All the preceding days were nothing in comparison with this day, and it was most probable that this day would be nothing in comparison with those to come.

On Monday morning the process of suffocation was speeded up. The temperature had grown hotter instead of cooler. Our throats were so dry that we could only whisper. Our bodies were raw, aching lumps of flesh. Our spirit was at its lowest ebb. We were utterly weary and no longer offered any resistance to death, who once more took possession of our dormitory.

Our agonized dying seemed to be an outstanding attraction in the camp. Every little while visitors came to watch us die. On the afternoon of September 27, the office senior, a typical SS man, arrived. He was an unusually big and burly fellow and he completely blocked the doorway in which he posted himself. He stood like a statue on the threshold, his fists planted on his hips, in dead silence. Only his eyes, which roved restlessly from one man to another, told us that he was flesh and blood.

The stinking cloud which streamed past him into the day room troubled him not at all. He was too absorbed in his mute contemplation. His silence and immobility did not deceive us. By this time we knew the mentality of the National Socialists well enough to realize that this calm only presaged a more violent storm.

Suddenly the motionless form in the doorway came to life. A plan had been hatched.

"Who is thirsty?" asked the SS man.

What a question! Our throats were burning with thirst, and we all cried: "I, I, I!"

But the SS man fell silent again and took up a statuesque pose on the doorsill. Many minutes crawled by. At last he spoke once more. "Any man who can drink up a whole bucket of water may step forward and he'll get a drink. But God help the man who volunteers and then leaves just one drop of water in the bucket!"

So that was the devilish plan! It did not require much penetration to see that death was the certain fate of anyone who took up this generous offer. None the less, one volunteered. He was a transport worker and had the strength of a bear. His massive frame had withstood all the beatings without too great injury. But for that very reason he suffered particularly from thirst and his thirst was stronger than all his power of reflection. The prospect of water had driven him out of his senses. As he sprang forward, there was a crazed look on his face.

The SS man was gratified to have found a victim. He gave orders to fetch a bucket of water and set it on a stool.

"Go to it!" he cried. "Now drink, you Polish swine! You are drinking for your life."

The prisoner rushed forward and seized the bucket with both hands. His head disappeared into the water; he had forgotten us and the SS man. Only the water existed for him.

The SS man looked on, fascinated. His body was tensed, ready to pounce upon his victim. There was triumph in his eyes. He had his prey safe, as safe as a fly that has blundered into a spider's web.

An oppressive silence reigned in the room. Only the victim's greedy lapping of the water made a rippling sound, as if it were not a man who stood there, but a horse at the watering trough. We listened in horror, waiting for the unavoidable catastrophe.

And the inevitable happened. In the act of drinking, the man collapsed unconscious. In falling he pulled the bucket with him, and the water poured over him and made a big puddle on the floor. Then the SS man cried out shrilly like a stuck pig: "So you thought you could put something over on me, you damned Polish swine! You guessed wrong that time, Jew!"

"Remove him to the day room," he ordered Paul and Rolly, who had come running in.

The two seized the unconscious man by the arms and feet and carried him to the day room, the SS man following. The door banged behind them. We saw nothing more. But we heard blows which sounded as if bones were breaking under them, interspersed with shouts: "Get up, you Jew bastard!" It was horrible to listen to. Still more horrible was the sight of the men near the puddle of water greedily licking up drops from the floor.

When we were driven out to the roll call shortly afterwards, we saw the body of the unlucky transport worker, battered out of all recognition, lying on the day-room floor. The pools of blood had been wiped up as usual, but the visible evidence told its own story.

At roll calls in the camp the bodies of the men already dead must be present for inspection, for the number must correspond with that of the prisoners listed in the report book at the previous roll call. So Paul and Rolly dragged the dead comrade out. The blockfuehrers inquired what had happened, and when Paul made his report on it, we all had to pay heavily for our comrade's thirst. There were many broken bones.

Strangely enough the dead comrade was not carted off after the roll call to the so-called "morgue," as was customary, but left lying in the washroom. Then a miraculous thing happened. Late that night the "dead" man awoke from a deathlike swoon, and when the memory of what had happened slowly came back to him, he summoned up all his strength and dragged himself into the dormitory. On the threshold he collapsed unconscious and fell across the straw sack nearest the door.

The two men asleep on that sack screamed loudly with fright, and in a few seconds all the occupants of the room awoke. We thought the blockfuehrers, who had visited us once that night, were back again. Great was our joy and amazement when we learned the truth.

By God's mercy Paul was so sound asleep that he did not hear the disturbance. When we saw that everything remained quiet, several comrades approached the unconscious man, wrapped him up in a blanket and crawled with him to the farthest corner of the room, where they laid him on a sack all by himself, in the hope that the blockfuehrers might overlook him if they came again. Fortunately they did not return, and the incredible vitality of the transport worker triumphed over death.

The following Thursday brought a new crisis. By early morning five more men were dead of suffocation, and we knew that it was only the prelude. Our lives were slowly flickering out. But as a candle flame flares up just before it expires, so the flame of life flared up once more in the eyes of the dying. Men who only a moment ago could scarcely move, whose voices were only whispers, suddenly got to their feet. There was anger in their eyes, and even rebellion. They began to mutiny and demanded that we smash the windows to let in air. They would not listen to the arguments that such an act of "sabotage" would only bring down the most fearful punishment upon all the Polish blocks.

A slight young man, who had not stirred for hours, suddenly sprang up. Before those around him could recover from their confusion, he was making for one of the windows. It was astonishing with how much strength his dying body could resist those who tried to drag him down.

Just at this dangerous moment Rolly opened the door. His gimlet eyes saw at once that something was up. At that, the resistance of the dying man collapsed. He let his comrades pull him quickly to the floor and lay there without making a sound. Half an hour later he was dead.

But the unrest had spread. Many of the men were openly defiant. Those of us whose nerves were still under control had hard work preventing trouble. Finally, however, the energy of the rebels wore itself out. Their resistance dissolved into helpless sobbing.

Instantly Paul opened the door and irritably demanded the reason for this "sniveling." We told him that several more men had lost consciousness. To Paul that seemed no reason for weeping and he threatened to see to it that more of us lost consciousness unless "that bawling" stopped at once.

Then, once again, an unforeseen circumstance came to our aid. The days had grown shorter, and since the evening roll call had to be held in broad daylight, on that day it was set forward one hour. The horrible sweating broke off an hour earlier and we had no more victims. True, eleven unconscious men were carried out to roll call; but the rest revived in the fresh evening air.

For the first time the blockfuehrers were impressed by the array of men laid out on the ground. "Things are beginning to look up. We'll get you yet. We thought we'd be finished with you sooner, but weeds are hard to uproot. From now on, we must work faster, until not one of you is left."

Then they trampled with their boots on the prostrate men and maltreated them in the usual way. Cold sweat broke out on our bodies as we had to look on helplessly at this scene.

After roll call the unconscious men were carried inside again. Since there was not room for so many in the washroom, we brought them into the dormitory. A sleepless night followed, broken by several visits from the blockfuehrers, by the groans of the men who had been beaten, the death rattles of those in their last agony and the desperate weeping of the rest, whose hearts were torn by the agonizing deaths of their comrades. To live through these shattering emotional convulsions without going out of one's mind would have been a test of strength for men in full health and vigor; and it is incredible that we—weak, broken, with our nerves utterly unstrung—ever lasted out that night.

During this night, six of the eleven men died without ever regaining consciousness. The other five, however, recovered toward morning. When they remembered the horrors they had lived through, a wondering, thankful joy took possession of them. They felt as if they had returned from the dead. Although, like the others, they had repeatedly wished themselves dead, they now thanked God for the miracle that had brought them back to life. The human will to live in spite of all suffering is one of the greatest mysteries of nature.

At the next morning roll call an unusually bright autumn morning awaited us. It was heartbreaking that the sky could be so radiantly blue, when war and destruction were ravaging the world. Flocks of birds flew over our heads, warbling with pure joy, as if peace and happiness reigned on earth and all men loved each other. The flight of the birds made me unutterably sad. They were so free! And we were so enslaved, we human creatures whom God had made to be masters over all other living things.

The blockfuehrers were slow in putting in an appearance that morning. When at last they did, their first question was of how many unconscious men had "croaked" the previous night. Paul pointed to the six bodies, which we had carried out, and explained that the other five had recovered.

"This race of traitors is as tough as bedbugs," grumbled a blockfuehrer; then, turning to us, he ordered, "Shout three times in chorus: 'We are traitors'!"

Automatically, without blinking an eye, we obeyed. Our sensibilities were so blunted that we no longer felt the humiliation. Our thoughts were concentrated on the barrack floor, on which we were longing to stretch out again as soon as possible. When we lay on our pallets once more, our brains rested too. We thought no longer, we wished no longer, we hoped no longer.

Paul was on his high horse that morning. It looked as if he wanted to impress Rolly and show him who was master in the block. This time he took the indoor squad in hand and announced that he was going to change some of the men. He picked out the ones he did not want and gave each of them the usual lesson in the day room. At intervals of a few minutes, filled with thuds and shrieks, bodies came flying through the dormitory door.

After Paul had "pensioned off" several members of the indoor squad in this way, he came into the dormitory to select substitutes. With his hands in his pockets and the air of a commander-in-chief, he stalked deliberately over us and decided on our fitness for the job. When his glance lingered on any individual, that man started up, only too eager, at a sign from Paul, to go into the day room and accept a duty that might offer him some relief and perhaps save his life.

"Lie still, *Hund!*" roared Paul every time. "A lot I'd get out of such a rattletrap!" Then he went on to the next. It was as if he were playing a game with us.

At ten o'clock Paul was unexpectedly interrupted. An unusually large number of blockfuehrers appeared in our barrack and ordered us to form ranks in front of our block immediately. Panic terror seized us. This was the end. Blocks 37 and 39 also hurried out. In front of our barrack stood about twenty blockfuehrers. Their large number and the unusual hour were proof enough that something extraordinary was afoot.

Minutes of suspense followed. All the comrades' faces were twisted with fear. Even the young ones looked like old men. On many heads the stubble of hair, which had begun to grow again, had gone gray in the last twenty-four hours.

Our knees were weak; our one wish was that what was to happen to us would happen quickly. But nothing happened. Strangely enough we were not once beaten, and I suddenly remembered that the shoves the blockfuehrers had given us as we ran out had been, in comparison to their usual blows, only child's play.

Paul and Rolly looked completely bewildered. They ran about

aimlessly and their faces showed a silent astonishment. This time they seemed as much in the dark as we about what was going on.

The sun's rays suddenly reached us, bathing us in warmth, but we could not give ourselves up to the sensation of comfort. Minute after minute passed. At last the group of blockfuehrers began to move; some distance away, the camp director was approaching, accompanied by a group of high officers.

Our suspense had reached its height. We sprang to attention. Our bodies grew rigid with expectation. The group stopped in front of Block 37, which was drawn up at a little distance from us. When, after a long time, they came to us, an unusual inspection began. The camp director, accompanied by an officer who we later learned was the chief camp doctor, paced along our front row. Several times they stepped forward and peered through the rows at each one of us. Then the camp doctor ordered the comrades who were most disfigured with wounds and skin eruptions to step forward, examined them thoroughly and let them resume their places in the ranks.

All this time the blockfuehrers remained in the background. The inspection lasted more than fifteen minutes, but no blow was dealt. That was more than we could understand. Our bewilderment grew. We stole glances at each other, every man asking his neighbor the same mute question. What did this peaceful inspection mean? Something told us that this time we had nothing to fear. When the party of officials moved on to Block 39, and the same scene took place there, our hearts suddenly began to beat with new hope. A sense of liberation took possession of us, and we lifted our eyes thankfully to heaven.

And then the thing most of us had ceased to hope for happened. Workers with carpentering tools suddenly approached our barrack, and the same hands, perhaps, which had nailed up our windows twelve days before now unfastened them again. The attempt at suffocation was over. Our eyes were glued to the windows, which in a few minutes stood wide open and let air flood into the tainted barrack. We would have liked to embrace each other, and could scarcely wait to be dismissed and give voice to our feelings.

Paul and Rolly were also overwrought, but their feelings were of a different kind. They stood motionless, not daring to exchange a word. Paul's face, which had become greenish yellow, as if all the bile had mounted to his head, and Rolly's red-blotched visage showed that the two were bursting with rage.

We had to remain standing outside until it was time for the noon roll call. But this time, standing did not tire us. From our new hopefulness we had drawn new strength, and everyone gave himself up to his thoughts, which were chiefly concerned with explanations for what had happened and hypotheses as to possible further relief, or even release. The noon roll call went like clockwork.

For the first time, too, everyone of us ate his noon ration. The thin soup and moldy bread tasted much better all of a sudden. This time it was Paul and Rolly who suffered from loss of appetite. Like beaten curs they cowered at their tables and could only get down a few spoonfuls of their soup. Evidently they had been forbidden to lay a hand upon us; for, although their eyes followed us with murderous glances, they did not touch us. The sudden restraint of these two criminals proved more conclusively than the events of the morning that an easier time lay ahead.

When the noon recess was over, Paul and Rolly rose from their places, took their bundles in their hands, and with reluctant steps the two accomplices in murder and crime slunk away.

Then the head room senior came in. He was a kind-looking, middle-aged man, himself a political prisoner, and had the supervision of all the room seniors in Sachsenhausen. It was the first human face that I had seen in the concentration camp. A kindly, understanding look came into his eyes as he stood in front of us, his legs apart and his hands crossed behind his back.

"You have a bitter time behind you, and those two scoundrels have much to answer for. But it will be different from now on. I have appointed another room senior for you. Wing B, too, will get another assistant, and you will all be satisfied with the change. You can sit on the floor now. Everything will adjust itself. And I'd like you to know that the room seniors and assistants in the other two blocks will be changed too."

With those words, he went on to Wing B, and within a few minutes all three Polish blocks knew of the change.

The sudden miraculous deliverance overwhelmed us. On that day, September 29, after sixteen days of bestial cruelties, of agonized deaths, a new regime was beginning in the three Polish blocks.

In these terrible sixteen days, with death at our side every second of the day and night, we had seen miracle after miracle. We had seen how, in defiance of all the laws of medicine, men afflicted with horrible wounds rolled in filth without perishing of blood-poisoning, how men believed dead had come back to life, how giants died like flies while weak, fragile men remained alive. Of what strange stuff human beings are made!

"What can have caused this unexpected right-about-face?" we asked ourselves constantly, when the first excitement had died down. And a lively discussion began. During that night and the nights that followed, I analyzed all the possible motives that might have put a stop to the butchers' proceedings.

It was not until after my release that I learned the explanation from my daughter.

When the death notices from Sachsenhausen reached Berlin in ever larger numbers, and our Swedish representatives still refused to intervene, Gucia decided to seek help elsewhere. The German press had hushed up our arrest; the neutral and Allied press seemed unaware that a flagrant breach of international law was being committed. If the foreign press were informed of the way enemy aliens were being treated in Germany, wouldn't the Gestapo, for the sake of appearances, reconsider its program of annihilation? It was worth trying. Gucia got in touch with Louis Lochner, the Berlin representative of the Associated Press, and asked his help.

Louis Lochner showed his sense of social responsibility. He not only passed on the news to the foreign press and to the British Broadcasting Corporation, but he did what our official representatives had not dared to do: at the next press conference in the Propaganda Ministry he asked if the German government knew what was happening to Polish enemy aliens in Sachsenhausen. This awkward question, asked in the presence of the whole corps of foreign correspondents, was followed by a relaxation of the regime in the Polish blocks.

# Part Two

In the reshuffling of supervisors Block 39 fared worst. Their new room senior and assistant were hardly better than their predecessors; both were brutal criminals and aped the blockfuehrers in every way they could.

Block 37 had better luck. Their room senior and assistant were criminals of a more harmless species: burglars, not murderers. Willi, the room senior, had an extremely irascible disposition but he calmed down as quickly as he erupted. Before his criminal career, Willi had been an ordinary workingman. It was more by accident than by design that he had been led into bad ways. Anton, the assistant, was a professional crook, foxy and cunning. He had the mother wit so characteristic of Berliners, and his most outstanding trait was his typical German thoroughness.

Willi and Anton belonged to the "Old Guard" of the camp. Neither had much hope of ever seeing freedom again and each had adapted himself in his own way to this state of affairs. Willi, as if he wished to spend the rest of his life as pleasantly as possible under the circumstances, took his duties lightly and left everything to Anton. Except to play chess with one of his colleagues during free time, he seldom lifted a finger. We nicknamed him "The Pasha."

Anton, on the other hand, took his duties very seriously, and before long he was in sole command of Wing B as well as Wing A. His efficiency eventually brought him recognition from the camp authorities.

While Anton was assistant in Block 37, the comrades under his control were the most fortunate of us all. He had a decided liking for young people, and these, by some chance, were all housed in his block. He also had an unexpected sympathy for the old and infirm. Most surprising of all, he showed respect for his charges' piety, and when they were praying, he would watch for the blockfuehrers' approach and warn them in time. Often he listened to the prayers.

Whenever there was "something cooking" in the camp and Anton saw the blockfuehrers approaching, he would suddenly begin to bellow and storm at his prisoners, cursing and insulting them in a way that would have done credit to the SS themselves. This convinced the blockfuehrers that he had matters well in hand, and they often departed without beating anyone. When the blockfuehrers were planning a surprise visit to the Polish blocks and Anton learned of it through his "connections," he took care to put the old and weak in the back part of the barrack, to protect them from the worst treatment. If there was time, he ran over to our block and warned our room senior to be on guard. On such occasions every object that could serve as an instrument for beating was put out of sight. For experience had taught us that the blockfuehrers would go away when they had broken their weapons and could find no substitute.

The room senior of our block, 38, was distinguished from his two colleagues by his quietness, decency and native intelligence. His name was Karl. Of working-class background, he was a thoroughly upright man, who had been sent to the concentration camp because of his radical, socialist opinions and his hatred for Nazism. His "education period" had lasted since 1935. But his sentiments were unchanged. Karl was one of the few inmates of the concentration camp who had no desire to be released. His great wish was to be in the camp when the day of reckoning came and to take vengeance on some of the criminals there.

In all those terrible months he was our only friend. The very first words we heard him speak filled us with confidence. "I know what it's like," he said. "Keep calm and try to maintain discipline. Have eyes in the back of your heads, for here danger lurks everywhere."

The words themselves were matter-of-fact. But his voice sounded so warm and understanding that a peculiar sadness filled us, half sorrow and half relief. Here at last was a *human being*. And from thankfulness and wretchedness we began to weep. Then Karl showed his quick understanding. He slipped out quietly and left us to our outburst of feeling.

We wept without restraint, like children; and, since everyone was weeping, no one needed to be ashamed of his tears. For the first time we were able to give way to our feelings without being punished. Now, as before, the door of our room was opened and a head looked in to see what was causing the noise. But this time it was not the dreaded murderer's face of Rolly, but the head of a comrade of the indoor squad, who softly closed the door again.

As our emotion subsided, everyone asked what was going to happen now. Karl must have guessed what was in our minds, for he came back and made us a short speech.

"You will remain isolated," he explained. "Your roll calls will be held in front of your barrack as before. You will not be sent to work. And you must spend the whole day inside the barrack. But from today on, you are to sit cross-legged, instead of lying on your faces. I suggest that you appoint one of yourselves as a foreman to keep order; this will save you from unnecessary punishments. And sit in properly graded rows across the length of the barrack, so that when you jump up at the command 'Achtung!' straight rows will be formed at once. The more military your behavior, the better you'll get on."

"But we're civilian prisoners!" cried several comrades at once.

Karl smiled indulgently. "Of course, of course," he answered, as one answers children. "But military drill is the backbone of German teaching methods, particularly in such an educational institution as this."

Then a storm of questions was unloosed upon Karl, who answered them patiently. He could tell us nothing about our status as civilian prisoners. But he promised to find out about medical care. As to writing, isolated prisoners were not allowed to communicate with the outside world for six weeks. So we had four weeks still to wait.

This first human interchange with a person in authority did more for the establishment of order than all the brutalities of Karl's predecessors. In a short time we had chosen a room foreman and were sitting in exemplary graded rows with our legs crossed under us, the old and weak in the background. Karl was more than satisfied when the room foreman invited him to review us, and he immediately proceeded to humanize our appearance.

The camp rules provided that each prisoner should have a shave every other day and a haircut once a week. But in the sixteen days of our imprisonment we had had only two shaves and one haircut. Karl appointed two comrades as haircutters and promised to get the necessary implements that very day.

The problem of shaving was harder to solve. There were no safety razors, and only one of us knew how to handle the old-fashioned kind. This comrade volunteered as a barber. Though his performance at the beginning was a bloody affair, he soon acquired professional dexterity. But to cope with the throng of customers from both wings he had to take on two assistants. They never learned their trade, and to be shaved by them remained an ordeal.

The whole problem could have been avoided if the camp authorities had allowed us to shave ourselves, but they did not want to let us have blades of any kind—the temptation to end our burdensome lives with one stroke would have been too great.

Karl's behavior had given us hope that we might have peace under his charge, but Franz, Karl's assistant, would not allow it. This man was a regular criminal, another member of the "Old Guard." He had abandoned his original occupation of farming for the more profitable one of horse trading, which notoriously has little to do with honesty. His machinations soon made him an habitué of various German prisons, until he finally landed in the Sachsenhausen camp.

This life history—of course, in an expurgated version—we heard from Franz himself. One day he found a former acquaintance among us and began to talk shop. To impress us, he pretended to have been a big landed proprietor and wholesale merchant who had done a large business with Czarist Russia. Later, our comrade told us the other side of the story and warned us of the braggart's sugar-coated malice and cunning.

At first, Franz pretended to be our friend and feigned sympathy, but gradually he dropped his mask and began to torment us with every sly trick he could think of. He paid us visits, on various pretexts, and always found something to criticize. He did not beat us; his rheumatic body was much too weak. But what he lacked in physical strength he made up for in meanness. His favorite way of bedeviling us was to drench us with water. When we went out to roll call, he used to take his stand in the doorway with several buckets of cold water and pour it over us as we ran past. In the winter of 1939-1940 the average temperature ranged from 14 to minus 4 degrees Fahrenheit. So the water froze instantly on our clothes and caused many cases of pneumonia, often with fatal results.

Another of Franz's fiendish ideas was his new rule for mealtimes. Even in the worst days under Paul and Rolly we had been able to eat sitting down. Franz decreed that we must do so standing. This often made it impossible to eat at all. The soup was frequently almost boiling when it was dished out and the thin bowls grew so hot it was difficult to hold them. Instead of using our short meal recess for eating, we spent it blowing alternately on our fingers and on the soup. By the time the soup had cooled, the meal recess would be over or part of the bowls' contents would have been spilled in the struggle. If some of us could not control our hunger and greedily swallowed the scalding soup, the result was burned throats, so that for days the men could eat nothing at all; and Franz would beam with satisfaction.

Strange to say, Karl never protested against Franz's excesses, and at first we often felt bitter about it. But the more we grew accustomed to camp life, the better we understood his behavior. Karl was no hero, but a human being with an instinct for self-preservation. He detested Franz, but he dared not check him, for in that case Franz would not have hesitated to report him for favoritism toward the "Bromberg murderers"—which would have been the end of Karl.

And Franz took advantage of Karl's passivity in many ways. One of his greatest pleasures was to report us to the office for such trifles as spilling water or misplacing a towel or tearing our clothes. This talebearing had a special purpose. Franz wanted to be room senior and he hoped to climb to promotion on our shoulders. But the head room senior could not endure him, so the only result of Franz's reporting was numerous Bunker punishments, blows and whippings for us.

When Karl took up his post, however, no one dreamed that the "new regime" would work out in such a way. The first day under Karl's charge had passed very calmly; even the blockfuehrers left us more or less in peace; they came a few times to inspect our new sitting formation, but although some of us, as usual, rose too slowly, the blockfuehrers dealt out few blows. The first roll call and the retiring for the night passed without incident. That night, for the first time, I lay alone on my straw sack. At first I had shared it with two men, then with one, and now both my sackmates were dead. My limbs had unaccustomed room, but I dared not stretch them out. How could I relax, knowing what a price had been paid for the extra space that was now mine?

The moaning around me kept me awake. Death had taken no notice of the new regime and had claimed its prey again. But tonight we could tend our suffering comrades, bring them water, give them air, prop them up. In this way we saved four whom we had given up for lost. One, however, died in spite of all our efforts. His death struggle lasted for hours and was unspeakably heartrending. Through it all he wanted terribly to live, and with the last bit of strength in him he whispered plaintively: "And just now, when everything is getting better; just now!"

The next morning Karl examined the comrades who were in the greatest pain. Some of them had internal injuries and spat blood; others had broken limbs and groaned at every movement. Karl picked out several, who needed help most urgently, for transfer to the infirmary, the so-called "Revier." He ran about the whole day, and, thanks to his "good connections," succeeded in having the sufferers admitted to the Revier. It was only much later, when I learned how the Revier was run, that I could appreciate fully what a miracle Karl had accomplished.

When Karl returned without our comrades we, of course, besieged him with questions. But Karl never boasted. "The main thing is," he said simply, "that the poor fellows are taken care of. It was high time."

Then he inspected our stinking straw sacks, sorted out the most soiled and had them replaced that same day. Only his smile showed that he was proud of his success in the Revier.

The next day was Saturday, and roll call took place at an unusually early hour. So there was some free time before the distribution of the evening ration. Karl made use of it to distribute clean underwear, which we were not supposed to get until Sunday. True, we had to put on the clean things over our filth-caked bodies. But Karl had at least saved time for the Sunday washing.

He had shown such understanding for our physical needs that we were surprised when he proved entirely without sympathy in a matter which to us was more important. There were many among us who wished to ease their souls in prayer. Since we had no prayer books, several comrades who knew the service by heart offered to lead us in prayer, and we formed small groups of worshipers. Once, when we were praying, Karl came in unexpectedly. When he saw a group of men with their caps on, he asked the reason and, suspecting no harm, we told him. His face grew white with vexation, and, in sharp words such as he had never used before, forbade us to pray in the future. In his radical Weltanschauung there was no place, of course, for religion.

But for us prayer was a deep emotional need, the only source from which we drew strength and hope. So we did not give it up. But we used the greatest caution thereafter and appointed several comrades to keep their ears open for Karl's footsteps and warn us of his approach.

Now the occupants of our dormitory formed a motley group. Many were not only vulgar but brutal and callous. They had always made fun of those who prayed and now they felt they had the whip hand over us. One of the worst was a malicious little tailor, who had charge of the sewing materials in our wing and had caused us many punishments by refusing to give us the materials when we needed them. He tyrannized over us with constant threats to report us to Karl for "sabotaging" the order against prayer. One day we boiled over and told the self-appointed spy we would beat him to a jelly if he ever carried out his threat. And to show that we meant it, we gave him a couple of blows "on account." After that we had peace from him and his like.

After the cramped lying position, sitting cross-legged was a relief, of course. But it was a hardship all the same; our legs became stiff and powerless from the unaccustomed posture. During roll call many comrades simply toppled over.

Then someone had an inspiration. We appointed several comrades to polish the windows, as the camp rules permitted, so that they could keep an eye on the approach to the barrack. As long as the coast was clear we relaxed, stretched our legs and moved our heads. When the window polishers announced the approach of the blockfuehrers, we resumed the prescribed position. Needless to say, we kept up the window polishing all day, and the polishers were more than willing. Many of them made themselves so indispensable, through their sharp eyes and constant alertness, that they demanded more soup or an extra piece of bread and got it without demur.

But the temporary relaxation was by no means an adequate remedy. We grew stiffer and weaker. And we would have given a great deal for the daily hour of exercise that even penitentiary inmates are granted.

Sunday, when I saw Karl sitting alone at his table during the noon recess, I told him about the condition of our legs and asked if he could get us permission to march or run for an hour, or even a half-hour, every day.

Karl gave me a pitying look. "Such a thing has never happened here, and do you seriously believe that they will make an exception for the 'Bromberg murderers'?" he asked bitterly. Seeing my disappointment, he added after a pause, "Perhaps it's just as well. If they gave you any kind of privilege—even one that the other prisoners shared—the camp authorities would turn it into anti-Semitic propaganda. That happened once before in these very blocks."

Thereupon Karl told me that Blocks 37-40 had been used to house the German Jews arrested on November 10, 1938, after the Second Secretary of the German Embassy in Paris had been shot by a Polish Jew. The German-Jewish prisoners, like the others, had been allowed to send for as much money as they wished and to buy all they wanted in the canteen. The prosperous ones had readily shared their money with the penniless non-Jewish prisoners. When this was reported to the office, it did not please the camp authorities at all, and they promptly arranged a countereffect.

Suddenly a hate campaign began throughout the camp, under the slogan, "Jewish benefactors." "First the Jews plundered you," it went, "and now they pretend to be your benefactors." It was not long before the poison worked. There were various demonstrations of hostility, and at last the non-Jewish prisoners attacked their Jewish campmates during the common work period.

The mention of the German Jews' arrest led us to speak of the pogrom of 1938. Karl asked me to tell him what had happened in Berlin on November 10. But it was not easy to talk about that horrible day. November 10 was the climax of the German prewar barbarity against German Jewry.

Several days before, every Jew in Germany had sensed some dreadful event impending. The Second Secretary of the German Embassy in Paris had been mortally wounded by a Jewish boy, and the Nazis had decided to make the dying official a martyr. Radio, press and posters were preparing the atmosphere. On November 9, when extras announced the death of the Legation Secretary and the obituary notice on the radio was followed by battle songs, German Jewry knew that its death sentence had been pronounced. While police trucks packed with Jewish men moved under cover of night toward various concentration camps, the most cold-blooded pogrom took place that world history had seen up to then.

That night, at a word from Adolf Hitler, members of the SA and other Party formations were suddenly ordered to their stations. There they were provided with benzine and other combustibles and finally with lists of names. The order was: Destroy every Jewish shop and place of business on the lists, set fire to all Jewish synagogues.

All night the streets of Berlin rang with pounding, hammering and the tinkle of window glass. On the morning of November 10 there was not a single Jewish shop in all Germany that was not wrecked and looted, not a single synagogue in Berlin, except those in private houses and the one in Oranienburger Strasse, that was not put to the torch at the stroke of 6:00 A.M.

The work was carried out with admirable efficiency and timing. The SA let nothing stop them. When a heavy synagogue door did not give way under the iron bars, the custodian was dragged from his bed and forced to unlock the door, then had to look on while the SA smashed the eternal light, poured benzine over the sacred Tora scrolls and methodically started a fire.

In many shops proprietors defended themselves against the looting of their wares. They were cold-bloodedly put out of the way. In smaller communities, where particularly conscientious Nazis even invaded private dwellings, the protesting householders were simply thrown out of the window. In many cities even the Jewish cemeteries looked as if a Vandal invasion had swept over them.

From early morning, the principal business streets of Berlin were packed with people, eager to watch the performance, while the radio broadcasted and the press printed eye-witness accounts from all over Germany on the "spontaneous vengeance of the boiling German folk soul." The streets looked as if a hurricane had swept through them. Mountains of furniture and glass were heaped in front of many stores, and shop-window dummies stripped of their clothes were scattered about the sidewalks. The shops were almost empty.

All day long in every street uniformed patrols were marching. They carried lists in their hands. Perhaps somewhere the job had been only half done? And the errors were corrected. When school was out, troops of children, many of them of kindergarten age, joined the patrols. They had clubs or pieces of wood in their hands and, driven by the child's love of destruction, they darted with howls of glee into the windowless and doorless shops and smashed everything that had been left unbroken.

The police, who stood around everywhere, were not allowed to interfere, any more than the fire brigade was allowed to interfere with the burning of the synagogues, although it had been summoned to the scene to keep the fire from spreading to "German buildings."

In front of the Jewish places of business that had recently been "Aryanized" special police detachments stood guard to see that the uninformed public did not attack "Germany property" by mistake; while the panic-stricken owners hastily put up on their windows and doors placards reading "Arisiert" or "Deutsches Eigentum."

But the pogrom did not end the Nazi reprisals. That same day Hermann Goering imposed a fine of a billion Reichsmarks on the Jewish community. The boarded-up shops, which for many days gave Berlin such a dilapidated look, had to be repaired by the Jewish owners at their own expense. Insurance payments were collected by the Reich. When the business properties had been put in order, they, together with all other real estate owned by Jews, were "transferred" to "German ownership" by a system which the Nazis called "Aryanization" and to which they tried to give an appearance of legality by much red tape.

Karl had listened up to this point without comment. Now he asked suddenly: "And the world—how did the democratic world react?"

"The democratic world reacted with expressions of sympathy," I explained. "Journalists wrote indignant articles; statesmen made speeches—very cautious speeches, of course. And then they did what they always do when they want to shelve a problem: handed it over to a 'special commission.' The eleventh hour, in which the world might have given help and saved so many lives, passed unused. Hitler was given a free hand in his war of annihilation against the Jews."

"The receiver is not less guilty than the thief," said Karl bitterly.

"What do you mean by that?" I asked, in surprise.

"I mean by that," he answered, "that the Nazis are no more guilty of the crimes they have committed and are going to commit than the rest of the world, which allowed such matters to come to such a pass."

Just then the dreaded cry, "Achtung!" rang out from a neighboring block and brought our conversation to a close. I ran hastily to my place in the dormitory and Karl followed, to see that everything was in order.

A few minutes later the blockfuehrers moved on to us and "amused" themselves with us in the usual way.

The day after this conversation, as if at a signal, hunger began to torture us all. Our calorie reserves had been completely used up. Our stomachs had not yet accustomed themselves to the starvation rations and grumbled audibly. We could think of nothing but food. With one of our comrades, a former cook, it became a downright obsession. All day long he used to talk to anyone who would listen about steaks, sausages, juicy drumsticks, stuffed turkeys, until the psychosis attacked one man after another. Whenever people talked together, the conversation always came round to the subject of food. This made our hunger even more agonizing.

It seemed to me that the only remedy was to divert our attention to some other subject. So I proposed that we hold conversation periods, to which everyone should contribute something—a talk on his field of knowledge, a story, a personal experience, an anecdote, or even a song or a poem. The proposal was received with enthusiasm, and Karl, who was always in favor of any kind of mental activity, immediately gave his consent. The window polishers undertook to watch for the blockfuehrers, and we kept the secret so well that we were not once surprised.

These conversation periods soon became the one bright spot in our despairing existence. Because of the varied character of our group, the most diverse problems were discussed. And everyone profited. The less educated enriched their general knowledge; the well-educated, their range of human experience. Some even learned new languages. Often when the wits among us were in good form there were moments of pure comedy which even the gloomiest could not resist. And sometimes there were moments of exaltation. When suffering was gnawing most sharply at our hearts, some comrade with a few inspired words might revive our failing hopes.

Later, when the influx of Polish prisoners from other parts of Germany and from Poland began, these conversation hours became general information periods, in which we learned about events in other German localities and in our native land.

Karl had not been in charge of us more than two days before the blockfuehrers resumed their former excesses. At first it was only beating. But it soon became murdering in the old style, which reached a climax on October 6, 1939, when the Allies ignored Hitler's peace offer.

We were already half asleep, when Karl suddenly opened the

door and cried, "Achtung!" Then a shrill whistle sounded, and a group of about forty elite prisoners rushed into the room, laying about them on all sides with their implements of murder. The group assembled in the middle of the room. Then came an order: "The whole pack run around in a circle!" We hastily formed a circle. There was not enough room to run, so we pushed, shoved and struck each other as we went around. And in the middle of the room, as in a circus ring, stood our tormentors, setting the pace with their weapons. When a number of men lay trampled or beaten to death on the floor, a second whistle broke off the hunt. The horde disappeared in a flash, and the circus act was continued in the other two Polish blocks.

Then Karl came in. "Always remember this," he said, in a voice that shook with indignation, "in the struggle between man and beast, man, in spite of many casualties, is victorious in the long run."

The blockfuehrers had come and gone so suddenly that the whole thing seemed like an apparition. Our minds were on the verge of madness. Karl's words of comfort had no effect. We were so shattered that we dared not even move and remained huddled together till dawn broke. Karl himself seemed to have taken little comfort from his words. When he came to us the next morning, he looked gloomy and depressed and avoided our eyes. The only one who had not lost his equanimity was Franz.

A few days later something happened that brought the war right to our doors. Shortly after midnight on October 15 we were wrenched out of sleep by the thunder of gunfire. In a few minutes the whole dormitory was aroused and all eyes were fixed on the sky, which was criss-crossed with searchlight beams.

We realized immediately that it must be an air raid somewhere in the immediate neighborhood. But it did not occur to anyone in those excited moments that the camp might be bombed and we ourselves killed. No one felt any fear. Instead, everyone whispered excitedly to his neighbor: "At last! The English are here! Or perhaps the French. Who knows—perhaps even our own Polish fliers!" Our eyes were fixed tensely on the illuminated sky. Our hearts held only one desire: Vengeance for Warsaw!

In case of an air raid on the camp, the rules prohibited the prisoners from leaving their barracks, even if the buildings caught fire; at the first alarm they must turn over on their faces and stay quiet no matter what happened. We assumed the prescribed position.

As I lay on my face and tried to prepare myself for the falling of the first bomb, my imagination worked feverishly. I tried to picture a bomb attack and the consequences. The wooden barracks would flame up like tinder. The camp authorities would be afraid that the fire might spread to the neighboring Gestapo settlement, and not only the fire brigade but all the prisoners would be put to work fighting it.

And then? Suppose the camp was burned to the ground? What would happen to us? Would we be free?

Free? What a foolish idea! Had not Hitler dotted all Germany with death mills? What would be simpler than to send us to another camp? For us the fire would have no effect except, perhaps, that we might take advantage of the confusion to settle some old scores. There were all the tormentors with whom we wanted a reckoning: the Rollys and Pauls, the blockfuehrers and elite prisoners. How good it would be to seize some of them, tear their throats, stamp on their skulls, as they had done to so many of our comrades! Our boots too were studded with nails.

All ethical concepts had suddenly faded from my mind. Retributive justice? World tribunal? All twaddle! Only naked vengeance! With our own hands!

But the English bombs, the prerequisite for the satisfaction of this primitive instinct, did not fall. Soon the gunfire died away. And even the searchlights, which were still exploring the sky for any suspicious appearance, went out one by one. A daydream had been dreamed out.

As always after any unusual event, Karl appeared on the scene. "The English evidently won't have anything to do with Hell," he said. Suddenly his voice grew grim and he almost screamed: "But this Hell will burn, never fear, burn to the ground. You can be sure of that." And he left.

Although we learned next day from the radio that the nocturnal gunnery had been due to a false alarm and that the flak had shot down a stray German plane, the "Bromberg murderers" paid a heavy price for the mistake of the German antiaircraft post.

The day after the alarm a terrific nervousness descended upon the camp personnel. Fear of a real attack, as Karl often told us with malicious satisfaction, showed through all their boastful talk. The authorities took the incident very seriously and began to institute extensive precautions against a real attack. All day long high officers and blockfuehrers inspected the environs of the camp and elite prisoners could be seen crawling around on the roofs of barracks looking for shrapnel.

One barrack had actually, in some inexplicable manner, caught fire, and though the fire had been quickly extinguished, the Kommandant was taking no risks. The camp fire brigade was turned out that very day for a drill lasting several hours. The waterworks were inspected with the utmost thoroughness; all the water pipes and fire hose were tested. Every block was ordered to form its own fire brigade, to which each wing had to furnish a contingent of ten men. And in each wing from now on two buckets of water, some sacking and a ladder had to be kept in readiness.

The drilling of our fire brigade began immediately and was frequently repeated. Of course, it was used as a new means of torment. When the order, "Fire brigade turn out," sounded, the fire brigade had to leave everything, snatch up buckets, sacking and ladder and rush outdoors, dressed or not. Our tormentors loved to call out the fire brigade at night, particularly in winter, and send them running out into the cold, half naked and barefoot.

Unfortunately it remained only a drill. Up to the time of my release there was not one single genuine alarm in Sachsenhausen. And I was not the only one in camp who bitterly deplored that fact.

The beautiful autumn weather, so exceptionally warm that year, changed in mid-October to piercing cold, and it was many weeks before we had adjusted ourselves to the new conditions.

We sat shivering on the cold floor and rubbed our numb limbs to keep them from freezing. Our imaginations were dominated by the stove in the day room, and every day we hoped that Karl would succeed in getting permission to light it. That would have given us a chance to warm ourselves a little, at least at mealtimes. But one day Karl, shaking with anger, announced the latest edict: it was forbidden to heat the Polish blocks.

We listened thunderstruck. There was scarcely a man in the barrack who had not already felt the effects of the cold. But coughs, sneezing and sore throats were only the beginning of our winter tragedy. Frozen limbs, gangrene, pneumonia and consumption would be the end.

Against this fiat Karl's ingenuity and his "good connections" were powerless. For a moment he thought of getting fuel secretly from his friends, but he quickly abandoned the idea. "You know," he said mournfully, "a lighted stove can't very well be made invisible."

Then he gave us a second piece of bad news. The "Bromberg murderers" were forbidden to have light. All the consequences of this order immediately rose before us. Since our preparation for the night had to be finished when darkness fell, the distribution of the evening ration would become a mad race. Soon it would be completely dark outside when we got up in the morning, and dressing, washing and leaving the barrack in the dark would be hopelessly confused. And the result would be punishment upon punishment.

Our faces must have reflected our deep despair, for Karl, who had remained in the room, suddenly adopted a casual tone, as if he wished to rally us from our grim thoughts.

"If we could complain to the English," he said, "about the ungentlemanly way the Nazis are treating their allies, perhaps that would help. The trouble is, we have no short-wave transmitter. But how would it be if we transmitted our complaints by telepathy? One thing is sure, if the Royal Air Force comes to Sachsenhausen, we'll get light and fire in abundance. Come on, let's try telepathy."

A lighted stove could not have given us more warmth and comfort in that bitter moment than Karl's half-ironic, half-serious words. Instantly a more cheeful mood took possession of the barrack. Some comrades eagerly took up Karl's proposal and began to "telepath" their wishes and complaints, not only to the English, but to various other addressees. To everyone's delight, one wit improvised a telepathic dialogue with Hitler, in which he spoke his mind to the Fuehrer with all the resources of his vocabulary, and Hitler, bursting into a frenzy, tried to answer him. This drama was acted in a whisper, of course. But it was a masterpiece of mimicry and so amusing that for a time our troubles were forgotten.

One night toward the end of October we were awakened by footsteps and whispers in the day room. At last Karl opened the door. "We have newcomers from Leipzig," he said, "forty of them, and each wing must take in twenty as quickly as possible."

Our ranks had been so thinned that housing new arrivals was no problem. We drew closer together and everyone who had a place near him reported it to the indoor squad. While the Leipzigers were being led to their places, stumbling and falling in the unaccustomed darkness, an excited whispering began among us.

This was the first time a consignment of Polish prisoners who did not come from the vicinity of Berlin had been brought to the camp; for the first time we were coming in contact with the outside world. What could be the reason for these prisoners' arrival? Would they be able to give us any news?

I too had received a newcomer as a neighbor. Like the other new arrivals he had no idea what kind of company he was in. I could feel him shaking with fear. In a few words, I gave him to understand that he was among his own kind and had nothing to fear. Helpless, despairing sobs were his only answer.

What could I do to soothe him? Words of comfort were too banal. Words of hope, in view of recent events, were hard to find. So I silently helped him to undress, and since I had grown used to doing things in the dark, I folded up his clothes in the prescribed way and put them under the straw sack. After that he slowly grew calmer and started to talk.

"After the reception they gave us here, I did not believe they would ever let us get out of their clutches alive. It is good to know that we are among our own people." And all his pent-up anguish found release in a flood of speech. But we were strictly forbidden to talk at night, and although I was burning with curiosity to hear some news, I had to silence my neighbor.

That was easier said than done. How could I speak to this terrified man of things "verboten"?

"Friend," I said, turning away, "I can readily imagine your reception. When we talk by daylight, everything will look different. But now let us sleep and gather new strength." Then we pressed each other's hand in silence and I turned over on the other side.

But sleep was not to be thought of. All my remaining hope of release or transfer to an internment camp had been smashed to splinters. Who could believe in any kind of alleviation, when new Polish victims were continually being offered up to the Nazi Moloch? Could there be the slightest doubt that we were lost, if the war did not end soon?

Fierce indignation arose in me. Why should we be lost? Would no human soul protest against these modern cannibals? Where were the Swedes? And where were our relatives? Where was Gucia? Had she tried anything? Was she at all aware of what was happening to me? Or had she submitted to the inevitable?

But no, that was unthinkable! Gucia and submission? The two things did not go together. Gucia would never submit as long as her mind was working and she had command of her limbs. I must possess myself in patience and go on trusting in her.

But what if Gucia was not free? What if the Gestapo had sent our women to a woman's concentration camp? As always when I thought of such a possibility, my self-control was done for. I tossed back and forth on my straw sack, and before my eyes unrolled a series of bloody scenes, with my daughter as the central figure. The phantasy images would not be driven out, but became ever more cruel, as if poison had been injected into my brain. It was hours before I calmed myself with the thought that perhaps the reports of the Leipzig comrades might give us some clue to the fate of our families.

The next morning began with a wave of terror. No sooner had we gone out in front of the barracks than the blockfuehrers appeared upon the scene. They took the new arrivals in hand and gave them a second baptism into the camp. The Leipzigers were assailed with a volley of questions, which they, unversed in the habits of the camp, could not answer correctly. That was the signal: the blockfuehrers ran riot. And one of them commented: "This is to remind you that you're in Sachsenhausen. This is no sanatorium. Here we have a crematorium."

After roll call, the Leipzigers were ordered to the Political Division. We had never been summoned to the Political Division, and we gave ourselves up to speculation. When the Leipzigers returned shortly before the noon roll call, they were so broken in spirit that we could get nothing out of them. It was only gradually that they recovered and told us what had happened.

They had been violently maltreated and then photographed in various poses. Some day their bleeding, anguished faces would illustrate an article on "the Polish beast men" or some similar theme in *Der Stuermer* or another of the infamous Jew-baiting publications.

"How could you ever stand it?" asked one of the Leipzig comrades. "You must surely have experienced something of the sort," and he and the others broke into wild sobbing.

With all understanding for their feelings, we could not help wondering at the naïveté of this question, and one of the "Old

Guard" answered ironically: "We just got used to it. Everything is hard to begin with, but you will get used to it, all right."

It seemed to me, however, that we ought not simply to dismiss the question. The state to which these three attacks had brought the newcomers was dangerous to their morale. Instead of accepting the facts as they were and rallying their strength for resistance, they gave themselves up to gloomy reflections and lamentations. Experience had taught us that this only undermined one's powers of resistance and hastened the end. If we wanted to help the Leipzigers over the critical first days, we must make clear to them what they had to expect and show them how to arm themselves. We must make it plain that whoever wanted to survive had to fight with all his spirit, hope and faith in God. I proposed therefore that we and the Leipzigers should exchange experiences.

After the noon roll call we had a short rest period at last and the Leipzigers gave us their report. As early as September 1, the Leipzig Gestapo had arrested all male Polish citizens over thirteen years old and sent them to Leipzig prisons. There the Polish Jews were immediately segregated from their Christian fellow citizens and made to do heavy work inside and outside of the prison. Toward the end of October, two groups were sent off to the concentration camps of Buchenwald and Dachau, and a few days later our comrades were shipped to Oranienburg to the Sachsenhausen camp. In the Leipzig prison there remained only a handful of old or particularly feeble Jews. At that time the Polish Christians were sent to a regular internment camp near Nuremberg.

After this report one of us took the floor and described everything that had happened to us since September 13. His speech was concise and matter-of-fact. But the very simplicity of his words made the story inexpressibly moving. We, who knew all these events from our own experience, listened in wonder. How was it possible that human beings could endure so much? In comparison, our Leipzig comrades' stay in prison was like a vacation. Even the newcomers must have felt that. When our comrade turned to them with the words, "Now you may decide if you are justified in despairing," they remained silent.

The speaker allowed a short time for his words to sink in. Then he continued:

"I have not told you of our experiences to harrow you, but to strengthen you, to show you how much a man can bear when his spirit and his faith are strong. It has always been the Jewish tradition to put spirit above matter. You must do the same. Remember, we are not the first martyrs and probably will not be the last. In this time of anguish, we must so live and, if need be, so die as to show ourselves worthy of our ancestors and give our descendants no cause for shame. This duty is ours, even if the world knows nothing of our sufferings and perhaps may never learn.

"But not only duty is ours. Hope is ours, too. Are we not in God's hands even here? Cannot God save whom He will? Cast doubt away, for doubt destroys you; build not on your own reason, for it must fail here; only hold fast to your trust in God and believe. For faith makes men strong."

A solemn stillness reigned in the room when he had finished. Deep faith in God welled up in our hearts. What else could we do but believe? According to logic and reason, should we not long since have been among the dead? What else but faith could give the answer, when logic and reason failed?

Again, as on the memorable night of the Feast of Atonement, a rare mood of devotion took possession of us. We were shaken, overwhelmed, filled with a sense of the inscrutability of God's will. It was as if the spirit of God had descended upon the room. Always, when I recollect the overpowering experience of such moments, I wish that I had the ability to put on canvas, for all the world and for all time, the exalted piety, the burning faith that I so often saw shining in the faces of my comrades. Could there be a greater proof of the indestructibility of faith in a Divine Power than the testimony of this deep religious feeling in a concentration camp?

Our exalted mood did not last long. We were all still under the spell of the moving speech when the guard at the windows suddenly announced the approach of the blockfuehrers. Quickly we straightened our ranks. Then they were standing in front of our windows, spattering us with the usual stream of filthy curses. That was only the prelude.

"Leipzigers step forward!" ordered a blockfuehrer as the band appeared in our dormitory. The Leipzigers carried out the order smartly. But that did not save them. Since their posture was too correct to be made the basis of attack, their appearance, which contrasted very favorably with ours, was used as a pretext.

"You full-fed swine," roared a blockfuehrer, "maybe you think that for all eternity you can fill your bellies with the fruits of German labor?" After this introduction, his club whizzed down on the man standing nearest to him. The blow was directed to such a vulnerable spot that the man collapsed without a sound and remained in a deep stupor. But the fists and boots of the blockfuehrers went to work unmercifully. It was not until many hours later that he regained consciousness. But he never recovered. He languished away, and one morning when we awoke he was dead.

As one day had followed another without news from our families, we had begun to believe that they too had been arrested. The Leipzigers had relieved our minds on that point, however, for they told us they had talked with their relatives just before being transferred to the camp, and we felt sure that the Leipzig Gestapo would not have let Polish women go free if the Berlin Gestapo had not set the example.

But the longing for a word from home consumed us, and, as time went by, the strain warped the minds of many comrades so that they succumbed to ugly doubts. "My wife," one of the overwrought men would say to his neighbor, "the devil only knows what's gotten into her. She can't be very much concerned about me if she doesn't take the trouble to send me one word."

Of course, the explanation was obvious to anyone who stopped to think. If we were forbidden to write, was it not logical that we were not allowed to receive letters either? But in their anger and depression the men were not capable of thinking logically.

One day the mounting indignation of those who believed themselves neglected burst out openly. Karl had brought a postcard from the office for a comrade whom we had never heard speak of his family and who did not seem at all moved by this event, which utterly overwhelmed the rest of us. "So then people can write to us if they want to!" the doubters cried out at once. "Do we need any more proof?" Men who until then had been quiet and reserved broke into outbursts of frenzy. Had they been able to go home, just for a few minutes, there would have been murder.

The arrival of the Leipzigers had caused the first stir in our block for many weeks, but from then on small groups of Polish prisoners from other German cities were brought in almost every day. The smaller the group, the worse they suffered; for in such cases the blockfuehrers could devote more attention to each one. The prisoners who were shipped in after the evening roll call had the hardest lot: by then the blockfuehrers' duties were over and they could give all their time to the newcomers. This sudden activity was not confined to the Polish blocks, as new transports of prisoners from all the occupied territories were continually arriving, and preparations were constantly being made for the reception of more.

Until the appearance of the Leipzig comrades, we had had no glimpse of any prisoners but ourselves and the occupants of the elite barrack, so effectively were the Polish blocks isolated. These three Polish blocks stood in a row. On the south a broad road lay between them and the rest of the camp; on the north a narrower path divided them from the three elite blocks opposite, which in turn bordered on the first inner wall of the camp. On the east a broad path led from Barrack 39, on the extreme right, to the storehouse barracks; while Barrack 37, on the extreme left, was separated from the Bunker only by a narrow ditch.

Thus we lived on an island, which the other prisoners were strictly forbidden to approach. One day, however, shortly after the arrival of the Leipzigers, we were startled to see a continuous procession of about 1000 prisoners making for the storehouses, from which they emerged in couples, carrying a straw sack between them. We craned our necks to see better. The majority looked terribly exhausted, beaten and emaciated. They moved with dragging steps, and although we could not hear, we sensed that they were panting under their burdens. The group was accompanied by foremen who mercilessly beat the human ruins when the work went too slowly.

When the men had finished transporting the sacks, they carried out iron bedsteads and the wooden slats that supported the straw sacks. Then came tables, benches, cupboards and other equipment. This lasted for several hours.

The sight of these prisoners immediately started a controversy as to whether it was better to work or to grow stiff from sitting. Most of us preferred any kind of work to doing nothing. But a comrade holding the opposite view broke in impatiently. "Are you all blind?" he shouted. "Can't you see from the faces and bodies of those poor devils that it isn't a question of working or being idle?

Here work is not done for the sake of work. Here work is only another method of extermination."

It was not until several months later that we learned from our own experience how right he was. The Gestapo did not make us work in order to obtain services out of us; if so, they would have done everything possible to maintain our capacity for work. Instead, they undermined our powers of resistance.

The question of drinking-water was the best proof of this. Where food was concerned, the SS might maintain, with a show of justice, that food was scarce and the German people must be fed first. But water was not scarce. Later, when we were sent off to work and were so desperate with thirst that collapse, and even death, seemed not far off, we had to watch a horse near by being watered. But instead of allowing us a reviving sip of water, the foremen beat us because we did not work fast enough.

The moving of the furnishings from the storehouse had, of course, made us wonder what new victims were expected. Karl brought us the news that two thousand Czech students and intellectuals had just been brought in. A few days later we saw the Czechs march past, close to our block. It was evident that by their arrest the Nazis had cunningly deprived the Czech resistance of not only their best brains but their best-trained bodies.

From then on we saw the Czechs almost every day, marching and running for half an hour in our district, until they were sent to work. They showed at that time no signs of mistreatment. Since they were allowed to receive packages of food and clothing from home, they looked comfortably warm and well nourished. They also wore regular uniforms and even overcoats.

The special privileges granted to the Czechs naturally created envy among the German prisoners. Could it be that the Nazis granted these privileges so as to kindle hatred against the Czechs and kill two birds with one stone? Yet the more I thought of the special position of the Czech prisoners, the more I became convinced that it was a stupid attempt to combine bribery with terror. And I was equally convinced that the Czech youth would not walk into this clumsy snare. Whenever I saw those splendid young men with their grim faces march past us, I could not help thinking of Gucia's and my last visit to Czechoslovakia, and of the anxiety and resolution we had found there. I remembered many little scenes, apparently unimportant, but, in the light of the contemporary political situation, symbolic.

It was in the autumn of 1937. We had been strolling at random near Wenceslaus Square, a part of the carefree crowd, letting ourselves be carried along by the waves of people. Suddenly we found ourselves in a completely strange neighborhood and quite lost. Then, as if summoned up from beneath the ground, a deus ex machina stood before us in the form of a stout, friendly-looking policeman.

"But we know no Czech," I said to Gucia, "so the policeman can't help us."

But Gucia began to laugh. "Now I'll prove to you that my *Collegium Logicum* diploma which you laugh at so much is of some use after all in practical life. Do you see his fat paunch and the many insignia on his uniform? That means he is at least forty-five, about twenty years in the service. So, since this is the year 1937, our policeman must have begun his career under their Imperial and Royal Majesties Franz and Karl von Habsburg. *Ergo,* he speaks German. We too can speak German. *Ergo,* we and the policeman can understand each other."

And before I could respond to this flood of academic verbiage, she addressed the policeman in German: "Wuerden Sie bitte——" But she got no farther. The policeman shrugged his shoulders, shook his head violently and made it emphatically clear that he did not understand a word.

Now it was my turn to be superior. "Hm," I said, "Collegium Logicum. A fine thing, provided the premise is correct."

Gucia gave me a disgusted look. Then suddenly another bright idea occurred to her. "The premise is 100 per cent correct," she cried. "Something quite different is wrong." And with the most disarming smile in the world, she spoke to the policeman in Polish. Then he grinned all over his face and said apologetically in Czech, "I thought you were Germans, and when I don't choose to I don't understand German." We spoke Polish and he spoke Czech; and we understood each other beautifully.

This apparently trivial episode made us thoughtful and we repeated the experiment. Wherever we went, we would speak first in German; instantly faces froze before us. Then we would speak Polish, and the faces lighted up. Prague in 1937 showed us, more plainly than any number of newspaper editorials could do, how the Czechs felt about the Germans.

That the Czechs were aware of the seriousness of the situation, an ordinary tourist guide had plainly shown us. We had made the grand tour of the city that year, as we always did, with a group of sightseers from all over the world. On top of the hill where the Hradschin stood, our guide had brought the trip to an end with these words:

"Before you leave this place, look down once more. At your feet lies the last democratic city in Europe east of the Rhine. If ever the fate of this bastion of democracy hangs in the balance, do not leave us in the lurch."

The influx of prisoners into Sachsenhausen was accompanied by an unexpected exodus. One morning Karl brought in a truly sensational piece of news. "The office has just announced that German prisoners whose political past is not too black may be released if they volunteer for service at the front," he said. "But even if they'd release me unconditionally, I'd politely decline. This war will last for years; and *the* scoundrel will put every available man into uniform —invalids, cripples and all. And am I going to risk having to fight for that bloodhound? No, I'm staying here; and when the time comes, I'll do my bit in the housecleaning."

In the toilet room, where we could talk longer and more uninterruptedly than at any other time, this piece of news, like all the latest events, was discussed and embroidered with all kinds of flourishes. Gradually a regular news service developed, which we dubbed "The Latrine Courier" and which soon came to have great influence. Anyone who had heard some bit of news or worked out a theory delivered his "copy" to the toilet room, from which it spread with the speed of wireless to both wings.

Little by little the indoor squad emerged as the news center and editorial staff. By staying in the day room, they had constant contact with Karl, and overheard his conversations with his friends. In the course of their duties, they often met the indoor squads of the other two Polish blocks, went on various errands around the camp with Karl and later alone, and in this way picked up morsels of news. The indoor squads of all three blocks exchanged their reports, and comrades whom they had appointed as "collaborators" spread it to the dormitories, via the toilet. In order to establish the reliability of their service, they alternately spread pleasant and unpleasant news, and since so many contradictory reports were in circulation, some of this could not help but be true.

Of course, a few of us pretended to have nothing but contempt for "The Latrine Courier." When a comrade announced that he had something of general interest to tell, they would say with superior shrugs: "Aha, a new latrine dispatch." All the same, they pricked up their ears and did not miss a syllable.

One day it occurred to me that we might use "The Latrine Courier" as a means of keeping up morale, and the indoor squad readily fell in with this idea. Often when the general mood had reached a dangerous low, we invented reports that dispelled the depression. Although the predicted improvements for the most part never came true, the men were so hungry for hope that they greedily swallowed the encouraging reports.

When Paul had assembled the indoor squad, he had picked out the scum of our company. Most of them became so successful in the role for which they were cast that one might have thought they had moved all their lives in Paul's and Rolly's sphere. Little by little even the more considerate ones followed their lead. There was only one whom they could not win over, the music professor D'Arguto, mentioned before.

He had not properly been chosen by Paul. One of the prisoners working in the office, who had once been a musician himself and admired D'Arguto, had asked Karl to put him into the indoor squad to make his life easier. From then on, the professor was a thorn in the flesh of the indoor squad, for he told them exactly what he thought of them. But from fear of Karl, none of them dared lay a hand on him. They punished "the crackpot" by ignoring him and went on doing exactly as they liked.

The key figure in the indoor squad in each wing was the food distributor, because, since he measured out the rations, he had it entirely in his power to slight or favor anyone—thus everyone courted him. The second most important figure in each wing respectively was the washroom overseer (Bademeister) and the toilet overseer, or "Scheisskommandant," as we nicknamed him. The bathmaster was chosen from Wing B. His task was to keep spic-and-span his half of the corridor connecting the two wings, the door and steps that led to his wing, and the washroom. This position gave him ample opportunity to torture the other inmates of the block. According to his mood, he harried us during the brief washing period so that hardly anyone could bathe, or let his favorites use the basins on the floor to wash their feet.

Since our wing adjoined the toilet, we furnished the Scheisskommandant. His duty was to keep clean our half of the connecting corridor, and the steps and door to our wing, and to cleanse the toilets three times a day. Out of pure, inborn meanness he used this position to torment us. Though he knew we could use the toilets only during recess, he made a point of doing the cleaning then and drove us out before we had a chance to relieve ourselves.

The Scheisskommandant not only jealously guarded the six toilet bowls which had to serve all the inmates, but also the water faucet in the toilet room. That was the only place where we could get water, except for the faucet in the washroom, which we could enter only in the morning when there was never enough time to drink. Although we knew that the water in the toilet room was not well filtered, and therefore unhygienic, everyone snatched at the opportunity of getting a drink. But when the Scheisskommandant began the cleaning, no one was permitted to go near the faucet. If anyone succeeded in stealing in there unnoticed and in his haste splashed a few drops of water on the floor, it was no laughing matter for the culprit.

The other members of the indoor squad were by no means backward either. Each of them tormented and tyrannized over us to his heart's content, and they had so intimidated us that we never ventured to single out one of the gang and make him pay for his meanness. The less we rebelled, the worse they tortured us, and this persecution by our own comrades was more bitter than the blockfuehrers' cruelties.

As long as Karl was our room senior, however, the indoor squad had to practice some restraint. Karl was the only one for whom they had respect and a certain fear. One of them, for instance, had appropriated some margarine and hid it; the rest of the gang, not being in the secret, reported the loss to Karl. Karl did not rest until the guilty man and the missing margarine were found, and he not only dismissed the thief from the indoor squad but beat him almost to death.

The others took warning from this example. They did not alter their treatment of us in the least, but they became more cautious and did everything in collusion. When Karl made a surprise search from time to time, everything was always in order. We—as the indoor squad knew only too well—were much too intimidated to open our mouths.

In Wing B things were still worse. There no one kept an eye on the indoor squad. By rights Karl ought to have seen to it, but he allowed Franz to do just as he liked, although he knew well enough that the other abused his authority. Franz used this freedom to further his own purposes. He had not been a horse trader for nothing. Since he never felt any too secure in his post, he took care to make as many connections as possible and used Wing B's food as bait. Always, when food was distributed in Wing B, a number of Franz's potential friends turned up to get their share. In this way a good part of the rations of Wing B found its way not only to the indoor squad, who of course took good care of their own interests, but to outsiders.

At the beginning Franz practiced his machinations secretly. But, when convinced that Karl was leaving him a free hand, he abandoned all caution. And the comrades in Wing B, who greedily picked up every crumb of bread from the floor, had to look on while their scanty rations disappeared into the mouths of other, better-nourished prisoners.

Bread was our most valuable possession and one of our greatest problems. Often, when sick and miserable and unable to eat the ration, many could not bear to give it away. The next day, perhaps, they would be hungry again, and how good it would be to have an extra piece of bread! So they hid the bread in their coat pockets.

It was not long before the blockfuehrers learned of this. One day at the noon roll call they searched every prisoner in all three blocks and collected the bread. Then a list of punishments came down upon us.

"Today the Polaks will go without food."

"And drink, ditto."

"The next time the Jew pack hides bread, they'll march to the Bunker or the punishment squad."

And then one of them had a more original idea. "The gang must have their coat pockets sewed up by evening," he decreed.

Franz welcomed the order as an opportunity to win favor with the blockfuehrers. As quickly as his rheumatic feet in their wooden slippers would carry him, he ran into his wing after roll call to supervise the sewing. Later he came to see how our work was getting on.

"In my wing they're already much further along," he said boastfully. "So they needn't sit so long without their coats and shiver like you. Here you need to get up some steam."

Karl said nothing and left the dormitory with a look that spoke his whole contempt for Franz. But Franz, pretending not to notice that Karl had cut him, kept a strict eye on the tailors. This made them very nervous, and one, who was always making funny remarks to cheer up the others, said to the air in front of him: "Who says I'm freezing? When that one watches me, I get hot all over and start sweating." The tailors who heard this remark began to laugh loudly and those who had not heard it followed suit. Franz turned red. "What is there to laugh about?" he demanded. But the men only laughed louder. Franz gave the tailors a baffled look, turned tail like a beaten dog and clattered out. Later, when the tailors reported to Karl that the sewing was finished, he remarked dryly: "There are some mouths around here that ought to be sewed up too."

In spite of Franz's parade of efficiency, the tailors in his own wing had not finished their sewing, so that at evening roll call he was in mortal terror that the blockfuehrers would hold him responsible for the failure to carry out the order. But the blockfuehrers had evidently forgotten about the pockets. A prisoner was missing, and the usual search had begun.

It was a cold night. We were hungry and frozen. From the assembly place the wind brought a peculiar noise, which we gradually recognized as the painful coughing of many thousand throats. We too were coughing incessantly—hollow, alarming coughs. And the standing continued for four long hours.

When at last we returned to the barrack, shivering all over and weary to the point of collapse, it was too late to eat. As we lay sleepless with cold and hunger, Karl came in and told us the whole story. The search for the fugitive had seemed hopeless until the blockfuehrers learned that the missing man had worked all day in a cellar. They searched it and from under a pile of rubbish dragged out the unfortunate man, who had lost consciousness from the confinement and shock. The blockfuehrers used their feet and clubs on him to such purpose that when he was carried to the Bunker for questioning he was already dead.

As the season advanced, the consequences of cold and undernourishment made themselves felt more and more. Our coughing never stopped, day or night, and for want of handkerchiefs our running noses became a real torment. The barracks were again overcrowded. This brought some warmth but increased the danger of infection. The rapidly spreading colds developed into cases of pneumonia; and we knew they would carry off many of us unless we got medical help.

Karl worked his connections for all they were worth, but his success was in no proportion to the need. All he could accomplish was to have a few of us treated in the Revier every day. And we had to decide, among the hundreds of pain-twisted faces, who was in most urgent need of medical help.

The Revier stood on the left side of the assembly square, an iron grating and iron gate separating it from the rest of the camp. It consisted of three wooden barracks, about 240 feet long and 33 feet wide, with deep cellars underneath. One half of the barrack on the extreme left contained the room of the doctor on duty, the treatment room for the prisoners, the file room and reception room. The other half had about the same arrangement; but as this section was reserved for the treatment of the camp SS, everything about it was cleaner, roomier and more comfortable. The treatment room was fitted with every conceivable apparatus: X-ray machines, ultra-violet lamps and short-wave equipment, a dental clinic and a very modern operating room.

At a distance of about fifty feet from the first barrack, across a wide lane, stood the second barrack, and a narrow path divided this from the third. The last two barracks contained only wards, and the hundreds of beds in each were always filled. All kinds of illnesses were represented there, including tuberculosis, dysentery and diphtheria.

The majority of patients brought to the Revier eventually landed in a fourth barrack that stood in the immediate neighborhood. This was the morgue, generally called "the storeroom." There, so I was told, the dead were robbed of their gold teeth and gold fillings. Later, whenever I worked there, I counted hundreds and hundreds of wooden coffins; there were even times when the storeroom could not accommodate them. During my last months in Sachsenhausen, when dysentery was making inroads in the camp and the coffin factory in the industrial section could not turn out coffins fast enough to meet the need, the corpses were stacked up in the cellar of the reception barrack until space was made in the storeroom for a new batch.

Disposing of so many bodies at last became such an urgent problem that the camp authorities—so the rumor went—considered building their own crematorium. But up to the time of my release no attempt had been made to carry out this plan. The bodies were left as before to one of the biggest cremating companies, which daily sent its huge trucks to the camp to collect.

Everyone who sought admittance to the Revier for treatment had to appear in front of the building at a prescribed time. Day after day, long lines of wretched-looking men could be seen in front of the big iron gate. Often they had to stand for many hours, and often, after hours of waiting, they were driven off again by passing blockfuehrers. The next day the waiting would begin anew.

Four doorkeepers stood guard by turns and enforced quiet and order. When a superior passed the Revier, the waiting men had to snatch off their caps and stand at attention—and smartly too. But crippled or half-dead men are not smart. So the gatekeepers punished the invalids for their "slovenly salutes" and, when it pleased them, sent the sick men back to their barracks. If they were alive the next day, they might try again. When one of the waiting men collapsed, exhausted by long standing, the doorkeepers took it as a breach of discipline. So blood often flowed in front of the Revier, and since the Polish Jews stood in a special line, their blood flowed most abundantly.

But even when everything went well outside, admission for treatment or reception into the wards was by no means guaranteed. There were so many prerequisites: the supervisor of the reception room must be in the right mood, the doctor in charge must agree with his decision, the sick man must have a fever of at least 102 degrees and there must be a vacant bed in the ward. If the supervisor chose to pretend there was no room, even desperately ill men were turned away.

Prisoners who were so sick that they had to be carried to the Revier by their comrades were immediately taken to the cellar of the reception barrack where a few temporary beds had been set up. They were then as good as dead. To spend time on desperate cases was considered a waste of energy. So many a man perished in the cellars when a little proper care and medical aid might have kept him alive.

As to the hospital fare, the only difference between it and the ordinary camp diet was that the prisoners received white bread instead of black and some generously watered milk.

One of the most shattering experiences in the Revier was the treatment received from the infirmary attendants. These were prisoners, most of them criminals. With few exceptions they seemed intent upon making the patients' lives as hard as possible and counted every bite that went into their mouths. For in the Revier, as elsewhere in the camp, food was one of the most important articles of trade; it might be exchanged for cigarettes and even cash. As long as a patient was seriously ill and had no appetite, the attendants could do business with his food, and everything went well. But when he was able to eat, the relations between patient and attendant became badly strained. Often the attendants revenged themselves by getting the patient dismissed while his condition was still critical.

Whatever treatment the prisoners received in the treatment room was supposedly carried on under the supervision of several assistant doctors, all of them just out of medical school, but was really left entirely to the attendants. The attendants were very poorly trained and frequently changed, and it was some time before the new ones were broken in. They had not the faintest notion of how to wash out a wound or put on a bandage, handled us clumsily and often changed our dressings with dirt-caked fingers.

The medicine that we were allowed in the Revier was limited to aspirin, charcoal tablets, castor oil and a mysterious white powder that we had to wash down with water and that none of us could identify. But often the assistants refused us even these. "First come the German front soldiers," they would say; or, "The sooner you croak, the better for you. What do *you* want medicine for?"

Absolute czar in the Revier was the head surgeon of the camp.

His activity was confined to treating the SS clan. Only when a particularly interesting operation or amputation was involved did he bother about the prisoners. The numerous cases of blood poisoning and gangrene gave him many such opportunities. He was far from regarding himself as a friend and helper of the suffering. He performed amputations, not to benefit the patients, but because amputating was his passion. To him the Revier operating room was an experimental laboratory, and the prisoners so many guinea pigs. No wonder that everyone called him "Butcher-in-chief."

My sackmate, Ring, had a typical experience with the camp surgeon. Ring had arrived in the camp with a double hernia and had guarded his truss like a treasure. One day, after a particularly savage attack from the blockfuehrers, the truss broke and both hernias burst out. Karl realized that Ring would be lost unless he received medical attention at once and, by pulling all sorts of strings, succeeded in getting him admitted to the Revier.

Although Ring's condition had been made even worse by his being moved, the camp doctor refused to operate until the next day. Lying on a hard, unfriendly bed, with an unknown fate before him, Ring during that night of waiting went through all the agonies of fear for his family, of vacillating between the wish to live and wish to die. When he was laid upon the operating table the next morning, his anguish of mind was too much for him and he began to weep helplessly. Suddenly the face of the camp surgeon bent over him.

"Are you afraid, Jew Polak?" he asked in a hard, cutting voice. "You're in luck, you fool. I won't let you croak. If I weren't so interested in double hernias, it would be different."

And Ring actually was in luck, as his attendant, who took particular pains with him, later corroborated. Most of the prisoners from the isolated Polish blocks waited for days before the camp surgeon condescended to operate on them. And then, in most cases, it was too late.

On November 8, after evening roll call, we were kept outside unusually long. Darkness came on quickly and we prepared ourselves to spend the whole night outdoors. Karl seemed particularly excited, and this increased our forebodings. But this time our fears were wide of the mark. When the blockfuehrers appeared they announced, after a suitable introduction of curses, that the writing veto had been lifted.

When we were dismissed into the barracks, it was quite dark. Drinking was no longer to be dreamed of, of course, and we had to lie down without eating. But no one gave a thought to this. The news had put us into a delirium of joy. Every man's head was whirling with the thoughts, hopes and wishes that he wanted to put on paper. What wouldn't we have given to be able to write down this crowd of feelings straight from our hearts!

Karl wanted to show that he understood. When everything was quiet he came in for a few words. "The fright was not enough," he said. "You had to go without your 'black nectar' besides. But I know *that* makes no difference tonight. The time has come at last! And tomorrow we'll discuss together how the writing is to be tackled."

After eight weeks of complete seclusion from the outside world, we could not only write ourselves, but receive mail from our families. In our excitement, few of us could close an eye, and we waited, tense with impatience, for the paling dawn to melt away the night. It was an overwhelming experience to see before us at last a morning with a goal and a purpose!

When morning finally came and Karl went to the office as usual, the strain of waiting became almost a physical pain. Since we assumed that we could begin writing as soon as he returned, we did not take our usual positions after roll call. Then Franz came into our dormitory and, seeing us standing, he went into a frenzy, shouted, boxed the ears of the men nearest him and threatened to report us to the office for lack of discipline. And he did not quiet down until he saw Karl running in.

Karl had run so fast that he had to stop and get his breath before he could speak. There was a glimmer in his eye that we had come to know; it meant that he had been angered beyond endurance. Something must have gone wrong at the office. Franz tried to sneak away, but Karl ordered him back and then told us what was the matter.

"I'm damnably sorry to disappoint you like this," he said, "but you cannot begin writing until Saturday after the noon roll call. You know, of course, that here the day is looked upon as working time, and although you do not work, your squatting counts as the equivalent. If we had electric light you could write after the evening roll call. But we haven't gotten that far, yet."

And without another word he went out with Franz. But the way he slammed the door behind him was sufficient comment on his feelings.

For a while it was so still in the room that we could hear each other breathe. The disappointment, after our overstrained expectancy, was more than men could bear. We went all to pieces. The fact that our senseless squatting was looked upon as work might have moved us to hysterical laughter if we had had the strength to laugh.

Karl, of course, knew exactly how we felt. He never said much, especially in the way of comfort, before Franz; but when he had got rid of his assistant, he came back and began to talk to us as if we were children.

"I can understand that you are beside yourselves at the sadism of that gang, but you must be reasonable. Keep your chins up. After all, it is only two days until you'll get your wish."

But we were too shattered to answer his well-meant words. We sat in utter depression, staring fixedly in front of us. Karl tried a different tack.

"Now that I come to think of it, it is better that you are not allowed to write at once. For here writing is a great art, you know."

With these words he disappeared into the day room and came back with a sheet of writing paper, an envelope and a postcard, which he had us pass around. The sheet of paper was white, about 8 by 10 inches in size and folded in the middle, so that there were four pages. Every page was ruled with fifteen red lines. In the upper left hand corner "Konzentrationslager Sachsenhausen" was printed in large red letters; below was an abstract of the camp rules. Next came a line on which a prisoner must write his prison number, block number and the designation of his wing. Envelopes and postcards also carried the abstract and the line for the prisoner's data.

After each of us had seen the stationery, Karl read the abstract aloud. It went about as follows:

"'Every prisoner may write and receive two pieces of mail a month: one letter and one postcard. The letters may not be longer than four pages and each page may not contain more than fifteen lines. The handwriting must be legible and may not go over the ruled lines. Erasing and crossing out is forbidden. It is forbidden to send packages of any kind to the camp. However, the prisoners may receive 15 Reichsmarks every two weeks, since everything can be bought in the camp. Upon application a prisoner can subscribe either to the *Voelkischer Beobachter* or to the *Angriff*.'

"So," said Karl, when he had finished reading, "you have heard how you have to write. Do you think you could begin your letters now?"

"Of course. Why not?" we all cried at once.

"All right," said Karl, "let's just try. I suggest that everyone compose a letter in his mind and that some of you recite your letters aloud. But before you begin, let me remind you of several things. Every letter sent to or from the camp is read by at least five censors. If it is not written according to regulations, they may tighten up on the rules or even forbid writing altogether. And since I assume that not only the 'A pupils' but the 'C pupils' wish to write home, I advise you all to impress these rules firmly on your memories.

"Well," he concluded, after he had given his words time to sink in, "who is ready?"

But now the writing did not seem so simple, and no one wanted to make a fool of himself. Karl prodded us several times and each of us prodded his neighbor. But no one had the courage to volunteer. It was like the old days in school.

Karl looked expectantly from one to another. If our indecision made him impatient, he did not let us see it. Finally, like a model pedagogue, he appealed to our pride.

"I spoke before of the 'A' pupils. Now I see that I rated you too highly."

But even this effort brought no results. We were all ashamed but we could not overcome our shyness.

Karl's patience seemed boundless. "How would it be," he suggested, "if I were to pick out one of you?" Overjoyed to be relieved of the decision, we all agreed.

Karl had a good idea of each man's qualifications. His eyes wandered from one to another as if he were considering carefully whom to choose.

"Patachon," cried Karl at last, "stand up and recite your letter."

We would have liked to cheer this decision. The choice of Patachon would assure us of some fun. In an instant the perpetual look of sadness faded from our eyes. All the faces relaxed. One could read in them how eager they were to laugh once more.

Patachon alone had become quite pale. But he said nothing, stood up instantly and began to recite his letter, as if repeating a monologue he had learned by heart. At first his voice was hoarse from agitation, but gradually it steadied itself. He spoke with a calmness and self-possession that amazed us. The letter was addressed to his wife and was impressively short and simple. Except for the information that he had caught cold, Patachon said nothing about himself. Instead he betrayed his great concern for the welfare of his family and urgently implored his wife to emigrate if an opportunity offered, without any delay on his account. Then he gave detailed directions about the settlement of family business and asked for news as often as possible.

Patachon, whom we had looked on as a comic figure ever since the affair of the tailors, gained stature in our eyes with every sentence he spoke. We suddenly realized that his comical behavior was no indication of the depth of his feelings.

Patachon was so exhausted by his first public appearance and so alarmed at his own boldness that as soon as he had spoken the last word he crouched down in his place as if he would have liked nothing better than to make himself invisible. But Karl had a triumph ready for him.

"Good, Patachon, very good!" he cried, "and I only wish you would all follow Patachon's example and write with as much sense."

There was only one thing in Patachon's letter for Karl to find fault with, the statement that he had caught cold. "In a German concentration camp you are not allowed to catch cold," he explained. "To croak, oh yes, you may do that here, and welcome; but to advertise the fact is 'verboten.' But," he continued, turning to Patachon, "that is not your fault. For I forgot to say that every letter must begin with the statement, 'I am in good health and doing well.' That must be written, even if the writer is at his last gasp. And, while I think of it, feelings are forbidden too; only good German matter-of-factness is allowed."

Now we realized that letter writing in a concentration camp was indeed a special art, which had to be practiced diligently. So the rest of us began to compose letters and submit them to each other for criticism. Only the men who had been so angered by the silence of their families failed to take part. To all our arguments they replied sullenly that they would not think of writing home before they heard from their families.

After the early Saturday evening roll call, Karl announced that we could begin writing and ordered the indoor squad to give out the materials. He himself went to the office to see if any mail had arrived for us. He had advised us that as many as possible should write postcards, to make less work for the censors and speed up the dispatch of the mail. No one wanted to write a mere card, but at last those who had no close relatives agreed to do so.

We waited in the greatest suspense for Karl's return. And Karl actually did come back with a bundle of letters and cards, among them two letters addressed to two of the most bitter grumblers. To our surprise, all the mail was written in a concise style and contained only factual information, as though our families had been instructed about the writing rules in camp.

Although the letters were of interest only to the recipients, they passed from hand to hand. Everyone tried to read them over again and to hold them in his hand as long as he could. It was as if the written pages had a magic power.

The two former grumblers who had received mail had suddenly become very subdued. And even the others were ashamed of their stupid unreasonableness. Avoiding our eyes, the whole group immediately asked for writing materials. We knew they were overcome with self-reproach and we were careful not to embarrass them any more.

As soon as the lifting of the writing ban became known, I had resolved to be in the first group of writers. But when Karl announced that he would see about incoming mail, I changed my decision. "Perhaps there is a letter for me," I thought, "and it would be better to wait and answer it."

Quivering with impatience I stood at the window and kept watch. The prospect of holding a letter from Gucia in my hand at last, of seeing her familiar handwriting, of trying to read important messages between the lines, made my temples throb with anticipation.

When at last Karl entered the barrack, carrying a pile of letters, we all rushed at him. But in our eagerness we only created confusion and delay. Karl had hard work bringing order into the swarm of overwrought men, all pushing and talking at once. But at last there was a tense silence and Karl began to read out the names on the envelopes.

I had pushed my way into the front row. Every time Karl picked up a letter, I stretched out my hand—this one was surely for me. The next one, then, must surely be for me. Suddenly doubt chilled my heart. "What gives you the right to be so sure that there's something for you?" it asked. Yes, why should I be among the first? And to guard against disappointment, I said to myself, "Nonsense, you will get no letter until you have written and Gucia knows that she is allowed to write." And to prove to myself that I was not counting on a letter at all, I slipped out of the front row and stood aside.

But my common sense had a hard struggle this time. I went on listening for the names that Karl read out until he had given out the last letter and there was no more doubt that I was not among the lucky ones.

My reflections were much closer to the truth than I guessed at the time: Gucia had had a reason for not writing. She knew from other cases that many an unauthorized letter sent to Sachsenhausen had ended the life of the recipient. So she preferred to disappoint me rather than put me in danger.

The hours until supper were filled with unaccustomed activity. The day room was given over to the writing, and a cheerfulness rare in a concentration camp prevailed in the whole wing. Karl watched this eager bustle from his table, where he was reading a newspaper, with an expression that showed how much he shared our happiness. When it began to grow dark, he ordered the men to stop writing so that we would finish our preparations for the night in time. The indoor squad was just beginning to give out the evening bread ration when Anton suddenly appeared in the day room, went up to Karl and whispered in his ear. Karl's face darkened instantly; he jumped up and left the barrack with the other man. We looked after them uneasily. Our consternation grew when Willi from Block 37 joined them outside and Anton also called out Franz from Wing B.

While we were still exchanging conjectures, Karl and Anton came back and Anton made a speech.

"Something's up," he said. "The brothers are going to honor us particularly tonight. So we had better make suitable preparations. All beating implements out of the way. Clothes put away in perfect order. Absolute quiet. And most important—at the word of command, on your feet like lightning." Then he went into the day room and gave instructions to the indoor squad.

This was the first time we had come in contact with Anton. We could see that he meant well, but his mysterious hints had plunged us into dreadful anxiety. The worst certainty would have been better than that nerve-hammering terror of the unknown.

Fortunately, Karl was a better psychologist. As soon as Anton left, Karl told us the whole truth. At the celebration on November 9 in the Buergerbrauekeller in Munich, where Hitler made an annual speech, a time bomb had gone off. True, Hitler had left the meeting earlier than usual. But the stroke was construed as an attempt on his life and was attributed to the British Secret Service.

"The affair smells strongly of the Reichstag fire," Karl commented, but he took it very seriously. "Of course, we have no English prisoners here," he said. "But we have England's allies. The murderers will exact payment from you.

"But you don't need to hang your heads so," continued Karl, when he saw the devastating effect of this news. "We've ridden out so many storms, we will ride out this one too. There's one comfort, remember; the arch-criminal can't feel any too secure if he takes refuge in such farces to put spirit into his dear German 'Volksgenossen.' But bluff won't help him forever," he muttered between his teeth, and went over to Wing B to say a few comforting words there, for he could easily guess in what fashion Franz had disclosed the impending attack to his flock.

Karl's words had produced only a superficial calm. The sudden transition from the joyful excitement of the afternoon to the expectation of new horrors was too great a shock to be softened by anything he could say. Even the efforts of our humorists failed this time; we could too plainly see the fear of death behind their forced, clownlike cheerfulness.

Mechanically we gulped down our food and stretched ourselves out on our pallets. Following Anton's advice, we kept very still. Only here and there some despairing man would give a sudden sob and instantly fall silent again. But our own hearts echoed the sobs, and the contrast between the dead silence and the occasional sounds of suffering shook us to the marrow. We lay there, waiting to be killed. Long before the murderers appeared in person, we endured their attack in our minds.

"If we could at least have fought for our lives," I thought, "like an animal when it is attacked." But the satisfaction of this primary instinct was not for us. We were not animals but men; and what distinguishes man from beast if not his sense of responsibility to his fellow men? Only this held us back from leaping upon our murderers and killing them as they killed us. We knew too well that for the life of any one of our tormentors we must pay with many lives of our fellows. Our highest law was still "All for one." We had no choice but to let ourselves be murdered unresistingly, however we might inwardly rebel.

Some day, however—this I felt quite certain of—when even the last of us had given up all hope, we would shake off this martyrdom. Our tormentors were still feeling safe, so safe that they never bound us or stunned us, as one does with cattle led to slaughter. They could still despise us for not resisting, still curse us as cowards while they were doing us to death. But some day, even in us, animal instinct would gain the upper hand. Then we would leap upon them and fight with our bare hands, not for our lives but for their deaths.

That night we waited long for the appearance of the blockfuehrers and did not notice their approach until the familiar glimmer of flashlights in the distance gave us warning. This time the attack began simultaneously in Blocks 37 and 39. We saw the lights flash out in both blocks and flicker into every corner; we saw the darting human shadows that flitted past the windows like ghosts. Complete silence accompanied this light-and-shadow play. Suddenly, as if by common consent, piercing screams broke out from both barracks. At the same moment a bumping noise was heard, as if heavy objects were being thrown around. Then came a clanking of metal.

In our block everything remained still. But the screaming of our comrades, which made us live through their mistreatment, and the waiting for our own to begin, put us into a state that seemed like the first stage of madness. Suddenly, as if at an invisible signal, we joined in the screaming.

Then Karl threw open the door. "Stop that screaming," he cried in a horrified voice. "Have you gone mad? Do you want to provoke the beasts still more?"

But we had lost control over our nerves. "Yes!" came confused cries. "We are mad . . . mad . . ." And instead of calming down we screamed still louder; and the howls that came from our throats had no resemblance to any human sound.

Karl made a last effort. "You are endangering not only your selves; you are bringing me in danger too," he cried, so loudly that he outshouted us all.

Then it was as if Karl had found the magic formula that transformed us from unreasoning wild beasts back into men. To bring him in danger—no, we did not want that—him, our only friend and comforter. And the roaring stopped as suddenly and simultaneously as it had begun. We could still reason. Certainly we were not yet mad.

Karl went out without another word and left anxiety and shame behind him. We were afraid that the blockfuehrers had heard us and our concern for Karl's safety was almost greater than the fear for our own.

At last the moment came. The lights in the other blocks went out. Only a few seconds later they flashed on again in our barrack. The blockfuehrers had divided themselves into two groups and each took one wing. Their number was unusually great. We were stunned, and Karl seemed as appalled as we. His voice trembled when he shouted, "Achtung!"

The blockfuehrers' lust for blood did not let them pause for the usual preliminary commands. Instantly they hurled themselves upon us. This time they had brought a special kind of club, which was bound with strips of metal. The metal cut into our bodies and mowed us down like withered grass. We let ourselves fall without a sound, but when they trampled on us and hopped from one leg to the other on our bodies, we began to scream with all our strength.

They had waited only for that. Now they began to curse us in chorus.

"This is the last time you'll ever scream, you English hirelings. Tomorrow you'll be hanged." And they trampled on us more furiously than ever.

But even the strength of blockfuehrers has a limit; so to give themselves a breathing spell, they made us run from one corner to the other. Suddenly one of them ordered: "Halt! To the wall with you, snouts facing it." They stationed themselves close behind us.

We huddled together facing the wall. The blockfuehrers behind us remained motionless for a while. For one brief moment we thought: "Now they will draw their revolvers and shoot blindly at our backs," and many a man was glad that a quick death was coming. But they did not shoot. Instead, one of them commanded: "Throw yourselves on your bellies without moving from your places."

We were pressed so close together that we could not move a limb.

How could we throw ourselves down? It was against the laws of physics.

But the blockfuehrers did not trouble themselves about impossibilities.

"Be quick, you miserable vermin!"

"Lively now, or there'll be fireworks in a minute."

Desperately we tried to obey the order. In vain.

"Sabotage! . . . Disobedience! . . . Mutiny! . . ." roared the blockfuehrers.

Then their metal-bound clubs whistled through the air. A dreadful cry of pain rang out. And in those few seconds we grasped the Satanic intention behind the order. We were to fall one on top of another, like a collapsing house of cards. As each row fell over, the pressure on the men below would be increased, and many would be crushed and smothered.

But the limit of our capacity for silent suffering had been reached. And as we had done once before with Rolly, we seized upon the only possible means of defense. We began to scream so murderously that we were frightened by the sound of ourselves.

The blockfuehrers had not reckoned with such a loud protest. At first they went on beating mechanically. But when our screaming did not stop, they suddenly broke off and went out to the day room, threatening furiously to pay us back for this mutiny. But this time the threats were lost on us. All right, let them pay us back, let them even return that same night. For the time being our united protest had defeated their purpose.

But they had to make up somehow for the loss of their game. For the first time the indoor squad felt the whole weight of their fury. First the blockfuehrers ordered them to climb up on the cupboards and jump down, then they had to get up on the cross beams which supported the roof and swing around on them, as on a horizontal bar. And since the victims were comparatively few and there was plenty of space, the blockfuehrers took good care that the orders were carried out correctly and that as many men as possible suffered broken bones.

When they had had enough of this they concluded their visit by knocking over and smashing all the cupboards. But the camp treasury did not suffer from the damages. They were charged to our account when the authorities took the usual inventory, which always ended in our paying several hundred marks for articles allegedly damaged and lost.

For the first time there was wild destruction in the day room. The floor was strewn with splinters of wood and squashed tin mugs, and it was a long time before the indoor squad could clear away the wreckage in the darkness and lie down on the floor for the rest of the night. In our dormitory there was the already familiar welter of straw sacks, blankets and clothes, into which we tried in vain to bring order.

The blows and crushing had left many wounded—how many we could not tell. They moaned pitifully and begged for help. We listened helplessly, wondering how serious their condition was and whether there were many dead. At first everyone tried at least to find out about his neighbor and an eager whispering began. But we soon realized that we must wait until morning revealed the full extent of the catastrophe.

That night Karl did not come, as he had always done before, to say a few words of comfort. What could he say that would not sound banal after the events of that day? Besides, he himself was at the end of his nervous strength. That night had been more horrible for him than all the nights that had gone before. At other times the blockfuehrers during their attacks kept him busy in various ways—would send him for beating instruments or had him light up the corners of the dormitory and peer under blankets and straw sacks. This time he had had to stand at attention by the door and silently look on at our sufferings.

We had a crowded day behind us, a day which had given us our first promise of happiness only to make us feel our misery still more. What had come of our anticipation? As the events of that Saturday unrolled before my eyes, I was seized with a more abysmal hatred of our tormentors and an infinite disgust for a world in which such monstrosities could happen and for myself who dared not give my hatred expression in action. The pain of my helplessness deepened. It was a pain beyond tears, which made me laugh from sheer bitterness. Only when I heard excited questions and my own name spoken around me did I realize I had laughed aloud.

All at once I felt completely exhausted. My body was so tired that I could feel the exhaustion in every single cell. My mind alone refused to tire, and I went on thinking. "So tomorrow we must write home,"

I suddenly remembered. "And every letter must begin, 'I am in good health and doing well'! Even if we were at our last gasp, we must be doing well."

An endless cold night was before us. In the stress of the beating, several windowpanes had been knocked out and a pitiless, cutting wind swept through the dormitory. Numbed fingers groped around on the floor for a blanket. It was a long time before each of us found one and covered himself adequately; and many had cut themselves badly on the broken panes of glass which lay about in splinters.

When at last the sky began to pale, the extra haste which always followed a night attack set in. The sacks and blankets must be hastily cleared away, the clothes sorted out, the wounded separated from the dead—and of these last there were many. The routine must go smoothly—routine "ueber alles." And there was so little time, and so few of us had any strength in their fingers.

An unusually cold November morning greeted us, when we carried out our dead to roll call. A gray-black wall of clouds hung in the sky and heavy drops of rain were beginning to fall. As if to complete the gloomy scene, a flock of crows circled above us and filled the air with their macabre crah-crah-crah.

Karl's face too was turned to stone as he stood before the long line of bodies. We could have cried out to heaven, not for help—that we had already done too often—but out of grief for our dead. But it was not granted to us to give voice to our feelings. And our grief became a solemn silence, the last tribute and the last honor that we might pay our comrades.

As we saw a group of blockfuehrers coming toward us from the assembly place, Karl, who had been pacing up and down nervously, went along our lines and whispered: "Pull yourselves together, as well as you can, so we won't have still more victims."

The blockfuehrers stopped first at Block 37 and there ran through the whole register of their cruelties, which ended with the usual "snouts to the ground" and "roll." Then they came to us. Karl ran toward them and to appease them delivered his report very briskly. But the blockfuehrers looked through him.

"Aha, there are the accomplices of the English," one of them bellowed. "And looking like innocent lambs, as if they had nothing to do with the crime in Munich."

Then another carried on the farce: "And we have to feed this bunch of spies. But not today; today there'll be no feed. And now down with you and roll."

We hastily threw ourselves on the ground and rolled in the November mud. Our eyes followed anxiously the struggles of the badly wounded who could make no progress. The comrades from Block 37 were also rolling in the dirt. And the wide lane that connected our two blocks was alive with human bodies that wriggled toward the assembly place as if they were creatures born to crawl, not to walk erect. Only when the trumpet from the Kommandantur tower announced the beginning of the roll call was the wriggling broken off. We had to form ourselves into line in the greatest haste. But many could not tear their bodies away from the ground and our efforts to bring them to their feet ended only in additions to the rows of dead.

After the latest events we expected the blockfuehrers to punish us by forbidding us to write. But Karl announced after roll call that we might begin writing. He had even settled the question of postage.

"I've already seen about your stamps," he said in his usual friendly way. "Tomorrow, everyone will have a mark deducted for postage, and of course I will keep accounts for each of you. Anyone who has no money in the office need not worry. His comrades will pay for him. And as for the writing, let me advise you again to write postcards. For I imagine you haven't the heart to write much."

Karl was right. We were not in the mood. The last few hours weighed upon us too heavily.

It rained unceasingly and the wind whipped the rain through the broken windows. In front of the barrack a number of comrades were silently laboring: the corpses, which still lay in parade order, must be carried to the mortuary. But we had scarcely strength to support the weight of our own bodies, so it took four men to carry one corpse. They laid the body in a blanket and each took a corner. At first the bearers tried to keep step, but soon their tired walk became an irregular stumbling forward and, at every step, the dead body on the blanket rolled from side to side.

There were only a few who could carry a body with the help of one other man, and only one comrade in our block could carry a corpse alone. He threw it over his shoulder and staggered down the lane with it, while on his back the dead man's head between its two limp arms swayed to and fro and rain water dripped to the ground from the stiff fingers. That was the last journey of our dead.

Meanwhile, inside the barrack the writing was proceeding according to rule. "I am in good health and doing well," everyone was whispering as the pens scratched over the paper. The death toll that Sunday had broken all previous records. The groaning and sighing around me never stopped. I myself felt so weak that I could scarcely hold the pen in my fingers. And the day was still far from over. But all that was not to be told. . . . "Dear Gucia, I am in good health and doing well."

Then followed four pages full of matter-of-factness, quite in accord with the rules. Had Gucia paid the fire insurance and made out my income-tax return for the last quarter-year? My shoemaker still had two pairs of shoes, which had long been waiting to be called for. The key of the house safe was in the upper little drawer of the desk, and the door key in the right pants pocket of the brown striped suit. Four pages of trivial details, in which suppressed feelings could find expression only in the last two words, "Your father"—words so simple that not even a concentration-camp censor could object to them, which held, concealed from the censor's prying eyes, a world of love and longing, a code of feeling that only my daughter could read.

The wounded were suffering dreadfully. But help was not to be thought of. It was impossible to be admitted to the Revier on any Sunday, let alone a Sunday after an attempt on the Fuehrer's life. However, Karl accomplished the impossible, though we never found out what it cost him to get a few of the most seriously injured from all three blocks admitted to the Revier.

A bloody noon roll call was before us, and when it was over, funeral processions again moved to the mortuary. The number of wounded continued to rise. They were in agony and could scarcely sit erect. They begged us to let them stretch out. But in the daytime we were forbidden to lie down. All we could do was to support them with our shoulders and backs, until it was time to bed down for the night.

Karl had collected the mail before the noon roll call, and stamped it immediately. But it was not sent off at once. The next morning Karl appeared with a man from the office and asked who wrote a good hand. When his companion had picked out one of the volunteers they both went off without a word.

It turned out that the camp authorities examined the correspondence between the prisoners and their families with the greatest care. Each block had to prepare a card file listing the name, birthplace and birth date, occupation, nationality and prison number of every inmate. We Polish prisoners had to fill out still more details: names and addresses of persons we intended to write to and names and addresses of those who wrote to us, dates of incoming and outgoing letters and statements of money received. Besides all this there was a blank space for memoranda by the office. Thanks to the efficiency of the volunteer scribes in all three Polish blocks, these complicated card files were set up in two days and the letters went forward to the censors, who kept them back another two weeks or so.

We who were still alive and had sent our first letters home looked on them as our last farewell to those we loved. What could we expect, when it suited the Gestapo to link us with the Munich attack? In vain comrades in our conversation periods drew parallels from history to prove that right *does* triumph in the end; in vain "The Latrine Courier" did its best to raise our spirits.

Then, just at the right moment, something happened which quickened our hearts with new hope. A postcard arrived for a comrade in our wing, a well-to-do baker. It was from his wife, who had learned that Polish prisoners might be freed, if they emigrated immediately. She had secured a certificate from the Palaestinaamt (Palestine Immigration Authority), guaranteeing his admission to that country, had filed an application with the Gestapo and was now awaiting results. A few days later the baker was released on the basis of his Palestine certificate. And within the next four weeks several other comrades were released on the same grounds.

Every one of us in his next letter home mentioned this possibility and urged his family to see about getting a similar certificate. It was not until after I was freed that I heard the whole story of this procedure from Gucia and learned the tragic fate of those we had considered so fortunate.

The president of the Juedische Reichsvertretung, a central Jewish organization of which all Jews, regardless of nationality, were required to be members, had been informed by the Gestapo that the Polish prisoners held in "protective custody" in Sachsenhausen could obtain release, provided they were able to emigrate to a neutral country outside Europe. It was indicated that emigration to Palestine would be particularly favored.

Emigrating to Palestine was relatively easy, since only a certificate from the Palaestinaamt was required, while for all neutral countries one needed entry visas and considerable sums in foreign denominations.

The Berlin Palaestinaamt immediately declared itself ready to issue certificates for the Polish prisoners if the applicants could pay travel expenses and had relatives in Palestine to look after them. The first applications were submitted to the Gestapo at the beginning of November, and the first releases followed within three weeks. Curiously enough, these applications were usually submitted not by the Jewish Community but by obscure individuals.

When the Nazis seized power, a new profession arose in Germany. Certain people, who had "connections" with Gestapo officials, would obtain the release of clients from concentration camps for a fee which varied from moderate to fantastic sums. When cash was not available, the fee was paid in kind: rugs, silver, jewelry. After the arrest of the "Bromberg murderers," these individuals automatically appeared on the scene, like earthworms after rain; and between November, 1939, and January, 1940, they succeeded in obtaining several releases.

The only man, however, who actually reached his destination by means of his Palestine certificate, was the baker mentioned. The others either were unable to leave Germany at all or were stranded somewhere in the Balkans. But all the Balkan governments concerned suddenly refused transit visas to the Polish refugees. After Italy had also refused transit visas and after long, fruitless negotiations with the Slovak and the Jugoslav consulates in Berlin, the Palaestinaamt decided to charter its own ship to take the refugees down the Danube to the Black Sea. But meanwhile the Danube froze over, and the last road to the Black Sea was cut off.

Thus the released men had no way of leaving Germany and the Gestapo threatened to rearrest them if they did not get out of the country somehow. So these unfortunates, with their wives and children, crossed the frontier illegally. Not only had the Gestapo deliberately provoked them to this, but some of its members even made a lucrative business out of acting as guides. Then, sooner or later, the fugitives were arrested on the other side of the frontier.

Gucia had sensed something wrong about the offer of release, and although she had obtained a certificate for me, she had not filed it. The thing was really too transparent. Here was the Gestapo emphasizing that only emigration to neutral countries would be permitted and at the same time encouraging emigration to Palestine, which was enemy (British) territory. Our release was therefore only a means to their own ends. For the influx of new immigrants was designed to stir up the Arab-Jewish antagonism, which had subsided after the outbreak of the war, and to serve as cover for the smuggling of German spies into the vital zone near the Suez Canal. Instead of depending on emigration to Palestine, Gucia had undertaken to obtain my emigration to Shanghai, a much lengthier process.

And it was not long before it became evident that this offer of release was also a maneuver. As soon as the road to Palestine was closed, though it was still possible to emigrate to North and South America or to China, the Gestapo lost interest in our release. One day a notice appeared on the door of the division of the Alien Police where our families used to submit applications: "No further releases of Polish Jews will take place. All inquiry useless."

When the first releases occurred we were filled with strength and hope; even the feeblest and most ailing revived visibly. Not even the excesses of the blockfuehrers, which increased daily, could undo this effect. We were all in a delirium of expectancy. "Perhaps help is really on the way at last," one or another would murmur aloud from the depths of his own thoughts. And his face would come alive at the mere thought of freedom. This hope of rescue even prolonged the lives of the dying; although they knew that they must certainly die, they wished to hold off death, to die at least in freedom.

From then on each of us felt next in line for release and we exchanged the solemn promise that each, as soon as he was free, would work for the freedom of the others; we memorized the addresses of several comrades, in order to seek out their relatives and inform them of conditions in the camp.

The releases always took place during the morning roll call. Their harbinger was a special runner, who brought the longed-for message from the office on a slip of paper and handed it to the blockfuehrer or room senior. The name of the fortunate man was called out, and if it was a blockfuehrer who received the message he screamed, "Off with the swine, at a gallop!" And then the freed prisoner had to run hell for leather; there was no pausing, no going back to the barrack for anything left behind, no turning around.

Thus the morning roll call became the high point of our schedule. All our thoughts were directed toward those fateful hours. The nights never passed quickly enough. From the moment that we took our places for roll call our eyes were turned in the direction of the Kommandantur building, whence the runner must come. If the runner actually did appear in the distance and a pair of sharp eyes spied him, the whisper flew along the rows: "A runner!" The blockfuehrers might manhandle us, make us exercise, beat us; we scarcely felt the blows. "A runner, a runner!" the words sang within us, until at last the messenger of freedom arrived and handed over the magic slip.

Then followed seconds of almost superhuman suspense. The saliva in our mouths ceased to flow. Our hearts threatened to stop. Our ears ached with listening.

Sometimes only one man was released, sometimes several at once. But even when there was no release, the candle of hope went on flickering in our hearts. We would put down the nonappearance of the runner to the delays of red tape. "It is purely a matter of luck," we told each other comfortingly, "whether a document awaiting signature on an office desk happens to lie at the top or the bottom of the pile. Tomorrow, let's hope, we'll have better luck."

The releases of the "Bromberg murderers" became a sensation in the whole camp. Every day different members of the "Old Guard" turned up to discuss the event with Karl. "It's unheard-of," they said. And since no one had a satisfactory explanation they fell back on the familiar anti-Semitic argument which is so often called into service when other explanations fail. "There's that Jewish clannishness again," we often heard Karl's friends say to him. Karl, who was puzzled himself, was, of course, too intelligent to let such remarks pass without contradiction. He explained to his friends that the power of Jewish solidarity was a myth and that the Gestapo was merely pursuing its own ends, which were shady as usual. But his arguments fell on deaf ears. "You've gotten absolutely Jew-minded yourself," his friends retorted. And hatred and envy ate into them deeper and deeper.

But the most enraged over the releases were the blockfuehrers. As if they had been robbed of their rightful property, their hate flamed up every time a runner handed over a release slip. "One more Ikey free," they spat. "But you can bet on this: one way or another you won't escape us."

From the moment of my arrival in Sachsenhausen, I had resolved to keep my eyes and ears open. Some day I would describe what I had seen, if I ever got out of this hell alive. That was a vow.

Once I had made this decision, a strange mood took possession of me, a mixture of despair, fear and boundless curiosity. So must an explorer feel who has fallen into the power of a cannibal tribe, hitherto known to him only through travelers' tales.

As long as the three Polish blocks were not sent out to work, I could form no conception of the details of the camp's arrangements. So I devoted my attention to observing the butchers who were our masters. I soon learned to know their idiosyncrasies, and from then on I never failed, while they were torturing us, to observe—often with great cunning and caution, often with great danger to myself—how they remained true to their own natures. Sometimes I felt like a man studying the effects of some dangerous and perhaps deadly serum on himself and those around him. Of course, such studies were very trying to the nerves. But I could not give them up, although later, as I grew weaker, I would gladly have done so. My brain had become too fixed in the habit of automatically reacting and recording.

After such scenes, I used to go over what had happened and impress it upon my memory. And each time my conviction deepened that the intense cruelty I had observed was not the result of National Socialist philosophy, but rather that National Socialism itself was the logical development of a pre-existing national character.

The soul of the camp was the Kommandant, an Oberfuehrer in the SS, who had practiced his profession in various concentration camps since Hitler came to power. The prisoners seldom saw him, usually only on special occasions, when schools of Gestapo officers, or Gestapo delegations from the occupied territories came to visit. Then the Kommandant, accompanied by his staff and unusually large details of blockfuehrers, would personally show the guests around. When there were visitors in camp the greatest excitement prevailed everywhere. The prisoners and their room seniors trembled with fear; even the blockfuehrers and guards, who usually kept out of the Kommandant's way as one avoids a wild bull, were in a high state of nervousness.

The Kommandant would show his guests all the attractions. The Bunker, of course, was a particular point of interest. But there were stops at other points as well: at the workshop, the horticultural sections, the elite block. And woe to those concerned if any place visited was not as neat as a pin, or if a hastily improvised performance went badly. Whatever happened, however, the result of such a Visitors' Day was always a toll of victims.

The Kommandant was never seen alone and seldom appeared at roll calls. But nothing that happened on the assembly place escaped his eye. He used to stand at the huge windows of his office in the Kommandantur building, which were decorated with handsome flower boxes, and observe.

It was a rule of the camp that each newly arrived group should not only be photographed—in repulsive poses, needless to say, as the pictures were to be used for propaganda purposes—but should present themselves at the Kommandantur, where the Kommandant made them a speech. For some unknown reason an exception had been made in our case, but the speech usually went something like this:

"Here you are not in a penitentiary or prison but in a place of instruction. Order and discipline are here the highest law. If you ever want to see freedom again, you must submit to a severe training. If we are convinced that our methods of instruction have borne fruit, that you have realized how false your former Weltanschauung and way of life were, then the gates of freedom may open for you once more. But woe to those who do not obey our iron discipline. Our methods are thorough! Here there is no compromise and no mercy. The slightest resistance will be ruthlessly suppressed. Here we sweep with an iron broom! Dismissed!"

This speech never failed of its terrorizing purpose. Every man who heard the Kommandant's address felt that he had been given a suspended death sentence.

The right-hand man of the Kommandant, and the next in rank, was the Lagerfuehrer. He was a sullen, silent man, with eyes which always looked hate and destruction. Important examinations and particularly severe Bunker punishments took place in his presence. When a prisoner deliberately ran into the high-tension wire, or invited death by a pretended attempt at escape, his blackened and bullet-ridden body could not be carried off until the Lagerfuehrer, with the camp doctor and an investigating committee, had appeared on the scene.

Usually one saw the Lagerfuehrer going around the camp alone. He would appear in the most unexpected places at the most unexpected times and poke his nose into everything. He was the only man in camp who possessed a horse, and he was never seen outside the camp without it. Once mounted on his lordly thoroughbred he was transformed. His gloomy expression brightened; his scowling face was almost friendly.

I often pondered on this change. There could be only one explanation. The Lagerfuehrer had a puny physique and was the shortest of all the SS officers. This had no doubt given him an inferiority complex, which vented itself in hatred and great brutality. But as soon as he sat high in the saddle and could look down on those around him, he forgot his complex, and his face assumed an almost human expression.

The Lagerfuehrer was a magnificent rider. But for us his equestrian skill was a source of great suffering. Sometime later, when we went to labor in the Klinker works, he used to supervise our march on horseback and accompany us for two kilometers to the bridge across the Oranienburg Canal. He rode back and forth along our marching columns, cantered on ahead and then waited to let us march past him.

The horse, however, was a wild stallion, and standing still did not suit him at all. He pranced around and struck out with his hoofs. And no matter how close to us the Lagerfuehrer stood, we dared not break our ranks to dodge the wild animal. The accompanying guards and foremen saw to it that our column was always straight as an arrow. Often the horse plunged into our column or reared up on his hind legs; and it looked as if the rider would land on our heads at any moment. But the Lagerfuehrer was much too good a horseman to be perturbed by such displays of equine temperament. He would get the beast on its four legs again and gallop proudly off. And we would be left with several wounded.

Often the Lagerfuehrer would ride out again in the evening and wait for us at the bridge. Then we suffered doubly, for we were utterly weary from our hard day's work. So it was always with fear that we marched back to camp, and we breathed more easily when we neared the bridge and saw no sign of the two beasts that harried us so.

The number of blockfuehrers and other superiors who tormented us, day in and day out, changed constantly. But six blockfuehrers were our steady visitors. Three of these six had the Polish blocks under them in turn. Of the other three, known in the camp as "the Trio," two supervised the notorious punishment squads and one belonged to the staff of the labor squads.

The members of the Trio, who were the terror of the whole camp, were commonly called "Iron Gustav," "Size Ten Gloves," and "Kopella." The other three, who were our blockfuehrers by turns, were called "the Saxon," "Schuschnigg" and Mueller.

The fiercest of all was Iron Gustav, although at first sight no one would have suspected his strength and his iron tenacity. He was about five feet six; his body was poorly developed; his dark eyes, hair and complexion and his stooped posture gave the lie to the myth of the Nordic German race.

Iron Gustav never spoke in a normal tone, either to us or to his mates; he screamed. Constant screaming had apparently affected his vocal cords, for his voice sounded hoarse and muffled. When he walked, he moved so irresolutely, with such convulsive nervousness, that his pace was more like skipping than walking.

Whether he came to us alone or in company, he always had some beating instrument with him; and whether it was a board, a broom, a wooden or iron rod, it was long; the longer the better; otherwise the beating would have been no fun for him. He used to rush in upon us with his hoarse war cry, a crazed glimmer in his eyes and slaver dripping from his gap-toothed mouth, striking blindly in all directions with his rod. The beating lasted until the weapon lay in splinters on the ground. On his face was the satiated look of a man who has just satisfied a great hunger with a hearty meal.

When Iron Gustav came with wooden sticks, the beating did not last so long. It was much worse when he had iron rods with him: iron cannot be broken to pieces on human bodies. So our sufferings continued until at last Iron Gustav saw the hopelessness of the task, hurled the murder instrument into our midst with a last exertion of strength and went off in a furious rage.

But beating with long rods was not the only torture we had to endure from him. He loved to ride through our ranks on his bicycle at a furious speed when we were lined up for the roll call. True, the group spattered like wind-whipped water. But there were always a few who were not nimble enough and they were ridden down. Iron Gustav himself had developed such skill on the bicycle that he never fell off.

Often, when the mud reached to our ankles, Iron Gustav improved on his trick. "Fall down," he would shout before he was anywhere near us. If he did not immediately afterward order, "Roll," we knew that as he rushed past us he would strike our heads with his long stick, without which he was never seen on his wheel, at the same time repeatedly yelling: "Lie there till roll call, Polish swine!"

Size Ten Gloves was outwardly a complete contrast to Iron Gustav. He was blond, blue-eyed and massive; his uniform coat was literally bursting from the pressure of his muscular chest. His walk had the firmness of a bear's; the unbelievably large hands that gave him his nickname had the strength of a bear's paw. In spite of his weight, Size Ten Gloves moved almost noiselessly. Like a cat, he would suddenly sneak up to our window. Often we did not know that he was there until he drummed on the pane like one possessed. Then we had to yank up the window as quickly as possible so that he could bound in and pounce on his victims.

In winter, when the windows were frozen, Size Ten Gloves, much to his annoyance, had to come in by the door. But this changed his procedure only slightly. "Stay sitting in the same position, or you'll catch it," he would order from outside. And we went rigid. For Size Ten Gloves had sharp eyes and a good memory, and woe to anyone whom he saw in one position when he looked through the window and in another when he entered the door.

Size Ten Gloves never indulged in promiscuous beating, but chose his victims individually. He never used beating instruments either. His hands and feet were so strong that they sufficed to break a few ribs or smash a skull. When beating, he did not scream, but carried out his crimes in almost complete silence. Before he dispatched a victim, he played with him awhile.

First he ordered him to stand up and lectured him on his misdeeds in a slow drawling voice. The accused, of course, was never allowed to answer.

After Size Ten Gloves had finished cursing, he swung up his great fist and landed his first blow. Usually it was aimed at the stomach or the liver and felled the victim to the ground.

Then began a scene which every time filled me with unutterable horror.

"Stand up at once," ordered Size Ten Gloves, knowing well that the man on the ground could not move. Then he walked up close to him, spread his legs, stuck both thumbs in his belt, bent down and asked in a tone just above a whisper, drawling every syllable, "So-o you-u won't—e-eh?"

But if the man with a tremendous effort had pulled himself up, he was laid flat again with a second blow. This was always directed at the same spot as the first. Then Size Ten Gloves walked nearer to the groaning man, his eyes fixed on him in fascination, drinking in every quiver of pain. "So-o you-u wo-on't, e-eh?" he asked again, in a voice that grew softer from moment to moment until it was only a whisper. Suddenly he straightened up.

"Stand up, you plague sore, you louse, you bastard!" he ordered. Then his feet took over the job. They worked with indescribable speed, treading on the liver, the stomach, the genitals. No vulnerable part of the body was spared.

As soon as Size Ten Gloves had laid a man flat with the first blow, the victim's neighbors on either side drew back, automatically making room for the murder. While their comrade was being beaten to death, they sat still, looking fixedly in front of them, intent only on making themselves as small as possible.

Twice my immediate neighbor was murdered in this way, and I still cannot conceive how I could have brought myself to look on in silence.

One of the most tragic murders perpetrated by this beast was the killing of a deranged man. The poor fellow had been in a critical mental state when he was arrested, and in the camp he had soon lost his reason entirely. His mouth was never still, and although we felt great sympathy for him, his senseless babble got on our nerves frightfully. But if we ordered him to be quiet, he became wild, screamed, struck out frantically and might have put us all in danger. So for the general safety we decided to let him have his way. It was especially pathetic, therefore, when he let Size Ten Gloves murder him without a sound or a motion of protest, as if in those last moments of his life he had recovered his reason and knew that resistance was useless.

Kopella, the third of the Trio, was, like Size Ten Gloves, a monster of strength. But he was out for amusement rather than murder. His jokes were always carefully prepared and he invariably brought a crowd of spectators with him. He would remain for a while in the doorway, his eyes darting critically here and there, until he had made up his mind whom he would have his fun with this time. Then he came forward. With long, springy steps and bent body he ran first around us, then between our rows. His arms swung to and fro like pendulums and, as if we were punching bags, his fists landed right and left in the stomachs of the men he had previously picked out. His ringing laugh accompanied every blow.

But that was merely the prelude. The real fun began when Kopella rejoined his laughing company at the door and ordered: "Roll."

The crowd made rolling impossible. But since we knew that if we did not make motions of some kind, Kopella's group would lunge upon us, we whirled around this way and that as well as we could, twisted, turned and wriggled over and under each other until we looked more like a writhing heap of earthworms than human beings. This was the effect intended and the high point of pleasure for Kopella and his companions. They bellowed with delight.

Usually Kopella let us "wriggle like worms" in this way for five or ten minutes; sometimes for fifteen minutes or more. Often, when he went off with his gang he ordered: "Keep at it, you stinking worms, till you turn blue." Then we had to go on squirming around without letup, for we never knew whether he would come back and look through the window. While Karl was our room senior, such degrading scenes were not unnecessarily prolonged. Karl knew Kopella's habits so well that he could tell by the direction he took whether he would return.

The Saxon, the first blockfuehrer in the Polish blocks, had received his nickname from us because of his ridiculous Saxon dialect. He was a young fellow, barely twenty, large, blond, blue-eyed—an ideal Germanic type—bursting with strength, health and the longing to distinguish himself.

His mistreatment had less method than that of the other blockfuehrers. Sometimes he only picked out individuals and withdrew their rations for a day or half a day. Sometimes he took a notion to drill us mercilessly. Sometimes he beat us, one after another, as if he wanted to test his endurance. When he was not in the mood for such trials of strength, he bombarded us with filthy curses. The flood of Saxon vulgarity was often so comic that it was hard to suppress our laughter.

Like all immature men, the Saxon had a tremendous craving for demonstrations of respect. He laid down a rule that the Poles must polish his shoes before roll call. The young people from Block 37 had been selected for this task and they had understood very well how to play up to the Saxon's weakness. When the Saxon came into sight at roll call, several of them would dart into the barrack and bring out a spotlessly polished stool, a brush and shoe polish. Then when the Saxon came marching up briskly, he would head for the stool, place a foot upon it, and with his under jaw stuck out and his hands on his hips, Mussolini fashion, would allow one of the young men who ran up obsequiously to polish his shoes.

As to beating, the Saxon was less dangerous than the other blockfuehrers, thanks to his lack of experience. It was not long, though, before he had learned so well that he was appointed blockfuehrer to the punishment squad, a post awarded to the worst brutes.

Our fifth tormentor, Schuschnigg, was the Saxon's successor. Despite the two stars on his uniform—most of the blockfuehrers had only one—he cut a pitiful figure. Everything about him was repulsive: his appearance, his nasal voice, his jerky movements. His head had an unusually elongated shape; his skull was covered with sparse, ashpale hair. His face was flat, without curves or cushions of fat; the corners of his mouth turned down sullenly. His eyes had a yellow, piercing stare and his nose was hooked like a beak, so that he resembled a vulture. This repellent head rested between bowed, hunched-up shoulders on a boxlike body with a pair of arms that hung down stiffly as if they did not belong to it and a pair of legs that looked as if they had been screwed on crooked.

Schuschnigg had no physical strength to speak of and was, as can be imagined, unskilled in beating. If one were nimble, one could dodge his blows. Nevertheless he had his part in our extermination. One of his usual punishments was to withdraw part of our ration once or twice a week and send it to the elite block or the Danzig criminals, who were being trained for future service in Poland.

Schuschnigg was particularly hard on us at roll calls. This wretched-looking, almost deformed creature had a morbid passion for military bearing. But the "Polish bastards" always looked like "jumping-jacks"; the good food had "made the pack too comfortable." So the food was reduced. Often when he came to the noon roll call, he shouted from a distance: "Today your fodder'll be cut in half." Karl would then try, by all kinds of devices, to save at least something for us. And when his maneuvers failed, he would not touch his food, but gave it to one of us who seemed particularly near collapse.

Mueller was the third blockfuehrer of the Polish blocks and still held this office at the time of my release. His specialty was to organize boxing matches and fist fights among us. For these amusements, he, like Kopella, brought a gallery of spectators. Of course, Mueller himself picked out the contestants. He always arranged it so that a son had to fight with a father, a young man with an old one, a strong man with a weak. And woe to any contender who did not strike with all his might.

Such boxing matches often lasted a whole hour and ended only when one of the partners was badly mauled and streaming with blood. Mueller rewarded the victor with a piece of dry bread. And it was heartbreaking when a victorious son sat down weeping beside his father and silently, as if asking pardon, held out to him the prize of victory; when the bleeding father comforted his son and both wept out their sorrow together, and together ate the bread that had been so dearly won.

Sometimes Mueller played another game with us. He and his train would bring several slices of bread with them. "Who is hungry?" Mueller would ask, pausing on the threshold. Of course, the answer was a unanimous "I!"

Mueller would throw bread into a corner of the room, and we would pounce on it like a pack of famished hounds. Then he threw more bread into the opposite corner. The human knot on the floor untied itself and lunged toward the other corner. We hurled each other aside, trampled and kicked each other. And all the time the room rang with bellows of laughter.

This "bread game" was one of the most degrading psychological tortures that were inflicted on us. It filled us with bitter shame. But we could not refuse to take part in it. Mueller had staged the scene, and no one dared spoil the show. Of course, the bread that Mueller used was taken from our allotted rations. At first we resigned ourselves to going without it. But as hunger tormented us more and more, we became so animalized that we gathered up the filthy trampled bread and devoured it greedily.

The only prisoners in camp who did not suffer from hunger were the room seniors, the foremen of the labor squads and the hardened criminals who were being trained for future service in the occupied territories and hence were particularly well fed. Many of the other prisoners were so wasted and enfeebled that they could not be sent out to work. So a special kind of occupation was created for these wrecks: "standing squads," in which they had to stand all day long. Several blocks near ours were set aside for this purpose.

The overseers of these squads were criminals picked for their strength and brutality, known in camp as the "barrack tramps." Their duty was to see that none of the prisoners sat down or even leaned against anything. They were equipped with extra-long truncheons. When a prisoner collapsed from exhaustion, the truncheons instantly went into action. After he had been bloodily beaten, he was driven out in front of the barrack where, with hands outstretched, he must do frog leaps and knee bending until he lay motionless on the ground.

Since all the prisoners in the standing squad were sick and consequently irritable, quarrels frequently arose among them. The settlement of differences was a duty of the barrack tramps. It was left entirely to their own judgment to inflict suitable punishment. And they saw to it that there was never a break in the chain of culprits exercising in front of the barracks. There was scarcely a day when a procession of dead and wounded was not carried out from the standing squads.

The prisoners in the standing squad suffered severely from the increasing cold. And several of them got the idea of wrapping a towel or one of the thin dormitory blankets around their bodies. As they were literally reduced to skin and bone, the extra covering did not show under their coats, and for some time the trick went undiscovered. But eventually the barrack tramps learned of it and promptly denounced their charges to the office.

From then on the blockfuehrers had a new amusement. Almost every other day body searches were held in the standing-squad blocks, usually under the direction of Size Ten Gloves. To make the inspection brief and impressive, Size Ten Gloves had all the standing squads line up along the whole length of the street that led from the elite blocks to the assembly place. "Unbutton coat and pants," he ordered. Then, while the wind blew through the unbuttoned clothing and the wearers stood with chattering teeth and shivering bodies, Size Ten Gloves and his companions proceeded at their leisure along the rows. Before any suspicious-looking individual they halted, surveyed him silently for a moment, then snatched his shirt out of his pants. Anyone found with forbidden covering on his person was beaten until he moved no longer and, if he was only half dead, further punishment awaited him. Many of the prisoners, in order not to look stuffed out, had torn off a piece of blanket and wrapped it around their bodies. These were promptly beaten to death as saboteurs.

Strangely enough, all these measures failed to intimidate. Every body search brought new "saboteurs" to light, and every time there were more dead. At first I was amazed at this. But when I tried to read the faces of those who were caught, I got the answer. These men suffered so much that they were beyond the fear of death. Indeed, they actually longed for it. Too weak to end their lives with their own hands, they courted death by disobedience. Every one of them knew that he must die. But as long as he was not caught, he might at least not freeze so terribly.

We too were emaciated, enfeebled and ill. We got less nourishment than other prisoners and so felt the cold more keenly. Moreover, we had no heat. We had been given the thinnest and shabbiest coats in the stock of clothing. And we were not allowed to wear overcoats outdoors except at work. Since we had been arrested in late summer, we did not have scarves, gloves and sweaters like most of the prisoners, and the warm clothing of those of us who had arrived later had been taken away.

It was to be expected, therefore, that some of us would also wrap towels or blankets around our bodies. But we knew that if any one of us was caught in such a crime, all three Polish blocks would suffer severely. So our indoor squad instituted a blanket-inspection service. Three times a day, before we went out to roll call, the towels and blankets were counted, and if the number did not check, there was trouble. Wing B and the other two blocks immediately copied this arrangement.

When Karl learned of our decision, he was very pleased and left the blanket inspection entirely to us. Franz, on the other hand, was far from delighted. He considered it his prerogative to discover the guilty and have a little private fun with them. So he forbade the indoor squad in Wing B to hold any blanket inspections. But the inspection was instituted nonetheless, and although Franz nosed around like a bloodhound, he never detected it in action.

In our wing no one broke the self-imposed rules except a few old people and a young student who had saved the lives of many of us during the suffocation period by opening the trap door in the roof. In a few months he had wasted away beyond recognition. After the old people had been caught and warned several times, they obeyed the rules. Only the student, who was almost out of his senses with cold, stubbornly persisted in his attempts. We applied all the arts of persuasion, tried to shame him and finally threatened him with punishment. But it was in vain.

Another of his fixed ideas was his sudden dread of cold water. Even in the worst cold, we tried at least to wash our hands and faces as often as possible. Only the student refused to wash at all. "I'm cold enough already without that," was all that he replied to our reproaches.

The student's refusal to wash was not obstinacy, but an infirmity of the nerves, which made him go to pieces under the effect of icecold water. Often when we had to stand stripped to the waist in the biting cold for fifteen minutes, until our turn came to wash, when our teeth chattered and we could scarcely hold the soap in our frostbitten hands, I understood myself what an effort of will it required to wash in cold water.

At first we laughed at him and called him water-shy. But when the crust of dirt grew fast to his body and he began to stink, no one wanted to sit near him, much less to sleep beside him. Karl more than once punished him severely. But even punishments were of no use.

One day Franz heard the story. He fetched some members of his indoor squad and they dragged the student into the shower room. In spite of his piteous cries, they pushed him under the ice-cold shower and scrubbed him thoroughly. But not even this could move the young man to wash of his own accord thereafter, so Franz took him unde his personal control. Karl acquiesced. "Do as you like with the fel low," he said; "I've got no more use for him." And the student wa transferred to Wing B.

Although the whole of Wing B always kept a watchful eye upor the student, one day he somehow managed to wrap a towel arounc him unnoticed. Luckily Franz became suspicious and searched him, shortly before we went out to morning roll call. And that very morning the blockfuehrers held a body search. When we learned of the fate we had escaped by a hair's breadth, we would have given the student a good thrashing but for the service he had done us.

Since the blockfuehrers had no success with their body searches, they sought new ways to embitter our lives. The camp rules provided that when prisoners stood outdoors they might keep their caps on until the counting-off began, but the blockfuehrers forbade us to wear caps at all. From day to day the temperature fell farther below zero, and the wind pierced our bared, shaven heads. Our ears began to freeze, and since to move was "streng verboten," we could not rub them.

"Just look at the Chosen People—they've got the jitters! These soft milksops ought to wear skirts instead of pants," jeered the blockfuehrers, as they came to roll call in their ear muffs, fur-lined gloves and warm winter overcoats with turned-up collars.

One day when the thermometer registered far below freezing, Kopella asked, "Would you like to hop a little, perhaps?"

Any kind of movement seemed to us the sum of all desires. "Jawohl!" we roared.

A volley of laughs answered us. "That would suit you pansies, wouldn't it? But we don't allow exercise in winter. Here everything is in its proper place. In winter you freeze and in summer you sweat. Next summer you'll have plenty of chance to hop."

Then the blockfuehrers developed a sudden concern for cleanliness. "The water-shy Polish hogs are stinking up the whole camp," they cried one day, when they came to roll call. And they hauled out several of us, drove them into the washroom, pushed them—dressed—under the ice-cold shower, then drove them out into the cold again.

From then on, "the cleaning campaign" became a favorite amusement. Since it usually formed the prologue to our roll calls, the victims often had to stand for half an hour or longer in the freezing cold. The clothes turned to ice on their bodies and caused pneumonia, usually with fatal results. Since the choice of victims had nothing to do with our actual condition of cleanliness, there was no way of taking precautions against it. And each of us had to face the prospect of being the next to suffer.

One day in November the food storeroom was broken into and a number of sausages stolen. That such terrorized, wasted remnants of men should find the audacity to defy the camp authorities was extraordinary. A rigorous investigation was then instituted. The room seniors and assistants from all the blocks were ordered to the office and informed that unless they produced the offenders within three hours, the entire camp would undergo standing punishment, even if all of them died of it.

The room seniors and assistants, who were trembling for their petty jobs, tried every possible trick to discover the guilty. But the burglars were old hands at crime. When the evening roll call was taken and the offenders were still undiscovered, no one was allowed to return to barracks. The standing punishment began. The Polish blocks had to spend some hours of the punishment lying on the icy ground.

Darkness fell quickly. It grew damp and cold. No one knew how long the standing would last; none could foresee how it would end. Karl ran restlessly up and down in front of us. Between his teeth he poured our curses on the camp SS. "You damned devil's spawn," he raged, "the war's not over yet. You'll land in the trenches before you're through. You skunks—some day you too will know what it is to tremble for your lives." Franz trotted after Karl like a shadow and his slippers klip-klopped an accompaniment to the curses, which were music to our ears.

From time to time the blockfuehrers put in an appearance, to see how lying on the ground agreed with us. Then the searchlights flashed out dazzlingly and their rays hung suspended on the patch of ground in front of our barrack, to which the scattered bodies gave the look of broken land. At such times we lay stiff with fear and did not move a limb.

At last they allowed us to stand up. When they had disappeared and the searchlights went out, we rubbed ourselves all over with stiff fingers, swung our crossed arms against our backs like coachmen and stood close together, side by side and back to back, so that we might get a little warmth from each other.

Long after midnight, after more than eight hours of standing, we were allowed to return to the barracks. We staggered toward them. It was as if our legs were made of an elastic substance which bent at every step. Beyond speech or feeling, we dropped on our straw sacks.

Not until the next morning did we learn how many dead the standing had cost.

But the burglars had not been found, and the patience of the camp authorities snapped. In the morning it was announced that the whole camp must stand all night long if the offenders were not produced by evening. After roll call, when the temperature fell several degrees, one of those in the secret betrayed the others.

A whole clique had taken part in the theft. They had stolen the sausages in their free hours after the evening roll call, when the prisoners were allowed to visit each other; smuggled the food into their barracks, hidden in their clothes; and eaten it in the dark, after everyone else was asleep.

The blockfuehrers made short work of them. Those who survived the blows and kicks were sent to the Bunker for several days, and any who were still alive after that were transferred to the punishment squad.

This was the first time that the sympathies of the prisoners were not on the side of the punished. As Karl told us, the theft aroused unanimous indignation. Everyone condemned the irresponsibility of the thieves, who must have known that their offense would come to light and that the whole camp would pay. And everyone held them responsible for the night's toll of dead.

After the example that had been made, we felt sure that such an event would never occur again. Only a few days later, the supply room was broken into again, and not only sausages but several pounds of marmalade were stolen. This time the burglars were quickly discovered, for their own gluttony betrayed them.

The marmalade, it seems, was of very inferior quality, and the quantity in which it was consumed did not go well with the sausages. The two thieves spent the whole night running to the toilets until they grew so weak that they could no longer drag themselves there. The disturbance, and the smell they finally spread through the barrack, awakened their fellow prisoners. When the theft became known next morning the thieves were identified without delay.

After the blockfuehrers had convinced themselves that no one else was implicated in the theft, they made an end of the culprits on the spot. That day we all had to stand outdoors for six hours and do extra exercises. Some of the room seniors and assistants were changed, and we were terrified that we might lose Karl. The entire camp was forbidden to write or receive letters for a week. In addition we were told that if such a thing ever happened again, the whole camp would stand for forty-eight hours on end, whether the thief confessed or not. Luckily, however, extra night watchmen were detailed to the food storeroom, and as long as I remained in camp there were no more attempts at burglary.

On the other hand, thefts occurred continually in the prisoners' barracks, ours as well as others. Hunger tormented us all incessantly and transformed men into irresponsible beasts. Even those who had formerly passed for honorable men stole from their comrades the bits of bread that many had laid by from their evening ration for the next day. By day, all with one voice condemned the theft. By night, the stealing was repeated, just the same.

In our conversation periods we sought counter-measures. We knew that the thieves did not realize the crime they were committing, for hunger had driven them nearly out of their senses. But we knew also that these bits of bread were the life-preserver by which we might keep ourselves afloat until the longed-for moment of freedom. And when we caught a bread thief, we punished him so severely that he lost his taste for stealing.

As the isolation district was enlarged, the street leading from the elite blocks past our barracks to the assembly place became a main artery of traffic. One day a special barrack was put up on this street for the military commission which was to sit every two or three months to enlist volunteers for military service. When the military commission arrived, Karl could not be pried away from his place by the window. The crowd of volunteers around the inspection barrack was always great, and Karl never took his eyes off anyone who went in or out. When the prisoners who were accepted came out of the barrack, joy overspread their faces. This had nothing to do with patriotism. But death in the trenches seemed infinitely more desirable than death in a concentration camp, and life was not too great a price to pay for even temporary freedom.

But these mass releases did not depopulate the camp. The Gestapo took care to supply replacements. One day a barrack in the isolated district, next to the elite blocks, was made ready. Like the barracks of the Bible students and the elite prisoners, it was guarded by a gate. Then we knew that some very special prey was expected.

The new occupants were about eighty priests of different orders from all over Poland. We saw them on the day of their arrival, when they were taken to the Kommandantur to receive the usual address from the Kommandant, and later, whenever they were marched off to the shower. Except for this, we never saw them. But we made Karl tell us how they were getting on.

On the whole their treatment was the same as that of all the isolated prisoners, except that they were not overcrowded and were permitted to wash properly and take a warm shower every two weeks. Three times a day, when we went out to roll call, we could hear the blockfuehrers taunting and mocking them, cracking vile jokes about their calling and putting them through all the ingenious humiliations of exercise. But the priests' self-command remained unbroken. Every time they marched past us, we were struck by the resolution in their faces.

Almost regularly, three times a week, our blocks received new recruits. Consequently the dreadful overcrowding began again. Often four men had to share a sack. Obviously the only way this could be managed was for all four to lie on their sides, and turning over was a great art. Death made several vacancies in our ranks each day. But the office kept a close census of the Polish blocks and took good care that there were always more arrivals than departures. The newcomers came from Germany, Poland, Czechoslovakia; from every place where Germany had planted its foot. But some good came of this constant influx. We always had new topics of conversation to occupy our thoughts. And that was to our spirits what oxygen is to the lungs.

When we had been furnished with clothing on arrival, many of us had received police or military coats with linings. During the sweating period, their possessors cursed them bitterly. But when the weather suddenly turned cold, the wearers decided they had been in luck.

Their luck did not last long. On November 24, after the noon roll call, Size Ten Gloves appeared in our barrack accompanied by six prisoners. At first he remained on the threshold and surveyed us thoughtfully, as if he were pondering how to carry out his task in the packed room. That he had come through the door and not through the window, quite like any ordinary human being, that he had not drummed on the pane with his fist, that he made no move to pounce on any of us was such an unusual departure from his routine that we all felt very uneasy.

While we were mentally trying to prepare ourselves for whatever was coming, Size Ten Gloves had worked out his plan. "Thirty men into the day room," he ordered.

The comrades nearest the door, who had to go out first, paled visibly. We could see them trembling as they obeyed and we too trembled.

Since the door had been left open, we could see all that went on. When the thirty men were lined up in two rows, Size Ten Gloves ordered, "Coats off!" Then he ordered the six prisoners to collect and examine the coats. The six "experts" inspected the coats carefully, turned the sleeves wrong side out, and examined the inside of the coat. And suddenly it dawned on us what it was all about: all the coats that had linings, even the thin ones, were being retained and piled on the floor.

"Dismissed," ordered Size Ten Gloves, when the experts had finished with the thirty men. Then the next thirty took their turn, and so it went on until all the coats had been inspected. Then Size Ten Gloves condescended to explain. "These coats here are to be taken to the clothes room at once," he ordered Karl. "There they will be exchanged for others." Thereupon he went on to Wing B, and there, as in the other two Polish blocks, the same procedure was repeated.

The men who had been robbed of their coats sat in their shirt sleeves and froze. We all looked toward Karl for an explanation. But Karl held his peace, and only his tightly compressed lips showed his thoughts. He briefly ordered several of us, whose coats had not been taken, to pick up a bundle of clothes and follow him. He himself shouldered the biggest bundle.

Suddenly an almost cheerful voice broke the gloomy silence. "I would have you know that you have just contributed to the clothing of the glorious German Army. Germany's clothing supply must be in a bad way. Isn't this knowledge worth freezing for? If only the foreign press knew of it! And do you need a better proof that the German General Staff is preparing for a long war than the fact that they are storing up reserves of secondhand clothing?"

This speech galvanized us like an electric current. If this were true, it *was* worth freezing for. If the Allies held out, even we might live to see Hitler's thousand-year Reich dissolve into sound and smoke.

But the general enthusiasm soon subsided. "Who's going to wear those old coats?" a voice demanded. "It's only another dirty trick on the 'Bromberg murderers,' and all these deep explanations are nothing but self-deception."

The first speaker would not be silenced. "Your little mind can't see beyond your nose," he fired back. "I'll bet anything that this time there's more behind it than a dirty trick."

When the debate had reached its height and we were all shouting excitedly at one another, the window polishers announced, "Blockfuehrers in sight," and we had to calm down at once. In a moment the blockfuehrers were at the window watching us. Our ragged aspect must have put them in high good humor, for they were still cracking jokes when they finally came inside.

We had had time to prepare, so we presented an exemplary front when the foreman shouted: "Achtung!" But the blockfuehrers for once had little use for military drill.

"See that—the bums have made themselves comfortable in their shirt sleeves, like in the middle of summer," said the Saxon.

And Schuschnig chimed in: "You must be hot today, eh?"

When the circumstances had been explained to them, the whole gang agreed heartily with the order from the clothes room.

"We have a better use for our uniforms."

"We must make the whole bunch run around naked so they'll freeze quicker."

Then Schuschnig had a brainstorm. "Which of you is freezing?" he demanded.

We did not answer.

"Haven't you washed your ears today?" asked Schuschnig, and his shoulders went up until they almost hid his head. His companions moved closer.

But we knew the trick, and by a tacit understanding we arrived at the right answer.

"No one," we all shouted.

Schuschnig was satisfied. He let his shoulders fall again and cried: "That's as it should be. Now shout three times in chorus, 'We aren't freezing,' and so loud the other bums can hear you."

We obeyed.

Then our visitors went off, to seek further diversion.

We were left in an extraordinary state of mind. The Saxon's singing voice and Schuschnig's wooden figure had diverted us highly. Some of us began to laugh and the laughter spread until the whole room shook with it. The indoor squad had hard work restoring order. When Karl returned with the substitute coats, we realized that we had entirely forgotten the cold.

Karl, of course, had tried to get back the coats that were whole, even if heavily patched. And he gave the warmest to the old and sick. It now appeared that in our former debate both groups had been right. For the clothes room had ordered that in the future lined coats should not be distributed to prisoners but sent to the military authorities in Berlin. Other prisoners, however, were permitted to keep the lined coats they had already received; we were the only ones deprived of them.

"But don't worry," said Karl; "the others will soon have to hand over too. The whole clothing-supply system in the camp is breaking down. I wouldn't be surprised if they gave us paper clothes before long. Oh, that gang is great at ersatz things, all right. Everything about them is ersatz: their philosophy, their New Order, their brown heroes. But that's the good thing about it. Ersatz doesn't last, so don't lose heart."

On November 29, shortly after the noon roll call, Karl brought us the shocking news that the entire faculty of the University and other academic institutions of Cracow had just been brought to Sachsenhausen. Even the dismemberment of Poland had not affected me so powerfully as this announcement. For Polish history had taught me that 122 years of alien rule had been unable to break Poland's resistance only because the Polish intelligentsia had understood how to keep her culture alive.

To all Poles, at home and abroad, Cracow was more than a university city which numbered the greatest Polish scholars among its teaching staff; Cracow had always been a symbol of Poland's greatness and creative spirit. It was the city where Casimir the Great had founded the first Polish university at a time when there was only one other university in Central Europe, Prague. Until the sixteenth century Cracow was the capital of the powerful Kingdom of Poland. And it was the city of Copernicus, whose astronomical discoveries revolutionized the thought and science and belief of the world. When Karl told us of the arrival of the professors, he could give us no details. All he had learned was that they numbered nearly two hundred and had been made to stand several hours on the assembly place before they were allowed into the shower barrack to be bathed and dressed in the usual camp style. I asked him to try to learn further particulars, but before he had a chance to find out anything, two of the professors were brought to our block and assigned to Wing B, where there was more room than among us. These two— Leo Sternbach and Joachim Metellman—were separated from their colleagues and sent to us because they were Jews. The other professors were assigned to a separate barrack in the isolation district, and we never saw them.

When we learned that the two professors must remain under Franz's care, we were all greatly alarmed. But Franz surprised us pleasantly. He treated both professors with the greatest respect and procured them as many alleviations as were possible in a concentration camp. He saw to it that they never suffered from hunger and that they ate at the table with the indoor squad. When linen was distributed, he gave them the best garments. He let them wash in a normal way and have to themselves the widest straw sack in the best place in the dormitory.

The other comrades, too, outdid each other in showing their esteem for the two scholars. Everyone considered himself fortunate if he could do them a good turn, and would gladly have endured all kinds of hardships if by so doing he could have saved them any suffering. The professors were deeply moved by these attentions. Professor Sternbach, in particular, never failed, at the smallest kindness shown to him, to murmur courteously in his warm voice a "Thank you, thank you."

And the reception of these thanks testified to the respect and pity which everyone felt for the frail old man, who looked as if a puff of wind would blow him away. In our brutalized existence, words of thanks rang false to our ears, and no one used them. When some newcomer did so he was bluntly told: "Man, there's no thanking here; that was before." But to the professor even the greatest boor replied promptly in a friendly voice: "You're very welcome, Professor. Don't mention it."

During roll call we all trembled for Professor Sternbach. Aside from the cold and wet which undermined his already delicate health, the severities to which we were subjected were a constant threat of death to a man of seventy-five. And we thanked God every time when roll call was over and he was safely back in the barrack. Then Professor Metellman—who was about twenty-five years younger and, thanks to the special privileges which Franz, out of respect for Professor Sternbach, extended to him too, was in a much better state of health—would instantly go to the old man's side, support him, help him to sit down, and try in every way to lighten his lot.

But no amount of kindness could alter the fact that Sternbach's health was growing steadily worse. Franz tried to find a remedy. When he learned that the professor's distinguished works had won him honors from Pope Pius XI, Franz, who was a Catholic, was still more concerned and found a way to send him to the Revier. He described the old man's plight to a Catholic friend, the room senior of another block, who had formerly been a doctor and was now practicing his profession in the Revier. This room senior saw to it that the professor received treatment, often coming himself for the old man. When it was cold, he brought an overcoat for the professor to wear on the way. This was a bold deed, for the doctor had removed the prison number from the coat, and every prisoner had to wear his number. But luckily the doctor, who was well known in camp, was never stopped and always succeeded in conducting his charge to and from the Revier in safety.

Since no pace was permitted except the double, the professor and his companion had to run to the Revier without stopping. It twisted our hearts every time we saw the old man return gasping for breath and sink powerless into his place. The doctor brought drops to strengthen his heart, but they did not help much.

Although Professor Sternbach never complained, we felt that he was marked for death. Not only was his body at the end of its strength, but his weakened heart could not endure the pain of separation from his colleagues, with whom he had worked all his life and from whom he was now parted in the hour of their bitterest trial. Several times, on Sundays, Franz and the doctor were able to arrange that Professor Sternbach and Professor Metellman could visit their colleagues for a short while. When the two came back, Professor Sternbach always seemed particularly depressed. He never spoke of it, but anyone with understanding could read the grief in his sunken eyes.

Of course, we were eager to learn from the two professors what had happened when the Germans marched into Cracow and how their arrest had come about. But it was hard to get speech with them. In a concentration camp public interests always come before private, and all conversations are public property. As soon as a comrade exchanged two words with either of the professors, a host of listeners would crowd around to take part in the conversation or at least to overhear what was said. Professor Sternbach would then become embarrassed and lapse into silence. He really never talked except when he was alone with Professor Metellman, for he knew that then no one would dare to intrude upon their conversation.

But at last Professor Metellman realized that the whole block was almost dying of suppressed curiosity and he agreed to give a talk on the events in Cracow. The comrades of Wing B passed on what they had heard to us. We would have liked the professor to come to our block and tell us himself, but Franz would not hear of such a thing. He took care that the professors never went to Wing A, and at first he would not allow the inmates of Wing A to speak to them. Here at last was his opportunity to settle accounts for a long-standing grudge.

From the beginning of our arrest, Block 38 had set the tone for all three Polish blocks. We were not only foremost in receiving blows, as we were at the near end of the blockfuehrers' line of march; we were foremost in thinking out measures of precaution and self-help, which were imitated by the other blocks. And of the two wings in our block, Wing A was the foremost; for by chance the most cultured, well-bred and intelligent men had been lodged there. Franz begrudged Karl the privilege of being room senior in such a "high-brow" wing. But with the assignment of the two distinguished scholars to his own wing, he had put Karl in the shade. And now he guarded his treasure proudly and would let no one share it with him.

But I would not give up and tried several times to talk with one of the professors during the noon recess. Such opportunities were long in coming, and even when I was successful I could hear the story only in installments, for the talks were interrupted by other comrades joining in. In the end, however, I got a complete account of the professors' arrest.

When the German troops invaded Poland on September 1, not even the greatest pessimist in Cracow expected the disaster that occurred five days later with the arrival of enemy forces in their city. But the professors quickly pulled themselves together, despite the shock of seeing German troops and swastikas all over Cracow. They knew that they, the representatives of Polish culture, must set an example to their countrymen.

The beginning of a new semester was at hand. Here was an opportunity to show that Polish intellectual life was going on, in spite of the national catastrophe. On November 2, all the professors, dressed in their academic robes, assembled in the university chapel for the usual opening ceremony.

The Germans reacted promptly. They invited the professors of all the institutions of learning in Cracow to a lecture in the university auditorium (the Aula) on November 6. The theme was: "The attitude of the German authorities to culture and learning."

When the rector of the university declared himself in favor of accepting the invitation, all the professors bowed to his decision. The professors' wives, however, had misgivings, and insisted on accompanying their husbands in the naïve belief that their presence might restrain the Nazis from carrying out any villainy they might have planned.

When all were assembled in the Aula, the head of the Gestapo, named Meyer, mounted the lectern and announced: "In view of the fact that the professors have opened the new semester without consulting the German authorities, whereby they have plainly demonstrated their hostility to the Reich, and in view of the fact that the University of Cracow has always been a bastion of Polish nationalism, all the professors present are hereby declared under arrest." And before the hearers had grasped the sense of the words, they saw themselves surrounded by Gestapo men.

The number of men arrested was 174. They included the entire faculty of the University of Cracow and several students who had stolen into the Aula out of curiosity. The prisoners were searched for weapons and counted. Then clubs and a rough "Forward march!" drove them outdoors. The faculty of Cracow University was herded into police trucks. The professors, many of whom had passed their seventieth year, had to climb onto a platform three feet above the ground, and any who were too slow were urged on by rubber truncheons.

After a night in the military prison in Cracow, and three days in barracks in a suburb, the prisoners were taken to Breslau. Immediately upon their arrival they were divided into three groups and taken to three different prisons, where they had to share a common cell with all kinds of criminals. A prison life with daily physical mistreatment began. At intervals one or another was summoned to the office and cross-examined by a Gestapo official. But the Polish professors had no information for the Nazis. So the questioning ended in more mistreatment.

After about three weeks of this, the professors were summoned to the prison yard. There a Gestapo man issued instructions: "Marching time must be kept up. No one may help another. Anyone attempting to escape or behaving suspiciously will be shot. Forward! March!"

In three columns the Polish professors marched to the railroad station through the city of Breslau. The inhabitants flocked to the curbstones to watch the procession. They were not only Hitler Youth, not only uniformed Party members; they looked like Germans of all classes, of all degrees of education, teachers, students. Yet they stood there, screaming filthy abuse at the Cracow professors, spitting in their faces.

When the three groups of professors met at the station they were all exhausted, soiled, battered and bloody. But the Gestapo had strengthened the guards, as if these enfeebled men could have planned any kind of violence. Their journey took them in an unknown direction. Only when the train stopped and the station signs announced "Oranienburg," did the professors realize that what lay behind them was only a drop in the cup of suffering that awaited them.

A guard of about one hundred men took them in charge at the station. Since it was raining in torrents, the country roads that led to the camp were reduced to slush. Walking in the mud was hard on weary legs, and many of the older men's gave way. But no one was allowed to support an exhausted colleague or help a fallen man to his feet.

The heavy downpour gave the professors a proper introduction to the camp. They were allowed to stand outside for several hours and get wet to the skin. It was not until then that a group of blockfuehrers appeared and began to ply them with filthy questions about their private lives. And many a scholar had to roll in the mud because he refused to gratify this perverse curiosity.

Then the subject was changed.

"If you had been illiterates like the rest of the Polish boors," said a blockfuehrer, "you'd still be able to sleep with your women."

And another chimed in: "Anyway, all you know is how to stir up revolt. But never fear, you scoundrels, we'll drive such nonsense out of your noodles and make you tame."

And a third took it up: "You and the cursed priests have brought all this misery on Poland. If you lice-and-bedbug carriers hadn't forced your seditious ideas on the race of serfs, they would have worked for us peacefully."

So it went on for an hour and a half. And the 167 professors, only three months before a power in the world of learning, helplessly endured these sallies.

Then the Kommandant appeared with his attendants to inspect the new arrivals. After he and his followers had amused themselves a while with questions and vulgarities, the Kommandant delivered his standard speech. But this time he added a special passage: "You were born in an unlucky hour. Poland no longer exists and will never exist again. From now on the Polish serfs will work for us and have no more need of professors. Germany has plenty of those. So we will re-educate you here and teach you German views. Henceforth Polish culture is a thing of the past."

But the words by which the Kommandant intended to kill their hope had the opposite effect. The men who had been bowed down by their country's misfortune lifted their heads again. The Germans were still Germans. They were doing what they had done once before, in the years of the Partition. But the Poles were still Poles. This time, too, Germany's will-to-destruction would only weld the Polish nation more firmly. The more mercilessly they ravaged Poland, the higher would rise the flood of Polish hatred, until it swept out the intruders as it had done in 1918.

It was not until I heard these words from Professor Sternbach's lips that I realized from what source he drew the strength for the heroic conduct which had so greatly impressed us all.

On December 2, Karl brought us a welcome announcement from the office. What was left of the money which had recently been deducted from our account and handed over to Karl to cover the cost of postage was now at our disposal for the purchase of shoelaces, toothpaste, toothbrushes, paper handkerchiefs and similar articles. But when Karl tried to list our needs—for in the Polish blocks these articles had to be bought by the room senior and not, as in the other barracks, by the prisoners themselves—an utterly insoluble problem presented itself.

After the cost of postage for the first letters was deducted, each of us had about 85 pfennigs left, and we had to save some of this for future postage expenses. But the price of articles in the canteen was double the usual market price, and there were comrades who hadn't a pfennig to their names, for whom we all must contribute. That meant that nobody's money would cover all his needs.

What should I buy with my few pfennigs? I reflected with anxious concentration. Toothbrush and toothpaste? I had not cleaned my teeth for three months. Or could I get along without a toothbrush and spend the money on handkerchiefs for my constantly running nose? Or wasn't it more important to buy shoelaces so that I would not stumble every time I ran? And all the others were making the same calculations.

Karl urged us to hurry. He wanted to be first in the canteen and have the best choice for his block. At last we decided to leave the selection of the articles to him. And Karl actually was the first in the canteen and bought up whatever he could get. Then he proudly brought his purchases back to the barrack and set about distributing them fairly. He made us all file in front of him, inspected us from head to heel, handed out shoelaces to those whose boots were flapping open, gave the few jars of stearine ointment, which was a rare luxury in the camp, to those whose hands were most chapped and swollen. The handkerchiefs went to the men who had the worst colds, and those who had no particularly pressing needs got toothbrushes and toothpaste.

Of course, the articles were of the most inferior quality, but we were overjoyed to have them. And we were satisfied with Karl's farsighted distribution. But our pleasure in our new possessions did not last long. Since the articles had to be kept in the common cupboards in the day room, confusion soon arose and, worse still, many were stolen, so that the purchase ended in bitterness and disappointment.

December 6 was the first day of the Chanukah, or Feast of Dedication, which is celebrated for eight days in memory of the liberation of the Jews from the Greek yoke and the heroic deeds of the Maccabees. In comparison with the observance of religious holidays and harvest festivals, the ceremonies commemorating the Chanukah are simple. The heroic side of these events is mentioned only briefly during the morning prayers; while the miraculous deliverance is commemorated by the lighting of candles, one being added each evening until there are eight. In addition, a special hymn of thanks and praise, recited only on the greatest holidays, is interpolated into the daily morning prayer. This hymn is the "Hallel," from which the word "hallelujah" is derived.

Since we knew that the Gestapo was very accurately informed as to the dates and significance of our holidays, we feared that they would make Chanukah the occasion for special tortures, as they had done on the Day of Atonement. For, besides its religious meaning, Chanukah had a marked national character and was regarded as a symbol of Jewish heroism.

At first our fears were not realized. But on December 12, the next-to-the-last day of Chanukah, when we were beginning to think we had escaped danger, the blockfuehrers appeared in force at roll call. They stopped first at Block 37. "Maccabees, accursed Maccabees!" we heard them shout. Then we knew that it had come.

After they had worked on Block 37 for a while, they divided into two groups and half of them started toward our block. "There are the successors of the heroic Maccabees!" they cried as they reached us. And then the old question-and-answer game began.

"Did the Maccabees stink like you plague sores?" asked Size Ten Gloves.

This question left no doubt that we had a black day before us. It was not enough that we must suffer for the crime of being born Jews and Poles, for the misdeeds of our English allies, for all offenses against Gestapo law within and without the camp. Now they were going to make us suffer for this also, that our forebears were heroes who would not be slaves. All that was dear to us they took away.

They stole our future, they laid waste our present, and now they were besmirching even our past.

A "Jawohl" would spare us many sufferings. But we could not bring ourselves to utter the word. Was it not enough that we had reviled ourselves as Jews and as Poles? Must we revile our forefathers as well?

"Didn't you understand the question?" I heard Size Ten Gloves ask suddenly, as if from far away. But the words did not reach my consciousness. My thoughts were busy with the Maccabees. What would they have done in a situation like this, they who had fought, without counting the cost, against a force many times their own? Would they have joined battle even here, with only their naked hands? Would they have sooner chosen death than suffer scorn and infamy?

A blow under my right eye startled me out of my thoughts. Now the blockfuehrers from Block 37 had joined the others and the whole group hurled themselves upon us. When the ground was sufficiently strewn with bodies, they broke off and went through the rest of their program.

"If you don't answer this time," said Size Ten Gloves, "the whole block will be declared a saboteur block and treated accordingly." Then he began again, "Did the Maccabees stink like you plague sores?"

Certain death faced us if we did not answer. And somewhere, perhaps in the near future, freedom was waiting. "Perhaps at this moment the order for my release is being signed," I thought. "Perhaps a runner will bring it tomorrow morning at roll call." And all the others were thinking the same thing.

"Jawohl!" we shouted in loud but hollow voices.

Then the game went on. "Which of you heroes can tell the story of the Chanukah?" asked Size Ten Gloves.

It could only be a trap. Nevertheless, a comrade volunteered. He was one of the smallest and weakest among us, but a good speaker and a profound student of Jewish history.

The blockfuehrers broke into laughter. "Look who's piping up," they cried. "That's a fine figure of a hero." And Size Ten Gloves remarked: "You must be a pocket edition of a Maccabee, eh?"

But our comrade refused to be put out. He was resolved to go through with his task as worthily as possible. Let the blockfuehrers make fun of him—it did not matter.

"Jawohl!" he answered loud and clear. But everyone who knew him could hear in his voice what joy it gave him to tell his beloved history of the Maccabees.

"Then go on," ordered Size Ten Gloves, "and show us how the Jews lie like their holy books have lied before them."

Without hesitation our comrade in a firm voice began his story:

"Some 165 years before the beginning of the Christian era, the Jewish nation was again passing through a period of persecution. Not only were they no longer masters in their own land, but the Greek tyrant, Antiochus Epiphanes, sought to take from them their dearest possession, their faith. In the Jewish Temple a statue of the god Zeus was set up, and the Jews were forced to bow down to this image. To refuse was death. But many preferred death to idolatry.

"At that time there lived in Medin a man named Mattathias, of the priestly house of the Hasmonees, and his five sons. They could not look on idly at the shame of their people, and as the Greek yoke became heavier and heavier, Mattathias and his sons rallied the remnants of the Jewish nation to fight their oppressors. And although they were only few, yet they succeeded in vanquishing their tyrants. Then the defiled Temple was rededicated. And in memory of that miraculous victory, the Jews have ever since celebrated the Chanukah, or Feast of Dedication."

"So even two thousand years ago you rebelled against the constituted authorities," shouted Size Ten Gloves and gave the speaker such a blow that he staggered and fell. That was the moment the blockfuehrer had been waiting for. His feet took care of the rest.

"This also is in memory of your miraculous victory," he screamed at the man lying motionless before him; "that is, if you ever remember anything again."

Now Kopella took the lead. "On with the sermon!" he ordered. "Who can tell now why the rebels were called Maccabees?"

In spite of what we had just witnessed—or perhaps because of it, to show them that we were not such cowards as they thought us—several comrades volunteered.

"What, so many?" cried Kopella in astonishment. For a while this boldness made him speechless. But he finally rallied. "All step forward!" he ordered. And when the comrades were ranged in front of him, he picked out the smallest and frailest.

"Here is the second volume of the pocket edition," he laughed uproariously. Then he ordered: "All right, talk!"

"When the Maccabees took up the fight," began our comrade, "they knew that the enemy was powerful and they were only a handful of fighters. But trust in God and the knowledge that their cause was just gave them courage. Firm in their faith that God would grant them victory, they took as their watchword the Hebrew sentence, 'Mi Komaucho Boeilim Adonai?'—'Who is like unto thee, O Lord, among the gods?' They wrote the initials of the Hebrew words upon their shields and banners and connected the consonants with vowels. Thus the word 'Maccabee' was created and they adopted it as their name, in token that they were God's warriors." [1]

Before the sound of his words had died away, the blockfuehrers were upon us like an avalanche. When they could do no more they issued the edict: "No food till tomorrow morning." Then we were released.

Everyone sat down, wherever he could find a place, to forget for a moment what had happened, if possible. Once again they had befouled us, inwardly with their beastliness, outwardly with the dirt we had collected on our clothes. And was that all for today, or would they come again? And what would tomorrow bring? We had still one day of Chanukah before us.

Karl's voice broke into our gloomy reflections. He called out a comrade's name. "Quick, quick!" he cried. "A runner is here."

That was the first time that a runner had come at such an unusual hour. It seemed to us a sign from Heaven that we were not forgotten after all. We awoke from the hopelessness that had enveloped us. One after another raised himself up as if we had passed the crisis of an illness. What could it be but a miracle, that on a day when the persecuting fury of the blockfuehrers had reached new heights of spiritual torture, a comrade should be set free? The flood of suppressed emotions found vent in loud sobs, sobs of deliverance and

---

[1] Maccabee in Hebrew letters is written thus: מכבי. The last letter, י, or Y (pronounced *yee*) is the first letter of the name of God, Jehovah. Since, according to Jewish teaching, only the High Priest in the Tabernacle was permitted to pronounce the name, Jehovah, in all prayers where the name occurs, other expressions such as "Our Lord" (in Hebrew, "Adonai") have to be substituted.

gratitude. And in the general convulsion of feeling a comrade found words for what we all felt.

"This is the Lord's doing; it is marvelous in our eyes," he recited, in a moved voice, the words of the "Hallel." "This the day which the Lord hath made; we will rejoice and be glad in it."

And we all joined in: "Save now, I beseech thee, O Lord; O Lord, I beseech thee, send now prosperity."

"The Latrine Courier," whose activity in the last few days had been almost dormant, seized upon the opportunity offered by the new release. At noon Karl had taken a man from the indoor squad with him to the industrial section on an errand. When the comrade had returned, rumors sprang up like mushrooms. The released comrade was already standing at the gate in his civilian clothes, reported "The Latrine Courier." Since prisoners released in the morning had to wait six or seven hours before getting their civilian clothes and leaving camp, this speedy progress seemed a propitious omen.

It was also reported that, from now on, releases would take place twice a day, and the attack of the blockfuehrers was ascribed to their anger over this fact. This news sounded credible, and since we were in need of hope, after what we had suffered, everyone clung to it.

A little later Karl came in. "I have something to tell you," he said.

We listened eagerly.

"The skunks are going to let us have light at last," said Karl, after a pause. "When it will be, I don't know. But I thought it would do you good to look forward to it. What light means to us, you know very well."

Oh, yes, we knew what light meant to us! Light was the best gift that could be granted us, next to freedom itself.

That this good news also should reach us on just this day seemed another good omen. We suddenly realized that we had not yet had an opportunity to commemorate the Chanukah holiday. Various proposals were made and at last we agreed that a fitting speech would best suit the occasion. The choice of a speaker fell unanimously on the comrade who had spoken so impressively to the Leipzigers.

The chosen man felt very weak, for he had suffered severe injuries in the attack on the previous day. But when we continued to press him, he rose to speak. Instantly there was dead silence. We knew that if *he* spoke to us, we should hear something worth hearing.

The speaker thought a few moments. Then he gave us his text, a sentence from the prophet Ezekiel:

"And when I passed by thee, and saw thee polluted in thine own blood, I said unto thee: By thy blood thou wilt live; yea, I said unto thee: By thy blood thou wilt live."

Our comrade let the full weight of these words sink in before he went on: "Are not these words meant for our generation too? Is not our blood a testimony that we too shall live on? Are we not living proofs of this miracle perpetually manifested in our people? And does not this miracle teach us that—although we have victims every day—we must not offer ourselves as victims; that is, we must not give up our hope. Hope is the greatest Jewish treasure, and faith in God is the key to it."

This introduction touched strange depths in us. We were transported from the world of every day into the realms of the unearthly and supernatural, into the mystery of the eternal Jewish renewal, which we had all experienced for ourselves. We sat rooted in our places.

Our comrade felt how mightily our spirits were stirred; and to give us time to recover he spoke now, simply but proudly, of the glorious age of Jewish life under the Hasmonees, up to the decline under the Greek yoke; of the battles and victories of the Maccabees and of the meaning of the Chanukah holiday.

Listening to this familiar story, we grew calm. But the speaker knew the whole gamut of human emotions and how to play upon them. This Chanukah was not a time for peace and contentment, but for meditation, for looking into our own hearts, for judgment and denunciation.

"Our sufferings are old, like our history," he continued. "For two thousand years, our blood has flowed in some corner of the earth. Our persecutors have been many, and the pretexts by which they sought to justify their murders have been many. And yet, not all their hostility, not all their contempt, not all their anger have availed to wipe us out. As if we still had a mission to fulfill on earth, we live on, as we shall live on forever."

Our comrade stopped to take a deep breath. "And now a new hater of our race has arisen, crueler, more dangerous, than any ever before. We were the ladder on whose rungs he climbed to supreme power. From this dark grave, I call to account the men responsible, the men, everywhere in the world, who let this happen without a protest. They left us to the vengeance of the power-hungry beast of prey, because they thought that as long as he had our bodies to mangle, the rest of the world was safe from his greed. But their silent toleration of this orgy has recoiled upon themselves. When the beast had torn us to pieces, he threw himself upon other victims, one after another, until the whole world ran with blood.

"Not until then did the world realize that Hitler's Jew-hate was merely a part of his world-hate, that he had chosen the Jews as his first victims because Jews are always hated by those who want to enslave a part of humanity as a step toward enslaving the rest; because to be a Jew and to love progress and individual freedom are the same thing. And now the beast of prey has become the victim of his own destroying fury. He has sown the wind and he will reap the whirlwind. The blood of those he has murdered, of those who are dying on the battlefields at his will, cries and smokes from the ground; and that blood will be upon his head."

The comrade seemed exhausted by his long speech, for he sat down to recover. We thought he had finished. But when several of us turned to him with words of thanks, he checked them with a lifted hand. "I am still far from done," he said. "Just let me gather strength for what I still have to say."

We could see that he was not merely tired. His compressed lips testified that he was suffering severely from his wounds. And we kept absolutely still, until at last he began again:

"During the last world war, it looked as if the sun had at last risen for us. The Entente Powers promised us Palestine as a national home. 'Why,' a few cynics may well have asked, 'shouldn't we make a pretense of generosity? The Jews will surely fail. How could these people, so long estranged from the soil, accustom themselves to agriculture? Are not money and trade their métier?'

"But we showed the world that it was they who had artificially estranged us from the soil. Undaunted we took up the battle with the desert and transformed it into a garden. We struggled with malignant diseases. We turned swamps into health resorts and established model colonies there. We created industries with marvels of technical achievement which gave a new impetus to the whole Near East. We built cities with hospitals, schools, universities, which could bear comparison with the most modern buildings of the kind. We covered an arid country with woodlands and orchards. And all this we did without foreign help, without foreign capital. And every bit of land that we cultivated we bought at an exorbitant price. Where else in history is there such an example of 'conquest of the land'?

"We stood our test. But we were not allowed to reap the fruit of our labors. When the mandate powers saw our achievements, they began to evade the mandate, which was drawn up in unequivocal terms and guaranteed by forty-two nations. They sent commissions to the country and issued a flood of reports, findings and White Papers. And the guaranteeing powers said nothing to this breach of their signed pledge.

"Where was justice then? And where is justice today? Twenty-two years ago, when our sufferings were light in comparison to the present, they promised us a national home; and in the era of Hitler, when we are literally being exterminated in one country after another, they are getting ready to take our national home away. And that, in a period when all the world talks of democracy, justice and freedom. How do those principles agree with their practice toward the Jews?

"But the period of our misery and homelessness is drawing to an end. All injustice, all falsehood, will be buried in the wreckage of the world that is now being smashed; and out of the ruins a new world will arise, a world which will give justice where justice is due. The promises given to us will be fulfilled. We will return to our country, as our prophets foretold and as we have never ceased to hope."

And with these words he struck up the opening notes of the Jewish *Hymn of Hope*:

> While yet the olden fires burn
> Within each loyal Hebrew breast
> And toward the East our eyes return
> With Zion still our only quest. . . .

And softly, but with enthusiasm, we joined in:

> Oh, then our Hope—it is not dead,
> Our ancient Hope and true
> Again the sacred soil to tread
> Where David's banners flew!

The speaker was silent, but his words went on working in our hearts and minds. And in tribute to his speech, we all maintained a thoughtful silence. Everyone clung to the belief and hope that his predictions would be fulfilled. Not until the next roll call did we talk together about this memorable speech, in which every sentence furnished material for conversation, and which for many days was the chief subject of discussion in all three Polish blocks.

One day after Chanukah, about an hour before the evening roll call, Emil, the room senior of Block 39, came in with a terrifically important air. We had never come in contact with Emil. But Karl had often told us how stupid he was, how he was always giving himself airs and being caught in false boasts.

"Important news!" called Emil, loud enough for us all to hear. His eyes roved into every corner of the room, as if he wanted to be sure we were all paying attention. "The Polish blocks will get light at last."

Emil looked at Karl expectantly. "Well, what do you say to that?" his eyes seemed to ask. "This time I know something you didn't know."

But Karl had nothing to say. Then Emil grew impatient. "Man, are you dim-witted?" he demanded. "We're getting light, I told you. It was no small matter to put that through, I can tell you. But I managed it."

Emil's stupidity stood out all over him—he couldn't have lured a cat from behind a stove. And he claimed that he had gotten us light!

Karl was answering him. "That we were going to get light I've known for a long time. The only news to me is that you put it through." And his tone added, "You, of all people, you idiot!"

But this was evidently one of Emil's brighter moments, for he sensed Karl's unspoken comment. He went red and shouted, beside himself with the affront: "You don't believe me. You think you've got all the brains. You think you're big here, and you won't grant me any success. You . . . you . . . you . . ." He began to stammer and lost the thread of what he was saying.

But Karl was much too prudent to humiliate Emil in our presence. And in a friendly tone, in which only we could detect the irony, he said: "What's got into you, Emil? I not believe you? Congratulations on your great success. I didn't know you rated so well with the blockfuehrers."

Emil looked at him doubtfully. Was this meant seriously, or was Karl making fun of him? But he had no opportunity to examine further. For Karl explained that he must hurry to the office before roll call and he disappeared.

When he came back, he had fuses with him. And after roll call, with official permission, we put on the light.

Light! For the first time in three months, light! Only those who have lived in darkness know what that meant. From the rafters of our dormitory hung two bulbs of about 40 watts each. But to us it was as if all the light in the world were concentrated there. We looked at each other incredulously and stared reverently at the shining bulbs, as if we had never seen such things before. When at last we found words for the overwhelming event, we began to make plans. Now life would be much easier. No more confusion in the morning when we dressed and left the barrack. We would no longer burn our hands when we set fire to the sheets of Karl's *Voelkischer Beobachter* and tried to hold them in our fingers to the last cinder, so that we could see to put the soup bowls on the table in the day room. And—God, what a prospect!—we would now at last be able to read. Karl had told us only that morning that we had the privilege of subscribing to certain newspapers and magazines. And we had laughed bitterly, for we were not allowed to read in the daytime, except on Sundays, and in the evening we had no light.

I began to make suggestions about what periodicals we should subscribe to. The *Wehrmacht,* the *Voelkischer Beobachter,* the *Schwarze Korps,* the *Berliner Illustrierte*—what difference did it make that these were all Party papers? We could recognize the news even in its Nazi dress, form a coherent picture, be less hopelessly cut off from the outside world. Karl made a list of our wishes— fifteen newspapers and periodicals altogether—and took down the names of those who wished to contribute to the subscriptions.

But the light proved a source of new troubles. Now, when the blockfuehrers visited us at night, they no longer needed to probe all the corners with flashlights for belated sleepers. With the touch of a finger they could light up the whole dormitory, and our invalids in the background were no longer any safer than the comrades in the front line.

As for the reading, we actually did receive the newspapers and magazines we had ordered, with subscriptions paid up for six months in advance. But the only readers were the indoor squad. For Franz, in order to dampen our joy over the light, not only ordained that we could no longer eat in the day room, but forbade us to stay there at all. And reading was allowed only in the day room.

When Mueller became our blockfuehrer, he made our wing his reading room, because of the unusually large selection of reading matter available. From then on he spent every moment of his free time there. While he was reading in the day room, we sat shivering with fear in our dormitory. For some of Mueller's cronies might happen to pass by and drop in to join him, and the whole lot of them might decide to pay us a visit before they left. Often enough it happened so. And after such a visit, all we wanted was to lie down as soon as possible and get to sleep, and the burning light was a torment.

Five weeks had passed since we had first written home, but most of us had not yet received word from our families. This made us very uneasy. On the previous Saturday we had begun to look with anxious hope for letters. And now it was Saturday again and once more our hearts beat expectantly.

Immediately after evening roll call, Karl went off to the office to see about mail, as he always did on Saturdays. This time we waited for him in the most perfect order, so that the distribution of the mail could be accomplished as quickly as possible. Karl came back with a big stack of letters. They had all been opened, and the censors had even removed the stamps on the chance of finding secret messages beneath them.

This time there was mail for almost every one of us. Each tore his letter impatiently out of the envelope. But I could not bring myself to read my letter at once. How long I had waited for this moment! And now that it had really come, I dared not even touch the treasure in my hand, for fear it would melt into nothing, and with it all my joy.

As I hesitated, a stream of thoughts and memories rushed through my mind. How much had happened since I had written to Gucia for the first time! All the releases, which had filled me, and surely her also, with so much confidence. Had she been able to get me a Palestine certificate or thought of some other possibility of rescue?

The letter which held the answer to these questions lay in the hollow of my hand. But I still did not read it. I looked at the envelope and a strange shock went through me. So I was a prisoner. Certainly, I had known that for three months now. But it had not really come home to me until this moment, when for the first time I saw on a letter addressed to me not only my name but a prison number. So I was no longer only Leon, or Szalet or Papa. I was also Number 9335.

But why had Gucia written to me on the typewriter? Had she not always said that a typewritten letter lost all its intimacy? But the question answered itself. Here in the camp there was no such thing as intimacy. My letter belonged to everybody, to my comrades and, above all, to the censors. Gucia had understood that. And more. "The writing must be legible," it said in the abstract of the camp rules. And suddenly I could not help laughing. What had Gucia's teachers always said? "Your handwriting is remarkably full of character; the only trouble is that nobody can read it." My daughter thought of everything.

But it looked odd on the familiar note paper and it disconcerted me. This was the note paper I had known for years. Silver gray with silver-gray lining. And inside, on the sheet of letter paper, I would see her name, printed in big white letters.

At that point I awoke to what was going on around me. It must have been only a few moments since I had taken the letter from Karl's hand, but the time seemed endless, like time in a dream. Someone was calling my name. A buzz of talk filled the room. Letters were passing from hand to hand; here and there comrades were clustered around someone reading his letter aloud.

Then at last I opened the envelope to read my letter. The blood rushed to my temples and set them on fire. Black and green circles danced before my eyes. Had someone played an evil joke on me or was I having hallucinations? The silver-gray lining had been torn from the envelope and instead of a letter it held a curt notice from the office: "Failed to comply with camp rules."

Empty of thought and feeling, I stood by the wall until Karl came over to me, took the letter out of my hand, glanced at the notice and the envelope and gave me the explanation. "Lined envelopes are against the camp rules, as they make the censoring of letters harder."

So that was it. A lined envelope had killed all my joy and hope. Why on earth had Gucia used her own stationery instead of ordinary business paper? But the next moment I realized how unfair it was to blame her. The abstract of the camp rules, her only guide, gave all kinds of directions about writing, but of lined envelopes it said nothing. No, she could not gauge the malice of the Gestapo. Even we did not yet know them fully, or this latest evidence of their mental cruelty—that they had kept back the letter, which was probably in order, and delivered only the offending envelope—would not have staggered me so.

This was the worst blow I had yet received. It hurt more than all the hunger and cold, all the blows and kicks, that I had endured. My comrades tried in the most moving way to distract my mind and to comfort me with the letters they had received from the released comrades, which hinted in veiled terms that they had reported our plight to the Jewish Community and that help might be near. But it was many days before I could reconcile myself to my disappointment.

In the third night after we had received light, we were wakened shortly before the rising hour by shrieks. At the same time searchlights flared out from the watchtowers and criss-crossed overhead. The beams paused awhile on Block 39. But when the guards had convinced themselves that everything within range was in order, the searchlights went out again. We had raised ourselves up and continued listening to the screaming, trying to guess from which of the other two Polish blocks it came. The halting of the searchlights on Block 39 showed us.

Suddenly the screaming stopped. At the same time we heard running and trampling close by. We could recognize the voice of Iron Gustav, who kept yelling: "Run quietly, you dogs, or your screaming will be over forever." Now it sounded as if the running was directly past our windows. We strained our eyes into the darkness, but we could make out nothing.

After about ten minutes, the trampling suddenly stopped, and a few moments later our alarm clock went off. When the light was turned on, it revealed our haggard faces, in every eye the question: "What is happening now?" But in the usual morning rush there was no time to ask questions. Silently, we dressed, put the barrack in order and made ready for roll call. But the unspoken question hung so heavily in the air that some of the indoor squad darted over to Block 39 to find out what had happened. Shortly before we had to go out to roll call, we were released from our suspense.

The comrades of Wing B in Block 39 had been startled out of a deep sleep by some blockfuehrers who dropped in on their way to their posts of duty. They claimed that clothes had not been properly put away, ordered the lights turned on and began a regular inspection. Of course, they soon announced that the occupants of the wing were a slovenly bunch, and put their truncheons to work, "bringing German order into Polish housekeeping."

When the "Polish pigs" had been suitably beaten up, the blockfuehrers had another idea. "The whole pack outdoors!" ordered one. Two others stationed themselves in the doorway, truncheon in hand, to welcome the victims as they ran past, and the rest stayed in the barrack to rout out the other unfortunates.

"Run three times around the barrack and keep quiet," went the order, when all were outside. And the chase that we had heard began. Since there was not even a moon to lighten the darkness, collisions were inevitable. Many men were knocked over, and as no one could see where he was going, the whole group ran over the fallen. The comrades were all barefooted and most wore only a shirt. A few, however, had slept in their drawers because of the cold, and since this was "streng verboten," they were afraid that on their return to the barrack they would be beaten. For a time they played with the idea of hiding, but they rejected the plan. For anyone who remained motionless in the damp, raw air was inviting pneumonia; and if their absence were noticed, they would receive still heavier punishment.

When the chase was called off, the blockfuehrers had the barrack lights put on again to make sure that all were present. All but two had dragged themselves back into the barrack. By the time the missing were found, almost trampled to death, and brought in, the blockfuehrers had to go to their posts, and luckily the drawers were forgotten.

We had a foreboding that this was some new form of amusement in which all three blocks would have a share, so we asked Karl what he thought.

"How do I know, any more than you?" he snorted bitterly. "We haven't enough imagination to figure out what goes on in the heads of those brown cannibals. Let's just be surprised."

The surprise was not long in coming. The next day, about 1:00 P.M., our window-polishing sentries announced an unusually large number of blockfuehrers in sight. Size Ten Gloves, Kopella and Iron Gustav were among them. They divided into three groups and each took one barrack.

"Achtung!" we heard Karl calling in the day room. Then, almost simultaneously, piercing screams broke out from the other two blocks. At the same moment the door to the day room opened. Size Ten Gloves stood in the doorway. His eyes were bloodshot. His huge hands seemed to have grown still more huge.

Fear jerked us to our feet, even before the order was given. But that was the worst thing we could have done. In our fright we had forgotten that Size Ten Gloves would not stand for any sign of independence. To anticipate his commands was as offensive as not to obey them promptly when they were given. "Down, you pests, snouts to the floor. I'll teach you to be uppity," he said in his almost noiseless voice, which oozed bloodthirstiness.

Instantly we threw ourselves down. We pressed close to the floor boards as if we could become one with them and thus escape the fury of this beast. We could feel his sharp eyes darting over our backs. For many minutes nothing happened. Perhaps they were only seconds. But the fear of death that we felt in that interval was the fear of a whole lifetime, of many lifetimes. Who would be first to die?

But Size Ten Gloves had changed his tactics. We first discovered that when the nails of his shoes, with the weight of his huge body behind them, bored into our backs. He ran over us in long, springy steps, and the rest of his gang followed suit.

I was no longer skin, flesh and bones, but one single wound, one devouring fire. I screamed. My neighbor screamed. Suddenly the whole room, the walls themselves, seemed to be screaming. I wanted to press my hands to my ears to shut out the sound of my own dreadful voice. But I could not move a muscle, and I could not stop screaming.

Then the voice of Size Ten Gloves cut through the uproar. "Everyone who screamed, stand up," he ordered. The shrieking stopped instantly.

"Stand up," he had ordered. That meant, stand up and be beaten to death. Nevertheless I pulled myself together and got slowly to my feet. The others had stood up too. What use in trying to hide? He would have found us all the same, and if not us, then others, who would have died in our stead. Suddenly I found myself thinking quite coolly: "So these are my last moments." Strange, how calm I was.

But we were not destined to die then. Size Ten Gloves had pondered too long. Suddenly something happened that diverted his attention. He looked out of the window and our eyes followed his glance. From the other two Polish blocks the comrades were pouring out. Once outside, they tried to form ranks. But Iron Gustav put a stop to that. He lashed at them with his long stick and drove the whole human mass around the barrack. The other blockfuehrers joined in, and in a few seconds a spirited chase was on. Size Ten Gloves could not bear to see his comrades get ahead of him and have all the fun to themselves. "Out with you!" he ordered. That saved our lives.

Outside, the blockfuehrers took us in hand, and in a few seconds we were a part of the human mass circling around the barracks. Our way led around Blocks 38 and 39. This was a distance of about 110 yards, and we were more than a thousand men. We pressed close to each other, not only for lack of space, but from the instinct to submerge ourselves in the mass.

The blockfuehrers had distributed themselves around the barracks, and all had pieces of rubber hose, threaded with chains to give weight to their blows; in the background more were appearing. Before all three barracks, groups of waxen figures were standing: they were the blind and crippled from each block. They stood rigid, and before each group blockfuehrers were shouting variations of the theme that "these crocks must be shipped by special train into the next world." Among those ghosts stood Professor Sternbach. I thought I saw new strength, new resolution, in that old, wasted face.

The prisoners on the outside, who were receiving the most blows, tried to press into the interior. But those in the middle would not let themselves be pushed out of their places, and a silent struggle began. The blockfuehrers noticed what was going on and changed their tactics. Instead of hitting the men on the outside, they swung out with their hose and brought them whistling down on the center of the running mass. The group scattered. Many were dashed to the ground. For a few moments the prostrate bodies dammed up the human torrent. "Remove that rubbish!" snapped the blockfuehrers. The dead and half-dead victims were carried before their respective barracks and laid out in a row with the stiffly standing invalids. The hunt went on.

Again a few quick-witted souls tried to evade the blockfuehrers. They split off from the mass so as to have more freedom of action and be able to dart past the danger zones. But the blockfuehrers guessed these intentions, took these individualists in hand and disposed of them. The rows of dead in front of the barracks lengthened visibly. More and more of the invalids collapsed. But, thank God, Professor Sternbach was still standing. He seemed to have a guardian angel.

We must have been running for more than an hour, and even the blockfuehrers seemed exhausted. But fate seemed to be against us. In the distance we saw Mueller, the Saxon and Schuschnig. Schuschnig ran as fast as his jerky legs would carry him and arrived first on the scene in a series of short, grotesque jumps. He was completely out of breath, but his frenzied eagerness to take part in the beating would not let him stop to breathe. He snatched the rubber hose out of the hand of the nearest blockfuehrer and swung it with all his might. But the swing was too violent for his feeble, ill-made body. The hose slipped out of his hand and landed wide of the mark. And Schuschnig himself spun around, staggered a few steps and fell flat on his nose.

This was the signal for a new climax in the beating. Whether the blockfuehrers wanted to cover up their colleague's disgrace or whether they wanted to show the newcomers in what good form they were, after a whole hour of this savage assault, they beat us with greater energy than before. This new outbreak of fury lasted only a few minutes, but during those few minutes more bodies were left on the ground than during the whole previous hour.

At last the beating stopped. They ordered us to throw ourselves down: "Snouts to the ground and no moving." And we had to lie that way until the evening roll call.

The next day Karl learned that this hunt had been organized by our six murderers as a farewell performance, so to speak, as they were going on Christmas leave.

At the beginning of November, we had noticed that the elite prisoners came back from exercise carrying rolls in their hands. This sight made us feel our hunger still more, and we asked Karl whether the elite prisoners were the only ones who got rolls.

Karl told us that the canteen had begun to receive a limited number of rolls for sale to privileged prisoners: the elite block and those who worked in the office, the Revier or the industrial section. If anything was left over, the room seniors and their assistants in all the blocks got their turn, and then the rest of the prisoners—except the Polish Jews, of course. There was a rumor that an unlimited supply of white bread would shortly be on sale. It appeared that the grain supplies which the Germans had appropriated from plundered Poland were greater than expected; the Reichswirtschaftsministerium (Department of Commerce), it was said, had decided to allow the whole population to buy bread without ration cards.

In December, the canteen actually did receive a small assignment of white bread, and the elite prisoners, of course, were again among the first to benefit. One day, we saw them with long loaves in their hands. This sight was too much for us, and from then on we avoided looking at them when they passed. But the elite prisoners knew very well how sharply we suffered from hunger and they always brandished the bread provokingly in the air to tantalize us.

The bread allotment increased from day to day, and at last all the prisoners were allowed to buy white bread. Only we were still excluded from this privilege. To show us his sympathy for us, Karl himself never touched a roll or a piece of white bread.

We were deeply affected by this latest proof of Karl's humanity, and since Christmas was at hand, we decided to give him some demonstration of our gratitude, as we had long wanted to do. Many plans were suggested, and at last a proposal was accepted with general enthusiasm. Provided that the blockfuehrers had not planned some special tortures for us on Christmas Day, we were to make Karl a speech expressing our thanks for all that he had done for us and present him with bread and salt.

The comrades in Wing B agreed to our proposal, but insisted that Franz must be similarly honored; otherwise his vanity would be offended and they would have to smart for it. It was plain to us, of course, that Franz could not be left out of the festivities, and we agreed to offer him a speech too, but we would not hear of giving him bread and salt. After all, Karl was a room senior and entitled to greater honor, apart from the fact that he had earned it.

The speech for Franz threatened for a while to endanger our whole plan, for who, with a clear conscience, could utter words of gratitude to Franz, who jumped at every opportunity to torment us? But a solution was found when a comrade proposed Professor Metellman, who could say a few kinds words to Franz without being hypocritical. Professor Metellman at once agreed, and when the indoor squad succeeded in trading a loaf of bread for a roll and in procuring some salt, our preparations were completed.

Of course, we could not keep our project a secret from Karl and Franz. In the first place, we did not know whether a celebration would be agreeable to them, and in the second place, we needed their permission, for we had planned that Wing B should come to our day room for the event. Karl grinned indulgently when we told him of our intention to hold a little celebration. "You have my blessing," he said, laughing. "But make it as short as possible. Brevity is the soul of wit, and besides we don't want to be caught out of our places."

A little later it appeared that Karl had also planned a surprise for us. We were indescribably curious to hear what was up, but did not want to ask him. Luckily Karl, who always knew what was going on in our minds, relieved our suspense.

"At first I didn't want to tell you what I and the other room seniors had managed to get for all the Polish blocks, until we had the treasure in our hands," he said, "although I know what anticipation means to you. For it seemed too risky to rouse your hopes and then perhaps have to disappoint you. But now it looks as if the thing is a certainty, so I won't keep you in suspense." Then he told us that for the first time every prisoner in all three Polish blocks was going to get a loaf of white bread, and that for this purpose a mark had been deducted from our accounts. The bread would not be distributed until the next day. However, we would get the next morning's bread ration with our evening ration, so that we could twice enjoy a larger portion of bread.

This announcement filled us with almost uncontrollable joy. A whole loaf of bread! And white bread at that, not the damp, sticky, brown mess we got every day. To eat almost our fill of bread for once —no, twice! It was more than we could ever have expected. We looked at each other and laughed blissfully; if we had not been too embarrassed, we would have fallen on each other's necks for joy. But since almost all of us were grown men and did not want to admit that the prospect of a loaf of bread could call forth such an outburst, we pulled ourselves together and began to speculate on what the bread would look like. For to abandon the subject altogether was beyond our power. What kind of loaves would we get? Long ones, like those we had seen the elite prisoners carrying, or round ones, or the angular wheaten loaves? And would they all be the same size? Bread was the theme which, in all its possible variations, dominated us until the beginning of roll call.

Shortly before evening roll call, Karl and his assistants returned from the canteen, laden with bread. Karl's face shone with joy and pride. Such a mountain of bread we had never seen—it made our heads swim. Our mouths began to water, and many of us besieged Karl with pleas to distribute the bread at once. But he remained firm: "No loaves until tomorrow, and that's that."

The evening roll call lasted fifteen minutes. Evidently the camp authorities were in a hurry to get to their own festivities, and we took this haste as another sign that we should be left in peace. When we returned to barracks, we ate our soup and the doubled bread ration with unusual speed. For the first time since we had been in Sachsenhausen, our stomachs were almost filled. To feel less hunger for once was such a strange and wonderful sensation that we were all in the highest spirits, as if we had dined on roast turkey and champagne. The day room and dormitory were straightened up in a twinkling, and our celebration went off according to plan. We formed an exemplary guard of honor for Karl; then Wing B marched over in parade style, and Karl and Franz and the indoor squads were escorted in. The comrade who was to make the speech stood ready beside a stool covered with two clean towels, on which lay a roll and a plate with salt, and addressed Karl:

"Lieber Stubenaeltester Karl, for a long time we have waited for a chance to express our thanks to you for all that you have done for us, and we are happy that this Christmas Day at last offers us an opportunity. My comrades have asked me to tell you, in the name of the whole block, that we consider ourselves fortunate to have you for our room senior. In these months of our greatest need, you have proved yourself a true friend to us, our only friend. You have, as far as it lay in your modest power, done everything to lighten our sufferings. When you could not help us, at least you tried to comfort us. We will never forget that.

"This is a Christian holiday. Unfortunately I do not feel qualified to speak to you of its meaning. Permit me, though, to mention a Jewish custom, which perhaps has something in common with the spirit of Christmas. From time immemorial it has been a Jewish usage to remember on certain holidays the friends and enemies of the Jewish people. We would like to assure you that if we come out of this den alive, we shall take that opportunity of paying tribute to you as our faithful friend.

"We will never forget that, in contrast to others of your comrades in this camp, you have been true to your convictions and never let yourself be deluded by hatred, envy and propaganda. We will never forget that when our food was taken away, you voluntarily went hungry with us. The latest proof of your solidarity, that you would not buy one piece of white bread when it was denied to us, has touched us deeply. Therefore we have decided, as a sign and symbol of our gratitude, to present you with a roll and salt, and we ask you to eat this roll, the first piece of white bread you have had for so long, in our presence."

With these words he handed Karl the roll and held out to him the plate of salt.

Karl seemed deeply moved. He cleared his throat several times, as if to gulp down his emotion. We saw that he wanted to say something, but the words would not come out. He silently took the roll, broke it in two, sprinkled it with salt, handed one half to the speaker and then slowly ate the other half himself.

We too were deeply moved. The whole ceremony had lasted only a few minutes, but they were minutes full of dignity and of genuine feeling.

Karl finally recovered and brought out a few words of thanks for the surprise. In his simple way, he said that he had only done what his conscience dictated and deserved no special thanks for it. But we could sense a suppressed happiness in the words.

We marched over to Wing B, where Professor Metellman was to make his speech. He spoke briefly about the meaning of the Christmas holiday and the hope of redemption for Franz, for us and for all mankind. Then he spoke of our sympathy for Franz's grief in being separated from his family on such a day. He asked Franz to comfort himself with the thought that although he was far from his loved ones, he was not forgotten, that his mother was surely thinking of her beloved son at this moment and praying that she could soon clasp him in her arms again.

The effect of these words was beyond all expectation: Franz was so touched that he burst into loud sobbing. Then we breathed more freely. For we had not felt altogether easy as we listened to Professor Metellman's phrases and could plainly see that he himself was not comfortable in his role. But Franz was wholly satisfied and remained dissolved in tears, we later learned, long after we had returned to our wing.

Next morning after we returned from roll call, Karl at last distributed the bread. He reminded us that we must eat it up by noon, since we were not allowed to put it away when we went out to roll call. One would have thought that this was an unnecessary warning—but not so. Only a few withdrew with their bread to a distant corner, like a dog with a particularly juicy bone, and did not emerge again until the last crumb had vanished. Most of the comrades simply could not make up their minds to eat. They eyed the bread lovingly, cradled it in their arms, walked to and fro with it as if they were having a private talk with their precious treasure. For so many months a whole loaf of bread had been one of their dreams and they wanted to enjoy it as long as possible. They would have liked to make the bread last for several days, to break off a piece now and then. The thought that they must eat it up at once, and that their dream would soon end in a full belly, seemed unbearable. Only after repeated urgings from Karl did they sit down and eat their bread, dutifully and without pleasure.

But in their stomachs too an unexpected reaction was taking place. For months these stomachs had cried for bread, and now that the bread was here, they became tied up in knots. The first half of the loaves went down with an effort, and the second half was eaten with actual disgust. Many of the weaker comrades even gave up the struggle and left the bread to the few gluttons.

On that Christmas Day there was an unusual atmosphere of excitement in the camp, which gradually penetrated to our barracks. At intervals, loud-speakers were turned on. First the annual Christmas message of Reichsminister Rudolph Hess to the Germans abroad was broadcast. Then came the tenderest Christmas carols, which played upon the feelings of the wretched, caged creatures torn from their families and crushed them. There followed a broadcast which seemed specially aimed at us and in which Polish megalomania and Jewish plans of world domination were held responsible for the war.

As though this were not enough, that afternoon a constant stream of visitors arrived with rumors that the Polish blocks were to be divided into squads and sent by installments to forced labor in the reservations set up in occupied Poland. Meanwhile, those remaining would be sent to labor in the dreaded Klinker works. Toward evening, some of Franz's friends, who worked as foremen of the labor squads in the Klinker, arrived with the same reports, and we could cherish no more doubt that, in spite of the peaceful Christmas, a black time was before us.

Then came New Year, 1940, and with it hatred and hounding again descended upon us like an avalanche. In all the official New Year messages, in the speeches of Goering, Hitler, Himmler, the Jews were again branded as the instigators of this war. We knew at once that the broadcasts would cost us many victims. And our foreboding was promptly realized.

As if to complete our misery, a heavy snowfall had set in on New Year's Eve. Then it began to freeze, and the snow became a sheet of ice. This gave the blockfuehrers further opportunities to torture us with chases over icy ground which resulted in a record number of dead.

If this was the beginning of the new year, what would be the end?

# *Part Three*

On the first Sunday of the New Year, 1940, the one hundred and seventeenth day of our enslavement, Karl returned from his usual trip to the office with such a troubled expression that I sensed some new disaster. Karl always used to inform us of the orders issued by the office each day; but this time he sat down at his table at once and set to work on his roll book and other records. Some time later he called a man from the indoor squad, told him to give out the instructions from the office and himself left the barrack.

Anxiety spread through the wing. One of the suspicions which forced themselves upon us all was that Karl had been removed from his job and was getting his papers ready to hand over to his successor. The thought of losing Karl plunged us into despair.

When we returned from roll call, Karl again sat down to his papers in silence, and we had to endure our suspense as best we might. Since this was writing day, a group automatically set to work on their letters, which we had almost forgotten in our anxiety over Karl. But no one could make headway. That morning our fingers stubbornly refused to put on paper the prescribed formula, which so belied our feelings. The foremen had to keep reminding us to hurry, so that the others could have their turn, but when these patient admonitions had actually got us started, the hard-won concentration was soon broken by one of the window watchers announcing that the head room senior, with several assistants, had just entered Block 37. Karl snapped his book shut, jumped up and cried out so loud that he could be heard in the dormitory: "Then it was true, what I heard this morning!"

The head room senior had shown that he was well-disposed toward us, so we knew that no immediate danger threatened from him. But a visit from him always meant that something out of the ordinary was impending, and Karl's troubled manner had made us fear that this time it was something very serious.

Since the head room senior was not alone, he did not greet us in his usual friendly way, but went straight to the point.

"Every time I have visited you," said he, "and seen you squatting idly, I have wondered if it would not be better for you to be at work. Now this question has been decided in higher quarters. From tomorrow on, the Polish blocks will be sent to work in the Klinker works. Each block must furnish two hundred men at once. Block 37 will be first; the next day Block 38 will follow, and the day after, Block 39. Of course, it is freezing outside. But you will get overcoats, gloves and ear muffs to work in. Your room senior will give you further particulars."

With these words, the head room senior and his companions went out and Karl followed. What we had so long feared had happened at last: we were to labor in the notorious Klinker works. And just at a time when the usual labor in the Klinker had been discontinued on account of the heavy frost! They would make short work of us; that was clear.

Karl's voice roused me from my thoughts. "To tell the truth, I'm glad that we finally know what's what," he said. "I've known for days what was in store for you, and early this morning the head room senior confirmed it. I hadn't the heart to tell you about it, for I know the Klinker only too well. I worked there myself long enough. There isn't very much to do there in this kind of weather, but those hangmen's lackeys will keep you busy."

For the first time Karl had not comforted us. The shock was so great that one comrade fell into a faint. Only then did Karl realize that his words had made the situation worse and he now tried to minimize the effect of his speech.

"I painted all that in the blackest colors on purpose, to prepare you. It is better to expect the worst than to let yourself be taken by surprise. I want you to take yourselves in hand now as you have never done before. Don't give them the satisfaction of seeing you suffer.

"As for the hundred men that your wing must furnish, I expect everyone who has some strength left to volunteer, so that I will be spared the unpleasantness of using compulsion. Those who are sick, or over sixty, need not report, of course. If we have more than a hundred men, we will keep the least fit in reserve."

These words shook us out of our despair. Karl was so right: we must deny our tormentors the gratification of seeing us suffer. They would attain the goal they had set themselves; they would destroy us. But when we died in this last battle, at least we would die on our feet.

When Karl saw that we had recovered ourselves, he called for twenty volunteers to accompany him later to the clothing room to fetch the extra clothes. He also asked those whose shoes were torn to report it, so that he might try to get them exchanged. Then he went over to Wing B.

It was, of course, quite clear in my own mind that I must volunteer for work in the Klinker, although I had a severe cold; I also reported for the trip to the clothing room. I knew we would have to stand outdoors for hours before the clothes were distributed. A keen wind was blowing, and my coat was thin and my cough bad. But my curiosity was beyond any thought of such things as lungs—it wanted only to see, to see through the walls, if possible; to take in everything. For somewhere inside me there was still the indestructible faith that on the day of reckoning, when the evildoers abased themselves and begged for mercy, these observations of mine might be cast into the balance.

When Karl left it was even harder than before to get the men to write. What was the sense of writing, now, when in a few days they might be dead? But the foremen appealed to their comrades' sense of duty, painted pictures of their families waiting with anxious hearts for a sign of life from them. This appeal worked. The letter writing was finished so quickly that when we came back from the clothing room Karl found even the list of volunteers already made out, with far more than one hundred names.

Now that I could think of it calmly, it seemed that the work in the Klinker might bring us some good after all. At least we would no longer have to sit in the icy water that began to run off the panes as soon as the sun shone on the windows. Perhaps the work might even restore the lost strength to our muscles, and when we had once regained the normal use of our limbs and familiarized ourselves with the lay of the land, we might have a chance for sabotage or even escape.

These thoughts and others like them must have influenced many of my comrades. Suddenly the mood changed completely. It was as if we had all agreed not to waste our strength in useless lamentation. When food was distributed, every man of us began to eat, at first with forced, and little by little with real, appetite.

Wing B, as always, tried to copy us. But it was a poor copy. Although Karl spoke to them as he had done to us, in Wing B a very different mood prevailed. For Franz had not kindled a spirit of unity and mutual responsibility, as Karl had done with us.

In the afternoon, those who had volunteered for work in the Klinker were supposed to try on the new clothes and shoes so that they would get those nearest their own size. Of course, heated arguments took place. Those who had shoes too small for them maintained that feet in small shoes would freeze worse, while those who had shoes too large maintained the contrary. Later we found that one was as bad as the other. The feet in the small shoes did freeze first; but the large shoes rubbed their owners' feet raw.

Our preparations were completed before evening roll call, so the Klinker workers presented themselves for roll call in their new overcoats, gloves and ear muffs.

The sky was cloudless, the air dry and sharp; the cold cut like knives. It was not comfortable to think that I was dressed more warmly than other comrades, who were more ill and feeble than I. I could feel how they were envying us. I could feel an invisible barrier growing between us and them. Here, for the first time, we were divided into two groups, which from now on would lead separate lives. One would continue the existence we all knew so well, squatting and freezing on the cold, damp floor. The other was going to an unknown, dreaded future but enjoyed the privilege of being more warmly clad.

The blockfuehrers made us wait unusually long. Around me my comrades were freezing pitiably. I could feel them shivering, hear their teeth rattling together. Karl too must have been dreadfully cold, for he kept running up and down in front of us, rubbing his hands.

The blockfuehrers noticed immediately that the Klinker workers were wearing their work clothes and flew into a rage. "Do you think standing for roll call is work? That would suit you swindlers," screamed Kopella, almost bursting his lungs.

And Mueller followed. "The rascals have made themselves snug. But not while I'm around. Gloves, overcoats and ear muffs are only for work, understand?" he roared at Karl.

"Jawohl, Herr Blockfuehrer," answered Karl, so loud that his words re-echoed from the walls.

The Klinker workers among us were actually relieved at the turn matters had taken, because the conflict in our consciences had thus been removed. At once the estrangement between the two groups melted away, envy disappeared, and the stolen glances we exchanged said that once more we were all equal.

When we were allowed to return to the barrack, we were seething inwardly at this latest malice of the blockfuehrers. But since we had resolved not to waste our energies in outbursts of emotion, everyone kept his feelings to himself. Karl alone could not restrain his anger and, when we had all lain down to sleep, he appeared, half undressed, in the dormitory.

"Klinker workers," he said, "I don't need to tell you what I think of those cannibals. And I don't need to remind you, either, not to wear your Klinker clothes tomorrow, so that they won't have an excuse to torture you. But I want to talk to you about something I've had on my mind for a long time and that some of you probably feel yourselves.

"This war will come to an end some day. Then, as once before, the Allied Powers will sit in judgment on Germany. If Germany is once again granted a peace which fails to punish those guilty of war crimes, that peace will contain the seeds of a third world war.

"We must not look on and say nothing. Every one of us must make it his duty, if he gets out of here alive, to force his way to the judge's bench and demand a seat on the jury. For only if the evildoers are judged by those who have suffered those crimes in their own bodies, will the sentence be just. If we neglect this duty, all our suffering will be in vain and our guilt in a future world butchery will be just as great as that of the deluded judges."

When Karl had finished and softly closed the door behind him, no one said a word. But the stillness was unnatural and uncomfortable. And since the dread, excitement and suspense that were in us had to find vent in some way, everyone began to toss and turn restlessly.

I too kept turning from one side to the other. My self-control was gone. My cough tormented me unbearably. It was deep in my chest and every coughing fit shook my whole body. What a day was behind me! And what days were ahead of me? How many would lay down their lives in the Klinker? Would I be one of them?

The fever pounded in my temples. My teeth chattered with cold. Had I caught pneumonia at last? My spirit sank; hope, my faithful companion since my arrest, threatened to abandon me.

Colored flames danced to and fro before my eyes, to and fro, and became letters that formed into words. I could read the writing plainly in the darkness . . . Pneumonia . . . Klinker . . . Pneumonia . . . Klinker . . . like letters on a moving band. Then the letters formed a name . . . Gucia . . . Gucia . . . Gucia. . . . Suddenly the letters began to spin like a wheel, faster, faster. I could feel my fever rising. If I could only have an extra blanket! I was so terribly cold. If this was pneumonia, what chance would I have in the Klinker? Fear and despondency overmastered me. I could feel their chill grip. It began at my feet and crept up my body. I must not let it reach my heart. If I once let go of hope, my chances of recovery and safety would vanish with it. And that increased my dread still more.

If I could only banish my gloomy thoughts and think of something cheerful! Surely that would cast out fear. Why not think of all the beautiful things that I had seen, of the countries and cities that I knew and loved. Why not go on a world tour in my thoughts and remember, remember. . . .

Think of Paris, I said to myself. . . . The Bois de Boulogne in the spring haze. . . . The banks of the Seine with the secondhand book stalls. . . . The Place de l'Etoile and the Tomb of the Unknown Soldier. . . . The light and movement of Montmartre and the peace of Sacré-Coeur close by. . . . The cafés with their tables on the sidewalks, where small braziers burned in winter and snugly wrapped patrons sipped hot coffee. And the stillness of Notre Dame, and the dome of the Invalides and Napoleon's tomb. . . .

What a wonderful trip! Let us go on farther, to Fontainebleau, Versailles, and further south . . . Marseilles. Ah, what a view! The Mediterranean and a ship on its way to the Far East. Then north again. This is Ghent, the city of Till Eulenspiegel. But what is that pyre doing in the market-place? An auto-da-fé? Yes, but the last pyre of the Inquisition burned itself out four hundred years ago. And what is this? The church of Notre Dame in Ghent? But it belongs in Bruges. I must go into the church; how could anyone visit Bruges and not go to see Michelangelo's loveliest "Madonna and Child"?

Well, since I am in Belgium, I might as well go to Brussels and see my friends again, and while I am there I can buy a new Brussels lace collar for Gucia's chatelaine dress. But where am I going now? This is certainly not Brussels. These green, lush meadows, that look like Ruysdael's pictures come to life, must be in Holland. How disappointed Gucia will be! I have written her about the lace collar; I must make up for it by bringing her a big box of Dutch caramels.

But what is this? Just now I was in The Hague, but this is Warsaw. How Warsaw has grown! Everything new and bright, and the elegant shops! How white and fine the sand is on the banks of the Vistula, how inviting the small excursion boats!

But how comes this dazzling light here, all of a sudden? This is not the Vistula Bridge any longer, but the arch of lights of the Margareten Bridge that joins Buda and Pest. And here is Vienna already, and the wheel of the Prater still turning, and the Viennese still sitting over their *Heuriger* wine singing, "Wien, Wien, nur Du allein . . ." And at the Opera House, *Die Meistersinger,* with Wilhelm Furtwaengler conducting. I must not miss that. But what is this —what is Furtwaengler doing in an SS uniform? What is an SS man doing in Vienna? There is something wrong here! . . . Yes, now I can see properly. Where were my eyes before? This, God help me, is Nuremberg, this is the Nazi Party Day! The *Meistersinger!* Hitler's favorite opera. This is Germany! Why did I come here? How can I get out again? Never mind where; just out—east or west, north or south—just out, out, out . . .

Praise God, there is a road. If I hurry and run fast, across the border to Italy, perhaps no one will see me. . . .

Oh, how good it is to be out of Germany! Here is Milan, Venice, Rome, Naples and Capri and the Blue Grotto. And song and dance and white teeth, waving hair, flashing eyes. . . .

Soon I will travel back, to gay Cannes, to Nice. . . . Oh, how sweet the air smells in Nice! How good to run through fields of flowers again, to feel the wind that blows the fragrance to the city! But what is this? There are no flowers here any more. There are . . . God help me, there are gallows and fixed bayonets growing out of the earth. What strange region have I entered? What is this thunder of cannon, these continual explosions? This is . . . yes, it is a battlefield. . . .

Soldiers hurry past me; medical orderlies dragging the dead and wounded go slowly by. The wounded are bleeding and moaning. I am growing faint: good that I have this tree to lean on. Dear God, that doctor must be mad; he is amputating arms and legs without anesthetics, and the nurses are washing the bloody stumps with iodine. And the cries of the dying! I cannot bear the crying any longer! They will not stop. They are laughing. They pour more iodine. Where have I heard that laughter before? Yes, in the Revier, in Sachsenhausen. Am I in Germany again, then? Yes, there is the head surgeon, there are the Revier guards. Out! Run . . . why don't you move? Run . . . run. . . .

They have nailed me to the tree so that I cannot move; they, the dead. Their eyes hold me, bore through me, as though they were nails. What do they want of me? Why do they hold me fast? I want to go, do you hear? I want to go!

Dear God, they are speaking. "You cannot go from this place until you have heard us. The time for half-measures is past. We are the fallen of this war. We do not want to have fallen in vain. From now on there must be world justice, or there will be world destruction. You must promise punishment for the guilty, or the blood of the innocent will never cease to flow. Promise us, promise us."

Who am I that I should promise you this? What can I accomplish against the will of the world leaders? I am only one man and they are so many. I cannot promise. Let me go from here!

Dear God, what rumbling! The ground is cracking asunder. The dead are swallowed up. Everything is crashing around me. Only my tree still stands and holds me.

In the abyss something is stirring. Oh, horror, these are mass graves! Men . . . women . . . children. . . . They rise in serried ranks, march through space. . . . The men have halters around their necks and carry gallows on their shoulders. The Nazis hanged them in Poland. . . . The women carry heavy shovels. The Nazis in Poland made them dig their mass graves. . . . The children are blue all over and have swollen bellies. The Nazis first starved them and then strangled them . . . and all of them are crying. Their crying fills the world. . . . If only I could get away! Their voices are growing louder. Ah, but I have heard these words before!

"You cannot go from this place until you have heard us. We are the murdered of this war. We do not want to have been murdered in vain. You must promise punishment for the guilty, else the blood of the innocent will never cease to flow. Promise us, promise us!"

They have all banded together against me, the fallen and the murdered. They cannot force me: I cannot promise it. Do they want me to go through the world and preach revenge? Who am I that the world should listen to me? . . .

Praise God, they are gone. They have given up. Now I can go away. . . . I see no one, but I hear a voice, plainly. Who are you, Voice?

"I am your conscience. I want you to promise what *those* enjoined upon you. You have seen the hosts of the fallen and the murdered. You know what they have suffered. It is your duty to speak for them, for they themselves have been silenced forever. I bid you promise, not revenge, but peace. All shall have peace—but the wicked. Do you hear? No peace unto the wicked! And now be on your way, for if you evade your duty, I, your conscience, will give you no rest. Your days will become black nights, and your nights wakeful days. So tarry no longer, but promise what they have asked, before the gong sounds. For the gong will seal your own and the world's destruction."

Well, then, conscience, I promise. . . . Oh, God, the gong! . . . Too late, then; my own and the world's destruction is sealed. Already I feel the chains on my wrists . . . and voices again. . . .

"What can be the matter with him today? Everybody's dressed already and he's still dreaming. Shake him again."

Only then was I aware that the gong I had heard was Karl's alarm clock, and the chains on my wrists were the hands of my comrades. I do not know how they got me awake and into my clothes that morning. I did not really come to until Franz ordered us out to roll call and poured water over us as we ran past him.

Outside it was still dark. But during the night the snow had spread a glimmering blanket over the ground. And after the snowfall an icy wind had blown up. The snow crunched under our feet as we ran to our places, and our breath rose like a long cloud of steam. Our eyes soon grew accustomed to the darkness, and I could make out that the Klinker workers were drawn up on the left flank of Block 37, so that they could march off without obstruction. That brought me back to reality.

As the blockfuehrers came in sight, the searchlights were turned on. The greenish-yellow rays, which held us like a vise, made our faces look still more starved and frozen. But even then we appeared too well-fed for Schuschnig's taste.

"Where the hell do you get so much resistance?" he yelled. "We're still feeding you too well. We'll try half-rations today, understand?"

With that, the official part of the roll call ended. The left flank of Block 37 marched off to the Klinker; the rest returned to barracks. Crushed, we sat down on the floor. Half-rations again, and at this time of all times, when only twenty-four hours stood between us and the Klinker and when we doubly needed every spoonful of soup. But none of the destined Klinker workers complained.

Instead, one of the others began to grumble loudly. "The Klinker workers are better off than we are. Our food has been docked. But the men from Block 37 will get their full rations outside."

An indignant murmur arose; whether it signified agreement or disagreement was not clear. Luckily Karl appeared in the nick of time to keep our feelings from boiling over.

"Aren't you ashamed of yourself?" he shouted at the disturber of the peace. "This evening, when Block 37 comes back, you will be cured of any trace of envy. But if you still think, after that, that the Klinker workers are to be envied, I'll gladly exchange you for one of them. In the meantime, help me to look after the drenched comrades, instead of stirring up trouble."

Then the grumbler realized how uncomradely his behavior had been, and when Karl came in with a bundle of clothes he had somehow managed to hold in reserve and began to distribute them to the men who were most soaked, the late malcontent eagerly lent a hand, as if he wished to make up for the injustice he had committed.

Since the bad weather had set in, the continual soaking, freezing and thawing of our shoes had imposed a severe strain on the laces, and they often broke. We knotted and knotted them, until they could be knotted no longer. Karl, of course, had tried to buy shoelaces in the canteen at every opportuntiy. But in January the canteen's stock was exhausted. When it was certain that we were to be sent to the Klinker, we were afraid that we would lose our shoes when running and have to march and work barefooted in the snow and ice, and be punished as well for wasting the property of the German state.

When we brought up the question, Karl gave a satisfied grin, disappeared and soon returned with a bag of varicolored pieces of string. He cut the string into the proper lengths and picked out those who needed them most. But much sooner than we would have thought possible, these substitute shoelaces also were worn through, and a piece of string became one of the articles for which we exchanged our precious daily bread.

The last day of waiting before the Klinker program was to start gave us too much time to brood, and in spite of all good resolutions, the general tension led to quarrels which the foremen could scarcely bring under control. The only remedy was to create mental diversion. I proposed that we should have some talks on subjects of general interest, and some comrades volunteered to speak. We announced the subjects and speakers, so as to arouse the interest of the whole room.

Only once was there difficulty, when a comrade in an advanced stage of tuberculosis offered to speak on "The safety and success of convoying by the U. S. Navy in the First World War." One of the doctors among us wished to prevent him from speaking, on the ground that he would scatter tuberculosis bacilli through the room. We were indignant. Among us there were many comrades with all kinds of infectious diseases. Not only did we sit and sleep in the same room with them, but our blankets, straw sacks and towels were constantly exchanged. We all washed with the same piece of soap, if there was any. Our dishes were washed in the same pan and kept in the same cupboard. Under such conditions any fear of infection seemed ridiculous. And in any case it seemed more important to hear our comrade's views on such a vital phase of modern warfare and his opinion on the possible entry of America into this war. For he was a professional journalist, who had lived in America for twenty years and been a correspondent there during the First World War.

The talks diverted us so completely that when we returned to barracks after the noon roll call we hardly noticed our half-filled bowls, so eager were we to finish eating and return to the lectures.

The speaker who received the most sympathetic reception talked on the topic: "Life after Death." Not only a brilliant speaker but a good psychologist, he took up the question with which our secret thoughts were constantly busied and gave us a deeply religious, comforting answer. As he talked, listeners and speaker became one. Dejection vanished. Even if the worst happened, what did it mean, after all? We would live on.

It was late afternoon when the speech was ended, and there was one more lecture on the program. But it was never delivered. As the new speaker rose, a comrade from the indoor squad rushed in and reported that a tool truck from the Klinker had just returned with two badly injured comrades of Block 37, who had been immediately sent to the Revier.

Karl at once ran to the Revier to learn more particulars but he came back unsuccessful, and we had to be patient until evening roll call, when all the Klinker workers returned. In the distance we could see them approaching in three groups. The first advanced at a fairly brisk double, though many had bloody faces. Some distance behind came a second group, men who limped heavily and had evidently received serious leg injuries. Then, far in the rear, came a smaller number, who were crawling and could only be forced on by the cudgels that descended on their backs.

The temperature was still below freezing, but I felt suddenly hot when I saw that group. I glanced at Karl. All the blood had left his face: we realized that a storm was rising within him. And since he could not shout at the blockfuehrers, he shouted at the miserable ghosts, who with all the strength left in them were dragging themselves to their block: *"Donnerwetter,* don't crawl like snails! Use your legs."

The injured men, startled, made a last effort. But only a few reached the block; the others collapsed. At an order from the blockfuehrers, some comrades hurried up and dragged off those who were lying motionless.

When the injured and the unconscious had been taken to their places in the ranks, the blockfuehrers made a rush for Block 37 and examined the Klinker workers with satisfaction.

"No more laziness now."

"Now you'll have to get used to work."

"Whoever doesn't put his back into it properly will be sent back —as a corpse."

"And in a month you'll all be done for."

Although our indoor squad tried to get in touch with the indoor squad of 37, no more details about the Klinker could be learned, and wild rumors began to circulate. But I refused to take part in the gloomy speculations. At all costs I wanted to go to sleep with thoughts of a more hopeful kind. The work in the Klinker surely had other aspects, if we would only think of them. Now, for the first time in four months, we would leave the walls of the concentration camp behind us. We would march past country roads and woods. Perhaps we would even see real homes and meet civilians. The march to the Klinker would be a foretaste of freedom. Already I was eager for that moment.

When Karl's alarm clock jerked us out of sleep the next morning, the Klinker workers became the privileged. We were allowed to wash first, were given our soup first, and Karl even had an undreamed-of surprise for us: an extra slice of bread which he had been collecting for three days for every Klinker worker.

When we went out to roll call, we were wearing our Klinker clothes. But although the temperature had fallen again during the night, this time none of our thinly clad comrades envied us. When the roll call was over, we joined the Klinker workers from Block 37 and marched with them to the assembly place, where this time, not the usual thousands, but a few hundred men were drawn up. The blockfuehrers assigned the men to working squads, but when they had finished we were not allowed to march off at once. For it was not yet light enough, and in the darkness there was danger of escape.

When at last the signal for departure was given, we again received final instructions for the march past the Kommandant and his attendants, who stood at the gate and watched the procession. "Quick step, hands on trouser seams, eyes right. And when you get out in the highway, at any suspicious movement you'll be shot without warning."

We had been counted several times on the assembly place by different groups of blockfuehrers. But as we passed the gate, another group counted us again. We marched in rows of five, and as we marched out, SS guards stepped forward and took their places at the right and left of every third row. The guards had guns with fixed bayonets. Some carried them over their shoulders, but most held them with the bayonet pointed toward us.

On our flanks marched the foremen of the Klinker labor squads. They were supposed to supervise us only during our work in the Klinker, but when we began to slip and fall on the icy ground, the foremen felt called upon—in view of the great number of guards, in view of the troop of blockfuehrers on bicycles, in view of the Lagerfuehrer, who, mounted on his steed, gave us the honor of his personal escort—to assist the armed guards with their fists. So we left a red trail on the dazzling white ground; and the tool truck, which brought up the rear of our column, picked up the injured who were left behind and later delivered them, dead or still alive, to the Revier.

We marched along a straight road until we came to a bridge, which crossed the Oranienburg Canal. About half a kilometer beyond, a dirt road forked off to the left, leading to the Klinker. Here guards were stationed at regular intervals, and no one was allowed to enter the road without a pass. On the right of this road lay an area of about 10,000 square yards that probably constituted an important military zone. The numerous buildings, the SS troops we often saw there and the shooting which we could hear all day long during our work in the Klinker, left hardly any doubt.

This whole area seemed to be surrounded by mystery, which appeared to center in a structure that looked like a rectangular mound of earth, sloping inward toward the summit and forming a plateau on top. The mound was overgrown with moss. There were doors in the side walls at intervals of about every five yards, and out of the plateau numerous pipes, about a yard in diameter, rose high into the air.

The Klinker works began where the road was barred by a turnpike. Behind it stood a special guard, who demanded identification cards from all pedestrians and vehicles before they were allowed to pass. Beyond the turnpike, the pace was accelerated until we arrived at the assembly place, where we were counted again. This huge area, which could easily hold six or seven thousand men, was divided into fifteen zones, where the labor squads had to assemble before they were marched off to their place of work. Here the prisoners had to go in the morning, before work began, to be counted; at noon to gulp their soup; in the evening, before the march back to barracks, to be counted again, and if there was any time to spare, inspected for dirty ears or dirty necks or lost buttons!

Usually several thousand men were at work in the Klinker, but during the severe cold and snow most of the work was at a standstill. So besides ourselves only a few hundred prisoners were marched out.

The first time I heard of the Klinker works, it called up visions of a model factory with the latest technical improvements busily turning out important work. In reality the Klinker was a stretch of waste land with working places scattered about it, where production was carried on, not for its own sake, but to kill the prisoners' time and embitter their lives. Before the outbreak of the war, when the importance of the war factories around Oranienburg increased, the SS decided to build a harbor connecting the Klinker works with the Oranienburg Canal so that the products of the war factories might be transported by water. At the same time it was planned to build new workrooms and barracks, in which, it was said, the workers were to be housed. But when I was there, the only structures in the area were a stone building about 12 yards high, 120 yards long and 150 yards wide, which later turned out to be the brickworks; a huge shed to the right of it, in which the tools were kept; and on the other side of the assembly place a few elongated barracks containing canteens, guardrooms, small workshops, a power station and some offices.

The Klinker was under the supervision of an SS Sturmfuehrer. He was assisted by twelve blockfuehrers and six prisoners, who were specialists in building and brickmaking. These six prisoners acted as absolute masters of the others. Since they could not, of course, attend to all the thousands of workers, they appointed squad leaders to carry out their will, and the squad leaders in turn gave their orders to the foremen of the labor groups. Thus there reigned in the Klinker not only the terror of the Gestapo, but the terror of our fellow prisoners.

It was an old Klinker custom that each newly arrived labor group should receive a Klinker initiation, which consisted in making the newcomers do the hardest work of the day. So the first day in the Klinker claimed the most victims. On our first day of work, we and the comrades of Block 37 were appointed to the harbor squad. Since the harbor excavations were covered with a thick blanket of snow, there was no work going on there at all, and we received our initiation in another way.

When the signal to break up was given, our squad leader stepped forward and ordered us to run straight ahead past the side wall of the brickworks. "And trot; we won't stand for snail pace here," he shouted.

"Ah, the same game as yesterday," I heard one of the comrades from Block 37 say, as we moved off. Trotting was not to be thought of, for our feet sank deep into the soft snow, and, of course, the foremen's truncheons were continually descending on our backs. As soon as we drew near the brickworks, catastrophe began.

Every few steps there were gates in the side wall of the brickworks, and from these gates in every direction ran rails, which were controlled by numerous switches and over which the cars laden with raw material and finished bricks were dispatched in and out. But the snow hid the rails and switches, as well as the bricks which were lying around everywhere. We first noticed the obstacles when we stumbled over them and fell in heaps on top of one another. The foremen charged into the human heaps. "Stand up, you scoundrels, form a chain and keep on running, or we'll make mincemeat of you," they screamed. The fallen pulled themselves up. Almost all had bruised their shinbones, many were bleeding.

We tried to plod on, only to stumble and fall again after a few steps. After this second crash, more men were left prostrate than the first time, and not even the truncheons of the foremen could rouse them. Then suddenly a realization dawned on us. Only a few of the comrades from Block 37 had fallen: evidently they had looked over the system of rails on the previous day and remembered where they were. And as if by common consent we stuck closely to the track of the men from Block 37, jumped where they jumped, swerved where they swerved and in this way got over the last few yards of the rail stretch without leaving as many comrades on the ground as at the beginning.

Once past the brickworks, we were again running on smooth ground. Suddenly the first rows stopped dead. In front of us a slope about twelve yards deep descended to the harbor. The slope was covered with an immaculate blanket of snow, on which there were no footprints to be seen. Only a path about three yards wide, which went steeply to the bottom, shone like a mirror, as if it had been deliberately stamped down and made slippery. This icy path the foremen ordered us to run down. Horrified we stared into the depths. Now we understood why the men from Block 37 had come back the previous day so dreadfully knocked up.

"Down! In quickstep, or there'll be fireworks in a minute," ordered the squad leader. But we stood as if frozen to the ground. One might ski down that slope, or slide down it or crawl down it. But to run down—that was absurd.

The squad leader ordered again: "Down, I told you! I'll count three, and if anyone doesn't pick up his feet before then, he's in for trouble."

But we still stood motionless. We knew that if we did not obey, something terrible would happen. But fear of the slope and fear of punishment paralyzed our limbs.

"One," counted the squad leader.

We still did not move.

"Two."

Still no movement.

"Three," yelled the squad leader, and at the same moment he seized the nearest man by the neck and gave him a kick that sent him rolling with incredible rapidity down the slope.

The shock had the foreseen effect. We began to move. The first row of the column ventured with cautious, experimental steps onto the icy path, and more and more followed their example. We made very slow progress, but by careful, mincing steps many actually succeeded in going down a few yards without falling. Only those who had leg injuries fell at the first step and rolled the rest of the way down the slope.

But this relative success infuriated the squad leader. "Do you cheats call that a quickstep? We'll soon show you what speed is. We don't waste time with mollycoddles." He signaled to the foremen who were standing around, some at the top of the slope and others on both sides of the ice path with their feet firmly planted in the soft snow. "Go to it!" he shouted.

Thereupon the foremen above pushed over the men who were just venturing onto the path, and the foremen on the sides pulled over those who were trying to inch their way down. In a few seconds a mass of bodies was hurtling down the slope, dragging with it those who had hitherto kept their feet. Twelve yards below, at the bottom of the hill, it came to rest in a human tangle.

It was a long time before we had extricated our limbs and could stand up. There was not one who was not bruised and there were some who had either broken or wrenched their ankles. With that our initiation ended, and the so-called work began.

"And now, trot to your places of work," ordered the squad leader, when he had formed ranks at the foot of the slope. He drove us across the harbor inlet, to a heap of sand, where shovels, picks and chests equipped with carrying poles were lying around. There the foremen divided us into three squads: choppers, shovelers, and porters, and ordered us to start work. The choppers were to chop loose the frozen sand so that the shovelers could shovel it into the chests. These the porters had to carry off at a run and empty at a spot about a hundred yards away.

There were not enough chests to go around, and some of them had bottoms knocked out or poles missing. But the foremen were not at a loss for a substitute. They ordered the porters who had no chests to hold up the left corner of their coats so that the shovelers could dump in a few shovelfuls of sand.

The sand removal proceeded at the usual quickstep, and the foremen's truncheons set the pace. Those comrades who had bleeding cuts from the fall bled still more during this chase, and those who had severe head wounds were so weakened by loss of blood that they were in danger of falling every moment. One of the foremen, a relatively "decent" man, who noticed their critical condition, withdrew them from the porter squad and took them to a barrack for bandaging. When he returned with them and found that they were still unable to stay on their feet, he even allowed them to sit down in the snow. This chance to rest was a boon to the injured men. But it was impossible to sit motionless in the snow for any length of time and not freeze fast to the ground. So they soon got up and began to totter slowly to and fro.

This infuriated the foreman who had taken charge of them. "So you were putting on an act for me," he raged. "You're by no means as shaky as I thought. Well, if you want to move, I'll soon give you enough motion!" And he drove them through the inlet and beckoned to the other foremen to join the chase.

Luckily, before the foremen had time to think up more mischief, one of the higher-ups appeared at the top of the slope and ordered the work stopped. We had to assemble again and climb up the hill. The climb was a hopeless struggle against the icy slope. We climbed and slipped, climbed and slipped. Finally the foremen had to recognize that we would never reach the top at that rate, and as we had to get to the assembly place on time, they allowed us to climb in the snow on both sides of the icy path.

The prospect of warm soup and a short noon recess quickened our steps. On the assembly place all the other squads had already arrived, and the soup kettles had been brought up. In front of each server stood a double line of men, and beside him was a pile of tin plates on a wooden stand. The distribution of food had been carefully organized. As each pair of men came up to the server, they had to form in single file, snatch a tin plate from the pile with their ungloved left hand, pass it over to their right, and hold it out to the server, who poured in a ladleful of soup. Then they went to their places to eat. The foremen and squad leaders always got a double portion of soup and a piece of bread besides. And after the others had been served, they could return for a second helping.

If the server was a decent fellow, he stirred the soup before he ladled it out. But if he wanted to cheat a prisoner, he dipped up the soup from the top, thus serving only water: the thick sediment stayed at the bottom for the favorites. But whether the soup was thick or thin, it was usually cold. The food was sent out from the camp kitchen in an open truck. Before the kettles were loaded aboard, and again after they arrived, they were left standing awhile in the open air. And when at last the soup was poured into the ice-cold plates, if there were any specks of fat floating in it, they had turned to tallow. Instead of warming us, the soup made us shiver still more.

When we had stacked up the empty plates again, the half-hour noon recess was over, and we had to return to work. The journey back once more led over the rails by the brickworks. But this time only a few stumbled.

When we reached the top of the hill, the morning's tragedy was re-enacted. Below in the inlet, the blockfuehrers had turned out in full numbers to witness our fall. When we had finally picked ourselves up and returned to our former stations, one of them said suddenly to a companion: "Just look at the delicate creatures shivering like aspen leaves. Hadn't we better warm them up a bit?" Then, without more ado, he yelled at us: "Forward, run! Like greased lightning."

We ran off in all directions. But the blockfuehrers soon brought system into the running. They had distributed themselves over the field.

"This way," called one.

We ran toward him.

"This way," ordered another from the opposite direction.

And "This way" and "This way" the orders criss-crossed back and forth, faster and faster. We got out of control. In the middle of the mass, where the press was thickest, the men's feet became hopelessly entangled. And, as always in such cases, when a halt was finally ordered, there were trampled bodies left on the ground.

We were not freezing any longer; we were bathed in sweat. But the blockfuehrers had grown cold from standing still and took themselves off. We began to work again, with a sigh of relief. For during the few moments that we had stood still our wet shirts had begun to freeze fast to our bodies. We knew the consequences, and everyone who still had the strength began to work as fast as possible, to keep himself warm.

It was customary in the Klinker for the blockfuehrers to make a round of inspection shortly before the end of the day's work. But since only a few squads were working that day, they came to us unusually early and gave us so much attention that the number of dead and badly injured who were loaded into a truck and driven back to camp rose to fifteen.

The march back to camp was worse than the march out. For we were weaker than in the morning, and the guards who again surrounded us had more work for their guns and bayonets. At the camp, the whole elite had once more assembled by the gate to inspect the returning column and assure themselves that our Klinker initiation had been duly carried out. The great number of wounded in our ranks evoked loud applause.

On the assembly place the whole camp was already standing in readiness for roll call. Our foremen and squad leaders left us to join their own blocks. We ran on alone to the isolation district. Our comrades were standing in front of the barracks. As we approached, Karl ran toward us, as if he were relieved to see us back at last. "Well, you've made it; soon there will be warm soup and a straw sack to lie down on," he called.

We were returning in three sections, just as the comrades of Block 37 had done the previous day. In the last section, the most severely injured were dragging themselves along. When they heard Karl's voice and felt his sympathy, their strength deserted them and they dropped to the ground: it was as if the motor which had hitherto driven them forward had been suddenly turned off. Alarmed, Karl ran toward them. "Pull yourselves together, quickly. Just for a half-hour longer. Then you can lie down." But the men on the ground did not move. Then Karl beckoned to some of the comrades, and by their united efforts they succeeded in getting the fallen men to their places in the ranks before the blockfuehrers appeared on the scene to finish them altogether.

When we were allowed to return to barracks, our first concern was to give instructions to the men of Block 39, whose Klinker initiation was still before them. If we told them about the rails and the slope and warned them to follow in our footsteps, we might be able to save them from paying the price of fifteen victims for their first day in the Klinker. So Karl sent a man from the indoor squad to Block 39, on the pretext of a message, to pass on our instructions. Not until then did he have the food distributed, and again there was an extra slice of bread for the Klinker workers.

When at last we were able to stretch out, our only comfort for the sufferings of the day was the knowledge that we had fulfilled our duty to the comrades in Block 39.

How absurd, in the light of our experience in the Klinker, seemed my hope that going out to work would be a foretaste of freedom! When we marched out it was not yet day, and when we marched back it was almost dark and bitter cold. So we had not met on our way any children, any signs of civilian life; only more barriers, more cruel tricks, more will-to-destruction. The hope of sabotage or flight, which many of us had harbored, now seemed very naïve. There was no real work going on in the Klinker, therefore what could we sabotage there? And the road to freedom was lined with spying eyes and bristling guns, just like the camp itself. For us there was no road to freedom.

But the next morning the gate to freedom opened, quite legally, for fourteen comrades in all three blocks. A runner brought the good news shortly before roll call ended, so that the lucky men from Block 39 who belonged to the Klinker squad did not even have to march out.

The blockfuehrers received the mass releases with a furious protest. "Don't get any rosy hopes into your heads. We'll take care that not too many will slip through our fingers." As we were marching out of the camp, they put their heads together with the blockfuehrers of the Klinker squad. And the latter went to work as soon as we had left the camp. The previous day many of us had slipped on the icy road. Since no one could help the fallen to their feet and the marching column was not allowed to stop for a moment, the fallen were trampled underfoot. Now the blockfuehrers hit upon a simple way to multiply these accidents. They ordered each row to link arms, so that every time one man slipped, four people fell at once and were trampled simultaneously.

In this way about twenty men fell out before we even reached the

Klinker. But the annihilation program really got under way when we arrived at the edge of the slope. We had to line up at the top of the icy path in a long double column.

"First five rows step forward," ordered a blockfuehrer. And when this had been done: "Right row, right about face."

The couples were still standing together, but now the partners were facing in opposite directions.

"Lie on your bellies," the blockfuehrer continued. "Turn on your left side."

The two partners in each row were now lying turned toward each other. But they had to adjust themselves so that the head of one lay by the other's feet and each clasped the other's feet in his arms. There were no further orders. When the men had taken hold of each other, the blockfuehrers advanced to the edge of the slope and with a mighty kick started the human bundle on its way to the bottom.

Those who let go as they fell were not so severely bruised when they landed. But the others, who clung to each other out of fright, and whose heads were knocked repeatedly against their partners' feet, were badly injured.

In the meantime, the blockfuehrers had divided themselves into two groups. One, on top of the hill, continued to kick down the couples. The others had stationed themselves in the inlet and made the fallen men climb up the slope again, as soon as they had gotten to their feet. So it went on, up the hill and down the hill. The men climbing up were often knocked to the bottom again by the men hurtling down, and if they succeeded in reaching the top, they were once more kicked down in couples by the blockfuehrers.

This human football game pleased its inventors so well that they resumed it in the afternoon. Later, when blockfuehrers from the camp came to find out the score, they were delighted with the results.

That was the way our days passed in the Klinker from then on. The day's program was freezing, being chased, falling down, crashing to the bottom of the slope, carrying sand or snow in our coats and being chased again. Only the order of events changed. Every day more of us were left on the field. Every day the dead were replaced.

What gave us, the survivors, strength to live through those January days was the newly quickened hope of release. From day to day we hoped for a miracle like that which had come to the fourteen comrades, until one day a new rumor brought all hope to an end. It was said that no more releases whatever would take place and that the Gestapo would not even accept further applications. For this, Gucia later gave me the explanation. The power of decision in all matters concerning Polish prisoners had been transferred to the Gestapa,[1] to which our relatives were referred, with cynical smiles, by the Gestapo. And in the entrance hall of the Gestapa office building was a big sign: "Entrance of Jews strictly forbidden."

The reported ruling was a virtual death sentence. Our hope wavered, and with it our powers of resistance. More and more men failed to return from the Klinker. Then, on January 24, something happened that kept us from being wiped out entirely. About eleven o'clock, while we were carrying sand, came an order to stop work and march back to camp. This unheard-of event revived us and we even hoped it might mean release. But when we reached camp, Karl told us the true situation. As the temperature had fallen to minus 22 degrees Fahrenheit, the blockfuehrers were too uncomfortable outdoors and had proposed a cessation of work until the cold abated.

In the meantime, an epidemic of dysentery had broken out in camp. It had begun toward the end of December with several cases and within four weeks it was raging in all the barracks. In the first stage of the epidemic we were granted a limited supply of charcoal tablets. But as the number of cases increased, our supply was drastically reduced and finally cut off altogether. "First the Germans get it, and then, if there's any left, the filthy Jews."

The lack of hygiene in our overcrowded barracks so increased the danger of infection that soon most of us had more or less serious cases of dysentery. This was just at the time the work in the Klinker began. Karl had kept the sick back from work as long as he could. But as the disease spread and the supply of healthy men ran short, the most he could do was to choose the mildest cases for the Klinker squad.

Even with a slight case of dysentery, the work in the Klinker was torture. At first the foremen allowed us to run to the toilets when we felt the need. But the toilets were at the opposite end of the area. Usually we could not make it but had to stop furtively along the road and, panicky as we were, crouch down in the snow. Of course, we took

---

[1] Gestapa stands for "Geheimes-Staatspolizei-Amt," of which the Gestapo was subordinate division.

care to cover up the traces. But the foremen found out. From then on, they forbade us to leave the place of work at all.

So, to the physical torture in the Klinker was added unspeakable psychological misery. Now, when need overcame us, we could not even stop our work, but had to relieve ourselves standing or running, like cattle. The excrement ran down our legs, soaked into our trousers and collected in our boots. But we went on working.

When the work in the Klinker was broken off, we sighed with relief: at least we would now have toilets at hand. But the cessation of work only made way for a chain of other hardships. First the blockfuehrers decreed that in all the Polish blocks the occupants of both wings must sit together all day long in one dormitory. This increased the danger of infection. A few days later the sitting was changed to standing, and we were ordered to use the toilets only at fixed times. We vastly preferred standing to sitting, although it drained our strength. For when the midday sun melted the ice on the windowpanes and the frost that had soaked into the wooden building, the floor was flooded and we sat in water. If we had only been able to use the toilets instead of covering the floor under our feet with excrement, we would have been quite satisfied.

In the fresh air, we had not suffered so much from the sight and stench of our own filth; but in the closed, overcrowded barrack, it was unbearable. One day Karl asked permission to open some windows now and then, to air the barrack. Thereupon the blockfuehrers ordered that all the windows on both sides of the dormitories in both wings, as well as all the doors, should be kept open for hours at a time. The stench was then not so unbearable, but icy winds whistled through the barrack from all directions. The cold pierced through our thin clothes, and hastened the progress of the disease.

At noon, when the sun shone on the windows, the cold was not so cruel. But then the water mingled with the excrement under our feet, and the disgusting brew ran across the floor to the side wall and soaked into the undermost of the piled straw sacks. We looked on sickened. And at night, when we lay down to sleep, everyone fought strenuously to avoid those infected sacks.

But the worst source of suffering was the lack of toilet paper, which we had already felt severely before the dysentery epidemic began. Toilet paper, in the form of old newspapers, was distributed to us daily by the Wirtschaftsabteilung. But the supply allotted was not sufficient for the needs of the dysentery sufferers. At this time the magazines and newspapers we had subscribed to so lavishly might have proved a blessing. But a camp rule decreed that all newspapers and magazines must be turned into the office in good condition. The result was that newspaper soon headed the list of articles for which we used to barter bread. Its price rose with the demand, until at last it became so high that even those who preferred cleanliness to food were forced to use their bare fingers.

One of those most severely afflicted with dysentery was Professor Sternbach. Although his friend the Revier doctor regularly procured charcoal tablets for him, his strength declined visibly. But in those days of illness, a transformation took place in him. Formerly he had kept himself apart, but now he tried with all his power to be one of us. He talked often and freely to everyone, told of events in his scholarly career or discussed the philosophic and religious questions that occupied our thoughts. And the more his body wasted away, the more brilliant grew his mind.

This change had begun after the first chase around the barracks. He often told us how, when he had had to stand among the other invalids and watch us being hunted, it came to him that we were all fellow travelers with one destiny and that no one should think himself better than the rest. And he told us, too, how much ashamed he was of the special privileges that had been given him. From then on he urged us to be brotherly, helpful and kind to one another. And he tried in every way to practice what he preached. He would not accept anything the others could not have too, and it took all the powers of persuasion that Karl and Franz could exert to induce him to take the charcoal tablets.

Such spirit brought the old man very close to us all. Those who before had merely honored and respected him now really loved him. We all tried more than ever, against his will and often without his knowledge, to do him services and favors. Although the frail old man had survived the sufferings of concentration camp life longer than many younger and stronger comrades, we knew that his days were numbered, and we all did our best to make his last days as easy as possible. To our great grief we could not spare him a final gross humiliation.

At the end of January, when the dysentery epidemic grew so bad that at night the sick could not get to the toilets in time and therefore soiled their straw sacks, the blockfuehrers ordered that the worst cases should sleep in the toilet room. The toilet room was built in such a way that the toilet bowls were against one of the long walls and a corresponding number of urine bowls against the other. The space between these walls was somewhat shorter than the length of a straw sack but about the same length as the benches in the day room. To fit the straw sacks into this space, the blockfuehrers ordered that the benches should be brought to the toilet room at night and the straw sacks laid out on them. In this way the head of the straw sack was on the urine bowl, while the foot hung down over the bench. Between the hanging end and the toilets there was only a small space, through which everyone who wanted to use the toilets at night had to squeeze.

Since the severe cold had set in, the water in the toilet bowls had frequently frozen at night. The contents could not be flushed down until morning, after the ice had been melted with boiling water. At the beginning of February, when the dysentery reached its climax, the bowls became so full at night that the contents overflowed. A horrible stench filled the narrow room, and anyone entering shrank back gagging. This was the place in which the desperately ill waited for death.

Led by Professor Metellman, we did our best to spare Professor Sternbach this degradation. We gave him a straw sack to himself near the door and, if the straw sack was soiled, we took turns cleansing it in the morning. But when the crisis came, and he was too weak to rise at all, he insisted on being carried into the toilet room. And we felt it was best to let him have his way.

The night that we left Professor Sternbach in the toilet room, deep grief reigned in the barrack. I could not close my eyes that night. I could not shut out the picture of the old man, trying to get up, trying to stagger to the toilet, and I had a foreboding that some accident would happen to him that night. At last I could not lie still any longer and got up to look at him.

All night long a light burned in the toilet room, behind blacked-out windows. When I reached the threshold and had accustomed myself to the pestilential air, I saw a pathetic sight. Professor Sternbach was sitting up on his straw sack, all huddled over, his hands outstretched before him. His face was smeared with excrement. His eyes were fixed unseeingly on the slime that covered his hands. In his body there was no movement at all, and for a moment irrational horror seized me. I thought he was dead, and I could not understand that he could be dead and still sit there. I wanted to go nearer, to make sure, and I did not dare. I wanted to summon a comrade from the dormitory, but my feet did not move.

But now life came into the seemingly dead form. Professor Sternbach turned his head toward the door, and when he saw me, he whispered, pleasantly and courteously as always, but in an almost extinguished voice: "Could you lend me a little piece of newspaper? I will give you twice as much tomorrow."

As it happened, I had managed to buy a whole newspaper that day, in exchange for half of my bread ration, and I ran into the dormitory to fetch my treasure from its hiding place in the straw sack. How frightfully he must be suffering from that foulness! If I could only get water for him. But that was impossible. At least I would offer to help him. But when I saw the poor smeared face before me again and laid the newspaper in the trembling hands, all I could say was a wretched, "Here, please."

Professor Sternbach tore off the first page of the newspaper and held out the rest to me. "Thank you very much," he gasped, and tears ran over his besmirched face. It was the first time that I had seen him weep, and my heart contracted. "No, it is all for you," I said and did not take back the paper. At that he stared at me in amazement and looked at the newspaper in his hand, and then again at me. "Really?" he asked, unbelieving. "Is it really all for me?"

Strangling sobs rose in my throat. But I would not cry; I gulped till it hurt. I wanted to say something, but I could not even bring out a "yes" and could only nod my head.

Then a blissful smile spread over his sunken face. He clutched the newspaper in both hands and said joyfully, with a liveliness unusual in him: "Ah, I am so very happy. This is something I will never forget. How much suffering it will save me! Oh, I cannot tell you how glad I am now."

That was too much for me. An old dirty newspaper had become the supreme blessing of a man who a few months before had been the pride of Polish scholarship, honored wherever learning is prized. I ran as fast as my feet would carry me, back to my straw sack, and my sobs were more like screams, and I could not master myself or give my awakened comrades a rational answer to their questions.

The next morning the friendly doctor succeeded in getting Professor Sternbach transferred to the Revier. We knew that he would never come back to us. When Karl told us, a few days later, that Professor Sternbach was dead, we did not ask about his last hours. We did not want to know about them, for we wanted to cling to the illusion that in the Revier he had at least died a cleaner death than he would have died among us.

After Professor Sternbach's death the attentions we had shown him went as a matter of course to Professor Metellman, who had been so close to the old man. This seemed to be the most fitting way we could honor Professor Sternbach's memory. Franz tried as long as he could to spare Professor Metellman; and when it was no longer possible to keep him from work he was, with Karl's consent, enrolled in the indoor squad. To the honor of Professor Metellman it should be said that he shunned no kind of work and that when there was any job to be done, he always volunteered.

The dysentery played into the hands of the Nazis. When, at the beginning of February, we reckoned up our victims, we discovered that half of our old guard had been wiped out. It was only a question of time until the rest would follow. During the days we spent in standing squads, we could watch death at work. We had accepted our fate as a settled thing, and everyone waited resignedly until his turn should come.

In vain were all the efforts of "The Latrine Courier" to shake us out of our lethargy. But one day, when that "news agency" claimed to have it from a wholly "reliable source" that the Cracow professors were shortly to be released, our indifference gave way to anger. We had too often cherished hope, only to see it end in bitter disappointment. So the report seemed not merely a clumsy attempt to cheer us up but a piece of downright sadism. To our amazement, however, Karl, who always used to take a noncommittal attitude toward the reports of "The Latrine Courier," declared that there might be something in it. Instantly the barometer of our hopes soared. A few days later, when the Polish Jews were put on snow-removal work in camp, we attacked the job with new courage.

Our task was to clear the whole camp area of snow and keep it clear. For the snowfall had broken all historic records for European winters. The snow lay almost a yard deep in places and the roads leading to the assembly square were blocked.

The equipment we were given for shoveling and carrying away

the snow consisted of a few shovels and some hastily knocked together wooden chests and sledges. The snow was first swept into piles, then carried from one place to another and finally pulled on sledges to the workshop section (Industriehof), where it was dumped into a huge pit. The sledges were always packed so full that it took six men to pull them, and the ropes were of thick, rusty wire. Under the weight of the load the wire cut into our hands, and the open wounds increased the danger of frostbite and gangrene. After a few days of snow hauling, we thought ourselves lucky when we were ordered to snow sweeping on the assembly place.

Instead of brooms and scrapers, we marched out to work in the morning with the benches from the day room over our shoulders. It looked supremely funny to see these "bench squads," as we nicknamed them, advancing on the assembly place with the benches, turning them upside down and pushing the smooth surface through the snow, two men to each bench. But the results were extraordinary. In a short time the assembly place was swept smooth.

The work was easy in itself. But the assembly place always swarmed with uniformed officials, and we were under observation from the windows of the Kommandantur building. This gave the foremen a chance to show their zeal and they made the snow pushing a torture.

Although we had grown used to seeing our comrades die in strange ways, the sudden death of a cantor from Block 37 moved us beyond all measure. He was nearly seventy when he was arrested, and behind him lay an illustrious career. His wonderful voice and simple, friendly ways had made him the favorite of his block. To the comrades of Block 37, the religious chants and folksongs that he knew how to render so well were comfort and refreshment, and he held a privileged position among them, like Professor Sternbach in our block.

One of the cantor's greatest admirers was Anton. He took the cantor under his wing and arranged that he was not sent either to the Klinker or, later, to the snow-removal work. But one morning, after a particularly violent snowstorm, when the office ordered that every man in our three blocks who could still crawl should report for work on the assembly place, Anton had to send out the cantor too.

We were uneasy when we saw him approaching with the labor squad. But the cantor himself seemed quite untroubled. As we set to work with our benches, I saw with satisfaction that I was placed in the row behind him and could keep an eye on him.

The cantor tackled his job with such good spirits that it looked almost like zest. He pushed with all his might, and as he worked he sang softly to himself the words of his favorite Psalm, the twenty-third. The blows that were dealt us automatically as we pushed our way past the foremen, he received unmoved, and as soon as he was out of the foremen's sight he began to hum the Psalm again.

But when we had almost reached the end of our stretch, the cantor suddenly collapsed and lay motionless on the ground. We had to go on pushing without taking any notice, but I could see the foremen running up and making the usual test with their boots. After a few minutes they were evidently convinced that the cantor was dead, and they ordered that four men should carry the body to the cellar of the Revier.

I reported immediately for this task, for it seemed impossible that the cantor should be dead. The Psalm I had heard him humming still sounded in my ears. Perhaps he was only unconscious and would come to himself if we shook him sufficiently. But in the Revier we had to recognize that our shaking was in vain. We laid him beside the other bodies, and our only comfort was the expression on his face: a look of sublime peace, almost of happiness, which not even the kicks of the foremen had been able to drive away. In memory of him, the Psalm most often chanted in our barracks was that which had been on his lips when he died.

During the weeks of snow shoveling, when cold and exhaustion made us an easy prey to tuberculosis, I was saved from serious lung trouble by an old pair of trousers. I had received them on my arrival in camp, and even then they were much too large for me. I had to pull them up to my chest, and during the sweating period in September, I had sweated all the more on that account. But when the cold days set in, I recognized the value of my old trousers. I had fallen off so much in the meantime that they reached to my armpits and I could almost wrap myself up in them entirely. In this way my lungs received some protection.

But the longer we remained in camp, the worse our coats and trousers were torn. Our tailors were continually patching them all over. Finally, when our clothes seemed to consist of nothing but patches, Karl contrived to get a few garments exchanged. But I refused to part with my trousers, although the head tailor in my block refused to take another stitch in them.

I had explained to the tailor, of course, why the trousers were so important to me. And my idea pleased him so well that he got himself an extra-large pair of trousers from the clothing room, to which, as a tailor, he had access, and padded them with patches all around, to make them as warm as possible. But the thought that another person should accidentally enjoy a similar privilege did not suit him at all and he stubbornly refused to give me needle, thread and patches when I told him that I would mend the tears myself. But not even this could induce me to give up. I bought myself patches, needle and thread from another tailor in exchange for bread, and held fast to my trousers, to which alone I owe the fact that on my release I was only on the brink of tuberculosis.

We had almost forgotten the rumor about the release of the professors when, on February 6, about one hundred of them were freed. Hope revived again; yet we were full of suspicion because only part of the group had been released. What was the basis for choosing who was to be freed?

When we learned from the *Voelkischer Beobachter* that the Bank Polski was to resume operations and that the governor of the bank had promised his cooperation with the Germans, the rumor went round that the released professors were ready to form a collaborationist Polish government. We were beside ourselves at these assertions. Professor Metellman in particular was enraged. He declared that the whole story was a low German propaganda trick to break Polish morale. "Polish professors have never yet been traitors," he said indignantly, "and they never will be."

But we never found out what really was behind the release of the professors or what became of them. Several of those remaining were let out at the beginning of March. The others, except for about ten, were transferred to the concentration camp of Dachau in April. Those left behind, including Professor Metellman, were still in Sachsenhausen when I was released.

On days when it did not snow so hard, only a part of us were ordered to the snow-removal work. The rest were assigned to all kinds of unpleasant labor, the worst task of all being to carry coffins to and from the Revier. As the coffins were made of damp wood, they were very heavy, and even when they were empty, the two bearers gasped under their burden.

The coffins were usually brought from the workshops or a supply warehouse to the cellar of the Revier. There they were lined up in a narrow corridor, from which one could see the bodies, naked and reduced to skeletons, lying on top of each other in heaps. When the bodies had been placed in the coffins, they were carried to another warehouse, from which they were later taken to be cremated.

Carrying the coffins was physically as well as spiritually the bitterest labor that we had to perform during our imprisonment. Not only were we completely shattered by the sight of the bodies, but the corpses, which had often waited for days to be coffined, had already begun to decay and even from within the coffins emitted a stench. Over and above this, the coffins had now become so heavy—as if each contained at least two bodies—that it took four men to carry one coffin. Even when we set the coffins on our shoulders, the strain was so great that we had to change every few yards from one side to the other. Since paint on the coffins was still wet, our hands, faces, and uniforms were stained black. The color would not come out with soap, and thus the blockfuehrers had a welcome opportunity to punish us as saboteurs for soiling our uniforms.

In the warehouse the coffins were piled up in long rows. Then, for identification purposes, a paper label with the prison number of the dead was attached with a thumbtack. But the tacks did not stick in the damp wood. Often when we arrived with a new load, we could see several labels lying on the ground. Which belonged to which coffin? We did not know. And after all, what did it matter? Probably the bodies were burned en masse, and the handful of ashes that the camp authorities "placed at the disposal" of the families did not even represent the last remains of their dead.

Whenever there were no bodies to carry, we were assigned to other work. Once when we were clearing out a tool shed in the Industriehof, we heard one of our comrades give a stricken cry. The foremen were driving us hard just then, and it was a long time before we found out what had happened. One of the comrades, in lifting up a board, had discovered four Hebrew prayer books. We could not believe our ears. How often had we longed to possess one single prayer book, and now, all at once, four lay within reach! Of course, we immediately wanted to secure the books and take them to the barracks. But that was easier said than done. Perhaps it was a trap and would entail terrible consequences. Would it not be better to discuss it in the barracks, work out a good plan and take the books away the next afternoon? But what if it were not a trap after all? And what if we were not sent to the same shed the next afternoon?

So the arguments went to and fro, in whispers and in telegraph style, accompanied by stolen glances. Finally two brothers let it be known that they were ready to take the risk. They would each rescue one book, and if they could not find two men to secure the others, they would let no one use the books they had saved.

After some hesitation two more volunteers were found. Then the problem was how to maneuver the books under their uniforms at the last minute. We agreed that when the order to cease work was given, whichever two of the comrades happened to be standing near the foremen at the moment would drop their load on the ground and on the foremen's feet if possible. While the foremen were giving all their attention to the culprits, the four rescuers could whisk the prayer books under their coats.

The trick went off according to plan. Happy and proud as children after a successful prank, we marched back to the barracks, yet with fear in our hearts that even now something might go wrong, that the books would show under our coats and be discovered.

When we arrived in the barracks and reported our great discovery to the other comrades, there was universal rejoicing. The discoverer of the books and the four rescuers were the heroes of the day. But it soon occurred to us that the real problem had just begun. Where should we hide the books? For hide them we must, not only from the blockfuehrers but from Karl, who would not tolerate the presence of such dangerous contraband.

After long discussion we agreed that the straw sacks were the only possible hiding place. As an extra safeguard we decided, reluctantly, to use the filthiest sacks. For the blockfuehrers, who were afraid of infection since the dysentery epidemic, would not search the soiled sacks, and the crust of filth would serve as a mark to show where our treasure lay hidden.

The news of our precious find spread with the speed of wireless. After evening roll call members of the indoor squads of the other two blocks came over on all kinds of pretexts to learn the particulars. And on Saturdays and Sundays, when, since we had been sent to work, we were allowed to visit each other, the comrades of 37 and 39 came in throngs to see us. They wanted at least to have a glimpse of the books and to hold them a moment in their hands. At first we refused to bring out the books, although we ourselves were eager to touch and look at them; for we lived in constant fear that their disappearance would be discovered and our barrack searched. It was only after some time had passed and nothing had happened, and after we had posted a guard to keep watch for the blockfuehrers and for Karl, that we dared to bring out the books.

Our barrack now became a regular shrine to which every Saturday and Sunday the comrades made pilgrimages. The four rescuers watched jealously to see that no one used a prayer book longer than a few minutes and that there were never too many visitors at once, so that we would not draw attention to ourselves. Finally, in order to lessen the danger of discovery and to give the other blocks a chance to pray too, we decided to let each of them have a prayer book and to keep for ourselves one book for each wing. With this, the prestige of our block rose enormously.

Those of us who knew the prayers by heart no longer had to recite the daily prayers with others who did not know them well enough. But one comrade would on no account release me from this duty: he was so old and nearsighted that he could not read the fine print of the prayer book. Until the day of my release he used to come to me every morning without fail, put his arm around my neck and ask with childlike trust: "Come, say with me the Psalm for today."

Our food, which had been bad enough to begin with, grew worse when the temperature fell below freezing and transportation difficulties arose. Now the scanty morsels of frozen, evil-smelling potato that floated in our daily soup grew fewer. The occasional portion of white cheese, which had consisted more of meal than of anything else, the marmalade, which used to be a mixture of potato syrup and a brown mess, we hardly ever saw—to say nothing of the luxury of a cube of so-called margarine or sausage paste. Only the black, sticky bread turned up faithfully, day in day out.

It was understandable, then, that some comrades who were assigned to work in the kitchen or the domestic department (Wirtschaftsabteilung) or in garbage removal greedily devoured every scrap of offal they found. This, of course, only made the dysentery worse and increased the number of fatalities. Later, when we were sent in large numbers to unload rotten vegetables, the temptation was still greater to hide some of them under our coats and eat them when we returned.

We sought means of relief. We pointed out to our comrades the consequences of their greed, which affected not only them but all of us, since it increased the danger of infection. When that proved futile, the indoor squad held body searches every time the labor squad returned to barracks and confiscated the hidden vegetables. But the result was that the comrades ate the vegetables on the scene of work. They had no illusions as to the consequences, but hunger was stronger than reason. It was indirect but conscious suicide.

Only once did a conscious, outright suicide occur among us. In my wing there was a comrade named Moritz, who had owned a small restaurant in East Berlin. He was a simple-minded person and in general rather silent. Whenever he did open his mouth, however, it was to talk about his two favorite topics: food and his heroic deeds in the First World War.

As Moritz had been born in Galicia, he had taken part on the Austrian side. But later, by his own account, he had joined the Polish Legion as a cavalryman and fought in the greatest battles, winning many medals for bravery. If anyone expressed disbelief in this epic, Moritz flew into a rage and sometimes came to blows. So whenever he embarked on his war stories, we used to steer him off to his other favorite theme. "Tell us about beef à la strogonoff, Moritz." And Moritz did not need to be pressed. We were instructed in the proper methods of onion frying and cream stirring; we were initiated into the mysteries of making sauce. Sometimes we listened with watering mouths. Sometimes we teased Moritz and claimed that his recipe was false. Then Moritz flew at his attacker like a fighting cock, but by and large the food theme was not as dangerous as that of the war.

But from the day that we were sent to work in the Klinker, a change came over Moritz. He became wholly silent and apathetic. Formerly he had been one of our most vigilant window watchers and had earned for this important service an extra piece of bread daily. Now his face wore an absent expression, which altered it completely. The worse our daily ration became, the more Moritz changed. Often he did not speak one word from morning till night. One day, when we did not have a single piece of potato in our midday soup, Moritz's feelings got the better of him. "I won't stand it any longer," his indignant voice broke into the monotonous lapping of the soup.

We looked up from our bowls, startled. Moritz's protest sounded so pathetic and, in view of our circumstances, so absurd, that it verged on the comic. We broke into laughter and he was chaffed from all sides.

"Yes, beef à la strogonoff would be better, of course."

"Moritz, get yourself invited to dinner by the Kommandant, for a change."

"And while you're there, get him to give you a leave of absence and to forget your address."

But Moritz only smiled an enigmatic smile that took us aback. He looked as if he had not understood the sallies at all.

We forgot the incident until several days later, when we were set to work in the Wirtschaftsabteilung, clearing out a cellar full of empty vegetable boxes. As we could see by the labels, they had contained southern fruits, vegetables and salads, destined for the kitchen of the Kommandantur. This sight, which brought so clearly before our eyes the contrast between the life of the Nazi elite and that of their slaves, filled us with bitterness. But the only one who gave voice to his feelings was Moritz. "I won't stand for it any longer," he cried, trembling with indignation.

That afternoon we remained in the barrack to mend and patch our things, as we always did on Saturdays. Moritz had once more gone out of our minds entirely, when we suddenly noticed him sitting in the farthest corner of the dormitory with a pile of short strings between his knees.

In those days string represented wealth to us. Immediately some comrades surrounded Moritz and begged him for string for their boots. At first he paid them no attention. But as they grew more insistent, he gave them a wrathful look and shouted, "Can't you see that this string is too thick?" It was true; the string was too thick to go through the eyelets. Still, it could easily have been unraveled and several shoelaces made from each piece. But Moritz would not hear of such a thing. His face grew threatening, as if he would jump at the throat of anyone who so much as looked at his string. Then the petitioners gave in and left him in peace, although they did not cease to curse his stinginess.

Moritz, undisturbed, continued to busy himself. He knotted the pieces together, testing each knot before he tied the next, and when he had finished with all the string, he rolled it into a ball. We watched this odd behavior uncomprehendingly and exchanged glances as much as to say that Moritz's mind was unhinged. The next day, Moritz seemed quite normal again and wrote to his family as all the others did. The following night he hanged himself in the day room.

This was discovered when Karl's alarm clock went off Monday morning and a comrade of the indoor squad sat up to reach for his trousers. He caught sight of the hanging man, shrieked out and fainted. Karl and the other comrades were on their feet in an instant. Karl took charge of the situation with his usual efficiency; he forbade anyone to go near the body and had some cupboards moved in front to spare us the sight. Then he attended to the man who had fainted.

In the dormitory we had heard the outcry and the moving of the cupboards and were in a state of intense excitement. When at last a comrade came to us and told us what had happened, we were paralyzed. Although there was so much to be done to get ready for roll call, no one made a move.

But Karl soon recalled us to ourselves. "I am as shocked as you are by what has happened," he said. "But we must pull ourselves together. You know that I must report the event to the office. The place will be swarming with uniforms until the body is removed. So I urge you, for all our sakes, to hurry even more than usual."

Then the work began to move automatically, and we soon saw how right Karl had been. A hanged Jew was a new attraction, and sightseers turned up in large numbers.

"There's one sensible Jew, at least," we could hear them say. "Let's hope all of you will follow his example." In this way they played on our feelings until the medical commission arrived and ordered the body cut down and removed to the Revier.

Although Moritz had not been a favorite in our barrack, his decision to end his own life made a profound impression on us, and we regretted the disagreements we had had with him. What hurt us most was that we had not taken seriously his intimations of his intention. Perhaps if we had taken the trouble to think about him, we might have reasoned out why he had obtained the string and stopped him in time. Many of us reproached ourselves that we had not told Karl about the string, although we knew well enough that no one would have consented to carry tales against a comrade.

Thus the weeks passed. The shadow of the hanged man lay heavy on our spirits, as if he were trying to avenge himself for all the jokes we had made at his expense. And worst of all, we lived in constant fear that Moritz's example might prove infectious among men whose despair deepened from day to day.

Since we knew that the Gestapo had determined to release no more Polish Jews, we were convinced that our relatives had resigned themselves to our destruction. But one morning something happened which proved to us that they had not yet given up the fight for our lives.

As the morning roll call came to an end, about thirty-five comrades from all three Polish blocks were summoned to the Political Division. To be sent for by the Political Division usually boded no good, and never before had so many of us been summoned there at once. We were amazed, therefore, when they returned with a look of joyful excitement. In the Political Division they had been received, not by blockfuehrers, but by a lawyer from Berlin, who had brought a pile of documents and photographs of their families and themselves. The comrades whose photographs he did not have were sent to have their pictures taken and given a civilian coat for the purpose.

The comrades were stunned when the close-mouthed notary finally informed them that he was there because of an application for their repatriation which their relatives had submitted to the Russian Consulate General in Berlin and which required the signature of the head of the family. More he would not say. But we could piece out the information with reports we had read in the *Voelkischer Beobachter*. The agreement between Germany and Russia provided for the repatriation of their respective nationals from partitioned Poland, as well as from the Baltic States. The Germans had gone to work at once and within three months had "brought home to the Reich" nearly a quarter of a million Germans, together with their movable property, from Russian-annexed Poland and the Baltic provinces.

The Russians, of course, could claim the Polish nationals in Germany who were natives of the regions annexed by Russia. Among us there were, including recent arrivals, several hundred comrades who had been born in the region claimed by Russia. The majority of these men were stateless, as the Polish Government, on one ground or another, had deprived them of their citizenship before the war. They were entirely without rights or protection. Their loyalty could not, therefore, be in question when their relatives undertook to apply for their repatriation as Russian nationals.

In the following months numerous applications of this kind were filed at the Russian Consulate General in Berlin and numerous signatures obtained in the camp Political Division. As Gucia told me later, this possibility of help seemed so credible that the Hilfsverein of Jews in Germany offered its facilities for investigating the families concerned and drawing up the applications correctly.

Our barracks during these months hummed with activity. There was a constant coming and going to and from the Political Division, a lively exchange of hopes and speculations. Every man who had been sent for expected his release from one day to the next. But the weeks passed and not one of the applicants was freed.

The Russian Consulate General in Berlin had at first shown so much good will toward the applications for repatriation that our relatives had been encouraged to take all the necessary steps. But when the applications had been presented and the time had come to act, the Consulate wrapped themselves in enigmatic silence, and the whole affair came to nothing.

The disillusionment smote like a hammer blow not only upon the men concerned but upon those who were not eligible for repatriation at all. This time it was more than personal disappointment. It was grief for the whole Jewish plight: "No one wants us; no one bothers about us; we can perish for all anyone cares." And it was true. When one thought of the powerful machinery that Germany had set in motion to bring home its nationals to the Reich, with what fanfare they were welcomed. . . . And with us it was a matter of saving our bare lives. If we had found only one friend among the nations, one country ready to take us in!

The families of the men who had suffered this bitter disappointment touchingly endeavored to give their men new courage. They always wrote as if there was still a good prospect of release and only the formalities were unusually protracted. But in the three Polish blocks there was no single person who put faith in these well-meant words.

While all this was going on, the dysentery epidemic and its victims wound its way through our existence. Then another and more terrible illness attacked us—dropsy. One morning when we woke up, the legs and arms of some comrades, and the faces of others, were swollen beyond recognition.

By that time we had become so familiar with despair that the stricken men were not even disturbed. They knew that under the conditions in which we lived, dropsy meant certain death. But since the repatriation hope had failed, they had resigned themselves to death in one shape or another. We others, however, who saw the progress of the disease in our comrades, were deeply concerned. It was not so much that their death was certain as that we feared the blockfuehrers, who always loved to pick out disfigured men as victims, would not even let them die in peace.

During roll calls we tried to hide the dropsy victims in the least prominent places. But if Size Ten Gloves or Iron Gustav was in charge, all precautions were in vain.

In those bitter days Karl was the prop to which we clung. Without making any fuss, or even showing that it cost him any effort, he succeeded in transferring to the Revier those dropsy victims in whom the water had almost reached the heart. We were moved; we were grateful; we were proud of Karl.

But it was just then that Karl was taken from us. One day, toward the end of February, when we returned from Klinker work, we were met by a "Latrine Courier" report that the room seniors in the Polish blocks were about to be changed. At the same time, Anton, who had previously shown much consideration for the prisoners, suddenly revealed another side of his character. He inflicted bestial beatings on the people in his block, including the old men whom he had previously protected. Not content with this, he suddenly appointed himself boss of our block and tormented us unmercifully.

Karl said nothing to this. Only after repeated urging could he be moved to speak. "Anton has great ambitions," he said. "You have heard, I suppose, that the room seniors in the Polish blocks are going to be changed, and Anton not only has his eye on a room-senior job but would like to be head room senior. Not even the Nazis would appoint a man as head room senior who can hardly write his name, but for a block room senior Anton has the right qualifications. And, as you see, he's trying to pass his examinations with the blockfuehrers. For which block he is a candidate, I don't know. But it is very doubtful if I'll be with you much longer."

We were thunderstruck. Karl was more to us than a friend: he was a symbol of endurance, resistance and an unbroken spirit. It seemed to us utterly unthinkable to go on without him. And because it was so unthinkable we refused to believe it at first. We comforted ourselves with the thought that nothing was settled yet.

But the next day removed all doubt. After noon roll call, we had scarcely finished eating when a horde of blockfuehrers descended on us. They set to work in the day room, called in Karl and Franz, heaped them with abuse, rounded up the indoor squad, forced them to climb up on and jump down from the cupboards and put them through hell. Then they began an inspection, searched the cupboards for bread and other forbidden objects, looked to see if the eating bowls were washed clean and the towels hung properly. And since, of course, nothing was in order, they blamed the "sloppiness" this time not only on us but on Franz, and on Karl whom they kept cursing as a "Jews' lackey," knocked over all the tables, benches, cupboards and buckets, and played football with the food bowls that rolled out on the floor.

We witnessed the tornado from the dormitory. Karl's removal now seemed certain. We only hoped that we would still have a chance to tell him how grateful we were for his loyalty; but we had no opportunity for that. When the blockfuehrers had finished in the day room, they came into the dormitory and drove us out of doors. The men who were ill with dysentery or dropsy collapsed almost at the first step, many never to rise again. Those who remained on their feet were hounded twice around the barracks until they fell unconscious. The other blocks were going through the same, which ended with the order to fall on our faces in the snow.

Our sweat-soaked bodies began to steam from contact with the snow. Then we grew chilled and stiff. But we scarcely noticed it. Our thoughts were busy with Karl. When would he have to leave? Who and what would succeed him?

We had to go on lying in the snow until evening roll call. When we were finally allowed to return to barracks, we were overjoyed to see that Karl was supervising the food distribution. We were eager to speak to him, to hear him speak. But Karl had put on a distant, unapproachable expression. It was his way of hiding his emotions. We understood and left him to himself.

The sound of Anton's incessant violence reached us from Block 37. One night still separated us from the decision that was hanging over us. We still had a breathing space. But at the end of that breathing space an unknown horror lay in wait. We could not escape it. We were riveted to an iron chain.

But the center of all my thoughts was Karl. What could be going on in his mind now? His life with us had often been far from easy. What were the privileges that he enjoyed as a room senior, compared with the anxieties and sorrows that he shared with us? Had he not often, perhaps, secretly felt his responsibilities a burden? Or had the respect and affection of the several hundred human beings under his care repaid his efforts? What moral strength he had! How often had I seen in his eyes the fanaticism of a missionary.

I do not know how many of us slept at all that night. Most of us lay awake, hoping that Karl would come in, as he always did in a crisis, and say a few words. But he did not come. Probably he too was overcome by his feelings and afraid that he could not find the right words of farewell.

While we were getting ready for roll call, Karl went to the office as usual to get the orders for the day. He had scarcely gone out when a group of night guards on their way through the camp dropped in on us, drove all the men out of the washroom half dressed and hunted them several times around the barracks.

As the time for roll call drew near, Karl returned. He was scarcely recognizable. He had not shaved that morning and his face was dirty and ash pale. His eyes were sunken and he avoided our gaze. This convinced me that his removal was a settled thing.

If we had any uncertainty left, Anton's self-assurance would have removed it. He ordered Block 37 around like a madman, while the room senior looked on, silent and powerless. When the blockfuehrers came in sight, he roared "Achtung!" with all his might, and no sooner had they reached the spot than he sprang forward and made his report as if he were already room senior. He was all on edge; he stuttered and stammered, and in his overeagerness to please the blockfuehrers he got the orders mixed up and created confusion. For a moment we took new hope. But the office did not care so much about smartness in the prospective room senior of the Polish blocks as about his being a man who could be depended on for brutality.

We still hoped up to the last minute that Anton would become room senior of Block 37. But after roll call, Mueller, who was our blockfuehrer just then, called Anton and both went into our barrack together. About ten minutes later Karl went out with his bundle and Franz trotted behind him. Our hearts contracted with wordless grief as we watched Karl go, and a dreadful fear seized us that some evil awaited him. In that moment we forgot ourselves entirely.

Anton's appointment upset his balance completely. Immediately after his installation—it was on Friday, March 1—he called together both wings into the day room of Wing A and let us know his intentions. "Here I am," he yelled, "and I can only warn you, with me you've got to make it snappy. If you don't come up to scratch, I'll make you wish you'd never been born. From now on I mean business. I'd sooner rub out all of you than have the office find fault with me. So now you know what's what; and now, Wing B, march back to your place." Anton had never, even in his good days as assistant in 37, spoken in a normal tone of voice. But since he had been promoted to room senior, his voice had gained in volume; from then on we never heard a quiet word from him.

No sooner had he roared out the last sentence than he started for the office. In a few minutes he was back with two prisoners, installed one as his successor in Block 37; the other he introduced to us as his new assistant. In Block 39 everything remained as before.

When Anton had finished with these preliminaries, he proceeded to introduce his new order. His first step was to transfer all the young people from Block 37 to our barrack, which confirmed an old suspicion of ours that his partiality for the younger men had a homosexual origin. Then he transferred another comrade, who had done clerical work in Block 37, and appointed him clerk in our block.

The clerk, whose name was Max, was the scum of the earth. He had no sense of solidarity with his fellow sufferers, reviled everyone and at every opportunity started quarrels which often ended in blows. When Anton was assistant in Block 37, he had kept Max in his place and had often brought him to reason with feet and fists. Now, all of a sudden, Max's qualifications seemed to suit Anton, and he chose him not only as his clerk, but also, so to speak, as his adjutant. Max eagerly seized the opportunity. With native slyness he figured that the more he imitated Anton and showed his zeal, the more privileges he would get. When the first noon meal was distributed, he spread a towel on Anton's table, took his food to him and stood beside him like a dog ready to perform at a signal from his master. Only a few weeks before, Anton would have called this sort of thing "sucker business" and put a stop to it. Now he visibly basked in it.

We felt at once that this sudden understanding between Anton and Max meant trouble for us, and we were not mistaken. Before long Max had become unofficial room senior in our block and did as he pleased. One of his favorite pastimes was to appoint himself as arbiter in the quarrels that often arose in our wing. He summoned the contending parties to him and held a regular hearing. Between questions he dealt out blows in a manner which he had learned from Size Ten Gloves. Often the hearings ended with the disputants lying unconscious or dying on the floor.

Max was, moreover, a sworn enemy of culture and learning and a "free-thinker" into the bargain. So the pious and all who held any kind of academic title were the targets of his viciousness. Not satisfied with all this, Max appointed himself the head of both indoor squads and forced them to adopt his own methods.

Our hatred for Max grew to staggering proportions: we even conceived the idea of murdering him. Often, when he had just finished one of his bouts of torture, groups of comrades clustered together and discussed quite seriously how to dispose of Max without terrible consequences for the rest of us. We finally agreed that the only safe method would be to beat him to death during work, if we ever got a chance to stage an "accident." But nothing came of this project, since Max was never sent out to work.

Anton had determined to give us no pause for breath, and as soon as the first noon meal was over, he began to pull wires in the office. When he came back, he once more herded us together and announced with great pleasure: "Tomorrow you'll have to hustle. The pipe must be cleared of snow, and everybody that can crawl has got to be there."

The so-called "pipe" was a part of the camp from which the snow had never been removed, and since it had thawed and frozen several times, the ice was piled high there. Chopping and carrying away the ice promised to be a hard task, but, strangely enough, no one was afraid of it. Since Karl had left, new resolution had entered into us. It was as if some unsuspected reserve of strength was making itself felt.

Anton, of course, had set his hopes on having the first day's work under his direction go off in a model fashion; and to show us that he was master now, he reorganized the indoor squads. He brought over the best beaters from Block 37 and substituted them for the former members. Luckily, however, he did not remove Professor Metellman and the musician D'Arguto from their jobs. The substitution was accompanied by incessant shouting, which got so on our nerves that those who were summoned to any kind of work in the camp were glad to escape.

The next morning, by agreement with Anton, we put on our working clothes. But since it was Saturday, the camp authorities had decided to postpone the work in the pipe. This was a terrible setback for Anton. He had already pictured to himself the first day's work, and its victims, as set down to his credit. So, when several foremen appeared and demanded recruits for the labor squads, Anton furnished them double and threefold. He got together a batch of workers indiscriminately, invalids and sick people included, and the foremen, when they got a good look at the human material on the way to the place of work, sent most of them back.

That was the second setback for Anton, and he gave the arrivals a suitable reception. After he had beaten them until he was breathless, he sat down to rest. When he had recovered himself sufficiently, he called us together and decreed that all who were not sent to work must stay either in the washroom or in the toilet. The dysentery victims all had to stay in the toilet, of course, and since the majority of those who did not go to work were sick with dysentery, the toilets were packed. This arrangement continued as long as the freezing weather lasted; later it was modified to the extent that whoever was not sent to work had to stand all day out of doors, rain or shine. This rule applied also to those who came back from work before the usual time.

Another of Anton's new regulations was that the alarm clock in the day room must have its face to the wall. The alarm clock had become an essential feature of our life; it helped us to get through the hours and to keep a certain order in our heads. It showed us when we would finally be able to go to sleep, when to expect our soup; and often when the time seemed to stand still, it gave us new confidence if we could steal into the day room and, by a glance at the clock, assure ourselves that time was passing after all. From now on we lived without time.

That Saturday the distribution of mail was due, but after what we had experienced from Anton, we did not believe that he would do so that day. So we were amazed when at noon he suddenly ordered us back to the dormitory and announced that there would be mail after roll call. We did not know how late it was and how long we would have to wait: the only comfort was that roll calls were held earlier on Saturdays.

When the mail was brought in at last, we saw to our delight that a big batch had arrived. But as the men's eyes searched through the pages for definite news, it appeared that the letters contained nothing but general words of comfort. I was the only one who had a message of hope. I read Gucia's letter once, twice, again and again; did not believe my eyes. There it was in black and white—"Everything is going according to my expectations. I hope that on April 11 we will sail together from Trieste for Shanghai."

I had hoped for such a message so long, and known in my heart that some day it would come. I had tried to imagine what feelings of dizzying exultation would overcome me when I learned at last that rescue was at hand. But now it was different. My feelings overpowered me so much that I could not shout for joy, could not even bring out a sound. But my comrades evidently read in my face that my letter contained something extraordinary. They surrounded me and demanded to see it.

Instantly a hot debate arose over Gucia's announcement. "So there is a chance of release, after all," said those who always insisted that their families were not sufficiently concerned about them. Others said that that was nonsense and that if I were going to be released it must be an exceptional case. But many protested at this. "Why Szalet in particular? Why should he have special luck?" And finally the majority agreed that Gucia was only trying to keep up my hopes and that if no one in the other barracks had received similar news, the whole story could be dismissed as an unsuccessful bluff.

The news of my letter reached the other barracks in a few minutes and immediately delegations from the other indoor squads appeared, to investigate the report. My letter passed from hand to hand and the discussion grew more excited every moment. Suddenly I was overcome by the excitement and confusion within and around me and I fainted.

When I came to myself and remembered what had happened, I begged my comrades to give back my letter and leave me in peace.

The letter was now badly the worse for wear, but I could still read plainly: "I hope that on April 11 we will sail together from Trieste for Shanghai." And *that* was only empty words of comfort? Absurd! Let the others think what they liked. I knew my daughter. She made positive statements only when she had good reason; if she had merely wanted to comfort me, her phrase would have been more general.

But how was it possible that, just at this moment when the situation looked so hopeless, I was to be released? Was Gucia the only one to succeed in putting through a request for release with the Gestapo? It sounded unbelievable and impossible. Then I remembered an expression that Gucia often used to repeat: "Impossible is a crutch that only the weak-willed lean on. "Weak-willed Gucia certainly was not. For her there was no "impossible." My doubts were banished, and I considered myself a certain candidate for an early release.

Only one fear beset me—that in the last few weeks something might happen to me, that Max and the other brutes among us would revenge themselves on me for the good news, and that my strength would fail at the very last moment. April was the messenger of rescue. Would I be able to keep my head above water until then?

Anton's intention of having us stand in the washroom and the toilet when we were not at work was frustrated when Sunday came around. No one went to work on Sundays, and not even Anton's malice could contrive to crowd all the occupants of the block into the toilet and the washroom. So each wing spent the day in a standing squad in its own day room. But Anton ordered all the windows on both sides of the day room opened, "so that the March wind will give you a good airing."

Still, Anton could not reconcile himself to the fact that we were "frittering away" time which might have been spent in useful work. When he suddenly left the barrack and went off hastily in the direction of the office, we knew that he had an inspiration. It was not long before he was back. The triumphant air with which he summoned Max told us that he had been successful. After the two accomplices had conferred, Anton threw open the door and came in noisily. "From now on there'll be no more hanging around on Sundays," he announced. "From now on Block 38 will carry the food to the whole Isolation District three times a day, so that you bastards won't be getting ideas in your heads."

Until now the elite prisoners had brought food to the Isolation

District. But on Sunday morning it had been announced that all the elite prisoners were to be released and incorporated into various Gestapo formations. Thereupon Anton had hit on the brilliant idea of offering the labor supply of his block for the vacant job.

Anton and Max then picked out the strongest men, and Anton personally escorted the squad to the kitchen to get the kettles. Of course, he saw to it that the comrades' task was made as hard as possible. But when they came back from work, they told us that in spite of everything, they preferred kettle carrying to the standing squad.

After this sample of Anton's conception of his job, many of us believed that the work in the pipe would be no worse. I could not agree; I remembered our snow-removal work in the harbor, and a terrible fear seized me. If we had to go through the same thing again, would I be able to hold out? Cold sweat broke out on my body when I thought that, with April so near, my strength might fail at the last moment. And I was not the only one to ask that question. The glances of my comrades seemed to ask ironically: "Well, friend, will you last until the great day?"

Anton could scarcely wait for the working day to begin. When the alarm went off the next morning, he was already half dressed and instantly rushed into the dormitory. "I advise you to move like greased lightning," he yelled, "or else the fur will fly." We hurried as fast as we could. When only half of us were finished washing, he drove us all out of the washroom and declared that the time for washing was over. And he closed the toilets earlier than usual.

Max supervised the distribution of food and, since everything had to go like "greased lightning," he suddenly announced that the time was up. He made us pour most of the soup into the toilets, so that the majority went hungry. After all this, there was still half an hour before the beginning of roll call, and we stood around, not knowing what to do. Then, when Anton finally drove us out to roll call, the blockfuehrers were not yet due. We took our usual places, but that did not suit Anton. He darted around us like a will-o'-the-wisp, improving the formation. "I want the healthy ones in front and the crocks behind, get me?" he yelled. "And if the counting doesn't go off right, there'll be no grub the whole day."

When roll call was over, each room senior led his block to the assembly place, where the labor squads gathered before marching to work. Even from a distance we could hear the voice of Iron Gustav, who was a member of the staff supervising the labor squads. "The big capitalists will finally learn what manual labor feels like," he shouted as he saw us marching up and laughed loudly at his own wit.

As we had feared, only the Polish Jews were sent to work in the pipe. Before we marched there, we had to run to the supply shed and fetch picks, shovels and chests. Then we were divided into three squads, choppers, shovelers and porters. The foremen in charge of us belonged to the notorious brutes of the camp, so we had several men wounded and one killed even before we reached the pipe.

The pipe was a zone about five yards wide, which encircled the camp. From there we had to carry away the ice to the Industriehof. To perform this work properly and quickly, we needed not only sound tools in sufficient numbers but intelligent supervision. Once again it was made clear that the camp authorities were not interested in efficient work but in extermination. Instead of distributing us into small groups at regular intervals in the pipe, the foremen herded us together so that the several hundred men got in each other's way. Choppers, shovelers and porters were tied up in a snarl; and the work hardly progressed at all. Furthermore, the chests were not equal to their task. They were crudely made and just firm enough to hold some sand. Under the burden of the lumps of ice with which the shovelers had to pack them to the rim, they broke to pieces. Every broken chest, as well as every involuntary fall, was the signal for a brutal beating, which cost the victim severe injuries or even his life.

I too came very near losing my life in the pipe. A comrade and I, who were carrying a chest between us, were waiting for the shovelers to finish loading it, when we saw several blockfuehrers approaching. The choppers quickened their pace. The shovelers shoveled with all their might. Our chest was packed to the rim. We heard the boards crack and were deathly afraid that after a few steps they would give way under the weight. With dread in our hearts we picked up the chest and moved off toward the oncoming blockfuehrers.

"Two lazy loafers for a nutshellful of snow," yelled one. "We'll fix that." And he picked up a huge lump of ice that lay in the path and threw it with all his might into our chest. The chest burst into its component parts and the lumps of ice rolled to the blockfuehrers' feet.

That was the moment we had feared. In an instant the blockfuehrers seized the scattered pieces of wood and fell upon us. I felt the wood on my head, on my neck, on my hips; I felt it break on my body and tasted my own blood that ran into the corners of my mouth, until I lost consciousness. When I came to I was in the Revier. My whole left side felt paralyzed. My shoulder seemed to be dislocated, my ear and the left side of my head were still bleeding, my left hip burned like fire, and I could not move my hand or arm.

My greatest anxiety at that moment was that I had some broken bones and that they would not be set properly, which would have meant the end of my chance of freedom—for cripples were not released to emigrate. But when, after many hours of waiting, my injuries were attended to, it appeared that, though I had dislocated joints and several hemorrhages, the bones had not been injured.

Neither Anton nor Max gave me a glance when I returned, heavily bandaged, to the barrack. But the next morning, when the labor squad went to the pipe again, and I had to be left behind, Max said: "Don't you imagine that I'll let you stand around here long on account of your fine bandages. In a few days you'll have to go out again, even if you're ready to croak." But my condition was so serious that he could not send me out. For several weeks I had to carry my arm in a piece of string, as slings were not furnished to Jews, and I was so handicapped that I could neither dress nor undress myself. During all the time that I was assigned to a standing squad in the toilet instead of going to work in the pipe, Max made me pay dearly for that privilege. But even so, I owed it to my misfortune in the pipe that I came out of the camp alive.

A few days after my accident Anton and Max at last allowed me to go to the Revier to have my bandages changed. As I stood waiting in front of the Revier, I suddenly saw a group of prisoners running in my direction. They were followed by a horde of blockfuehrers, who fiendishly hounded them to and fro for about an hour. Then the blockfuehrers drove them into a side lane near the Revier, which was piled high with snow along its entire length; the prisoners were driven into these masses of snow. Under the snow were lumps of ice. The prisoners slipped on them as their feet sank into the loose snow, and the men fell forward on their faces. The blockfuehrers laughed ringingly as the sweat-drenched men got a cold plunge; and with that, the penal exercise, as this man hunt was called, ended.

I had been covertly watching these proceedings, and suddenly I noticed Karl in the group. My heart began to beat wildly, for this was the first time since Karl's removal that any of us had had a glimpse of him. When I returned to the barrack, I told my comrades of this unexpected meeting and what Karl and the others had suffered. The whole barrack received the news with the greatest excitement, and it was decided that we must try to get in touch with Karl somehow and find out what was happening to him.

The next day a comrade was able to steal into Karl's barrack, and he learned that several heavy punishments had been inflicted on Karl. He had been enrolled in a dangerous labor squad, had to undergo penal exercise twice a day and, in addition, had been forbidden to send or receive mail for a month. Though he spoke of his own fate calmly and without bitterness, he was still the old Karl when he talked of our lot and flashed out in hate and anger.

When Anton took over Karl's job, a welcome legacy fell into his lap. Shortly before Karl's removal it had been announced that every prisoner would soon be allowed to buy extra bread and other necessary articles in the camp canteen. "It looks very suspicious to me that the boys are so big-hearted all of a sudden," Karl had said when he told us, "but let's wait and see." Unfortunately we did not see until the time of Anton's regime, and Anton promptly made use of the new regulation for his own ends. He decreed, on his own authority, that every prisoner must withdraw the maximum sum permitted. If anyone had less than 15 marks to his credit, he had to withdraw all but one mark. The money must be handed over to Anton, as he had to effect the purchases, and woe to anyone who tried to cheat and claimed that he did not possess 15 marks. Max underlined Anton's orders with comments of his own, and when both had finished, we had no doubt whatever that we would get little return for our money.

A few days later extra bread supplies actually went on sale in the canteen. In principle, we, like the rest of the camp, were entitled to buy bread through our room seniors, but in practice we only got what was left over after all the other blocks had supplied their needs. So a good deal of our money was left for Anton and his accomplices. Anton had, meanwhile, acquired a new assistant, who was one of the oldest residents of Sachsenhausen and an international burglar. This creature succeeded in concentrating the purchasing and distribution of food for the whole barrack in his wing. From then on, the greater part of the money that we were allowed to draw out was systematically dispensed for the benefit of Anton & Co., as we nicknamed the gang. Later, when there was plenty of bread on sale in the canteen, we did not have enough money to buy it; when every prisoner was permitted to buy two cigarettes a week, we hardly ever saw a cigarette. But except for Max, who used our money to buy himself a pipe which from then on hung constantly from the corner of his mouth, Anton & Co. smoked cigarettes like chain smokers.

Since Anton & Co. had several hundred marks in their possession, they were able to live like lords at our expense. By connections and bribery, they not only got margarine and sausages in the canteen, but even procured themselves some low-grade alcohol. After we lay down to sleep, regular orgies were held in the day room. The assistant even forced the strong and healthy men of the indoor squad to have homosexual relations with him, and Anton behaved with the boys as before.

In this way, our block, which had formerly had the highest moral standing, became a center of depravity. We were very bitter about it, and one night we complained in whispers to each other. This was reported to Anton by a spy. And the next morning a strict investigation began, which lasted for weeks. When we stood firm, Anton & Co. borrowed the hostage system and at every hearing picked out several men at random whom they beat till they were nearly, or quite, dead. We could not find out who the spy was and from then on we lived in constant fear.

The transactions of Anton & Co. continued unhindered until my release. Theoretically, the blockfuehrers were supposed to supervise the withdrawal of money, as well as the expenditures. And they did supervise. But Anton contrived to arrange matters so that all the accounts checked. We could never agree whether he accomplished this by fooling the blockfuehrers or by bribing them with our money.

It was always a puzzle that, in spite of the filth that surrounded us, we suffered comparatively little from vermin. This was due in part to the fact that, at the beginning of February, Karl had succeeded in getting us permission to take showers every two weeks. Although the SS men in charge of the boiler took pleasure in turning on us either a scalding-hot or an ice-cold stream, so that we could not stand under it for more than a few seconds, and we had no soap, the showers served to keep the parasites in check.

But shortly after Karl's removal a regular epidemic of vermin broke out among us. Whether it was owing to our stay in the filth-smeared toilet or to the constant influx of prisoners from the occupied territories, crab lice suddenly appeared. They multiplied with positively uncanny rapidity. The itching never stopped. Many of us, who continually put hands to faces, transferred the crab lice to eyebrows and eyelashes, and when we began to scratch, caught horrible eye infections.

The appearance of the crab lice filled Anton with fear and rage. Since the whole indoor squad could wash regularly and always kept their blankets and straw sacks separate from ours, the personnel of the day room had until then been free from lice. Now the danger of the infection spreading to them was increased. Therefore, Anton took care to get us a fortnightly shower. But at that time there was allegedly no coal in camp, so we only got cold showers, which did not bother the crab lice at all.

Then Anton tried in his own way to remedy the evil. He had us line up in the day room, stripped to the waist. Then, with Max and one of our comrades who was a doctor, he went along the line, ordered each of us to raise his arms, lower his trousers and bend over, searched the hairy parts of the body and beat the breath out of everyone who was heavily infested. When this proved ineffective, Anton got us a vermin-exterminating salve from the Revier. The salve stank so overpoweringly that it almost knocked us out, but it had no effect whatever on the lice.

Two weeks had already passed since I had received from Gucia the announcement of my approaching release, and nothing more had happened. My wounds had in the meantime almost healed; only my arm was not yet well and I still had to wear the sling. One afternoon when we were standing in the toilet, it suddenly occurred to me that my injuries might endanger my release. Injured men were not released for emigration. The eleventh of April was near; moreover, it appeared from all the newspapers that Italy's entrance into the war was impending. With that, the last sea route to China would be cut off and all hope of freedom would be over for me. For we had learned from some recently arrived prisoners that the Russian Consulate had refused some Polish women transit visas through Siberia.

Anxiety and the pestilential stench were making me so dizzy that I thought I was going to faint. But a sudden din outside recalled me to myself. The door was thrown open, and several blockfuehrers appeared on the threshold. They yelled like drunken men: "To the floor with you."

We hesitated a moment. But the blockfuehrers struck the men near them so that they fell like logs. Some fell with their faces in the full toilet bowls, others fell flat on the floor and the rest threw themselves down on the prostrate men so that those underneath were in danger of smothering beneath the pressure.

Luckily, however, the stench was so overpowering that the blockfuehrers could not stand it. They cursed us, ordered us to stay as we were and vanished into the washroom, yelling and blustering. From the washroom we could hear the raging of the blockfuehrers and the screams of our comrades.

We could not get up, of course, but at least we could move and give the men on the floor some air. "For the first time, staying in this stinking toilet turns out to have advantages over staying in the washroom," one of the comrades suddenly whispered.

"I'll take the disadvantages without the stink," countered another, who had fallen with his face in the toilet.

And a general lament began. "How long is this going to go on? How long can a human being stand such hell? How long can we keep on hoping?"

These questions were spoken in whispers, and in the screaming that rang from the day room they were almost drowned out. Suddenly I heard a voice near me. "For us there's no hope; the only one who has reason to hope is Szalet."

It hurt me that the prospect of my release had aroused such ill will, and most of the comrades appeared ashamed of their enviousness. After the blockfuehrers had gone, they took to task the comrade who had made the remark, and for the rest of the day I was left in peace.

The next day the distribution of mail was due, and the whole barrack waited in suspense for my letter. I continually heard whispering around me and felt curious glances resting on me. When at last the distribution began, a group of the curious hung on my footsteps in order to be on the spot when I opened my letter. But this time there was no letter for me, and, since I showed no disappointment, they had to content themselves with meaningful looks and more whispering.

One evening in the third week of March, when we had lain down to sleep, Anton suddenly came in with his assistant and Max. "Stay as you are," he barked, and turned on the light. Then, without a word of explanation, he began to walk along the rows and take a good look at each of us. His companions followed. From time to time, Anton would stop before one of us. "Name and number," he ordered, and Max, who followed at his heels, noted the information on a long list. Twenty comrades were listed, and I was among them.

Since Anton had become our boss, we had grown used to viewing every unexpected occurrence in the darkest colors. The next morning our fears were confirmed. In Wing B, Anton had picked out fifteen men, and it was said that the selected group constituted the first Jewish contingent to be deported, probably to Poland.

This rumor brought me to the verge of despair. My release was at hand, and just then, when it might be ordered any day, perhaps any hour, I was to be deported.

Max was bustling around officiously and dealing out orders and blows. Perhaps, I thought, the rumor wasn't true after all; he would surely know. I swallowed my contempt and went up to him.

"Max," I asked, "is it true that we are to be sent to Poland?"

But Max ran on as if he were deaf and blind.

"Max," I tried again, "please answer me. Is it true that we're going to be deported?"

Max would not grant me a word. He ran back and forth diagonally, and let me run after him, as if I were a troublesome dog. But I gulped down my pride.

"Help me, Max, please. You know I'm expecting my release; can't you see to it that I'm taken out of the group?"

Then at last he stood still and laughed in my face. "You surely don't think I'm such a fool as you and believe in fairy tales."

Let him curse me for a fool and laugh in my face, if he would only give me a word. "It's true, Max, please believe me; my daughter definitely . . ."

I did not get any further. Max's fist felled me to the ground. I heard him still laughing as I dragged myself, bruised and despairing, into the dormitory.

A few minutes later Anton came back from his morning trip to the office and announced with the air of a general: "All those slated for the deportation squad aren't to go to work any more. They wait in the dormitory in their work clothes, ready to march off. Anybody that's got a toothbrush can take it, but letters and that kind of trash must be left behind. And anybody with torn boots can get them exchanged."

An excited murmur arose. It was true, then. Even in the eyes of those who did not belong to the deportation squad I could see panic. They knew that sooner or later the same fate awaited them.

"But where are they sending us?" an anxious voice asked. Anton, who was on his way out, turned, leaned against the wall, folded his arms, and said in an amiable tone such as I had never heard him use: "Ah, children, that's the only thing I don't know. But I think it'll be a much nicer place than here, where they'll serve you crisp sausages and sauerkraut for breakfast and a big bottle of beer for lunch. I tell you, children, it'll be a regular health resort."

This answer confirmed our worst fears. All at once I lost my self-control and began to sob. I was lost.

But I would not give up yet. Was it not my duty to try everything? What was the sense of showing pride toward these creatures? Perhaps I might manage something through Anton.

"Herr Stubenaeltester," I said to him, "I have received word that my release is impending in the immediate future, and I beg you, in view of that, to take me out of the deportation squad."

Anton looked at me thoughtfully for a few moments and I began to cherish hope—but too soon.

"Man, don't get any bees in your bonnet. The gentlemen of the Gestapo wouldn't even let a Polish louse crawl out of here, and you think they'll let such a juicy morsel slip through their fingers! And *if* they want to release you, do you think they'll need a microscope to find you again?"

"But Herr Stubenaeltester," I protested, "I have . . ."

"But, but! Here there's no buts. You stay in the squad and that's that."

When we ran out to the morning roll call, Anton did not fail to remind us that the deportation squad must report to the dormitory at once, in order to be ready to march off. Outside, we soon discovered that no deportation squads had been formed in the other two blocks. That gave us new hope. Perhaps the deportation was only one of Anton's bright ideas, and in that case there was a chance that it would come to nothing.

We spent the whole morning waiting in the dormitory. Our conversation was like the reading of a last will and testament. From time to time, Anton and Max looked in on us, but they said nothing. Again in the afternoon we had to hold ourselves "at the ready." But again nothing happened.

When we ran out to the evening roll call, we saw by Anton's sour expression that his plans had been crossed in some way, and slowly hope began to stir in our hearts. Still, we did not close an eye that night. The next morning we waited with thudding hearts for Anton's return from the office. And as Anton avoided looking at us, we felt that the danger was growing less. However, Max enjoyed our bitter anxiety far too much to free us from it. Not until after morning roll call, when we returned to barracks, and the deportation squad prepared to take its former place in the dormitory, did he rush in and spit out an order to take off our work clothes and beat it to the toilet. The deportation had been postponed for several days.

I was one of the first to reach the toilet room, which all at once seemed a wholly desirable place to be. I did not notice the stink at all. My only thought was that the danger had been averted. My ship was to sail on April 11, and it was now almost the end of March; my release could not be deferred much longer. For me the danger was over.

Anton did not once refer to his new come-down. But we could see that it had cut him to the quick, for from then on he mistreated with particular meanness the men who had belonged to the deportation squad. One of his nastiest acts was forbidding us to write home on the next writing day. "It would be a sheer waste of paper," he answered to all our protests. "You're soon going to be deported anyway, and then you can write your precious relations your new address right away." We pleaded with him to let us send at least a card, but he was deaf.

This mental torture was not the only revenge that Anton had in store for us. He ordered the two doctors in our barrack to keep watch on the toilet at night and to report to him everyone who visited it. The men who were reported he pronounced sick with dysentery and banished them to the infected toilet. There the healthy men indeed got dysentery and soon went the way of the other sufferers.

Then shortly before Easter there occurred an attempt at escape which was surely unique in the annals of Sachsenhausen. The fugitive, who had spent six years in the concentration camp, knew all the roads in camp and was familiar with the habits of the guards. One day, shortly before evening roll call, when traffic in the camp was particularly heavy, he obtained an SS uniform by a carefully prepared plan and left the camp dressed as an SS man, without arousing the suspicions of the guards. But at roll call his absence was noticed, and within half an hour the SS had put a cordon around Oranienburg and the false SS man was recaptured. At once there began a search for possible accomplices, which dragged on for weeks. The whole camp was ordered to stand for several days in roll-call formation, in order to set an example. But at 1:00 A.M. the order was revoked and we were allowed to return to barracks. The guards who had let the prisoner slip through were sent to the front as a punishment, and the prisoner himself was assigned to the punishment squad, which meant his certain death.

This attempted escape occupied our minds for weeks. It was completely incomprehensible to us. For the prisoner was to have been released at Easter. His family had worked for years for that moment. He himself had borne his six years' imprisonment with surprising patience, but when he heard of his approaching release he suddenly could not stand it any longer. For six years he had held out, but the last few days of waiting were too much. Although he knew what was in store for him if his foolhardy enterprise failed, he risked the attempt at flight. We could not understand his curious psychological processes, though we felt the greatest sympathy when we heard of his fate.

The attempt at escape had disastrous consequences. To avenge themselves for the punitive transfer of their SS comrades, the block-fuehrers began a reign of terror. The punishment squads got the worst of it; and one day the despair and seething hate of the punishment-squad men boiled over. A prisoner who had been inhumanly mistreated by one of the foremen hit his tormenter over the head with a spade and dangerously injured him. Thereupon the other foremen fell upon the culprit and beat him to death on the spot. The rest of the punishment squad was sentenced to penal cells for mutiny and was probably soon finished off there.

The rain, snow and cold winds that succeeded each other by turns kept us from realizing that by the calendar it was already spring. Immediately after Easter the camp authorities began to incorporate the human material of the camp in an expanded work program for the spring months. Thanks to my injured hand, I was not assigned to any particular labor squad, but was used to fill in wherever there was a vacancy. In this way I at last became familiar with the whole camp and could form a picture of its layout, as few comrades, even after years in Sachsenhausen, were able to do. Only after I had worked in the most widely separated sections of the camp did I understand how its different divisions were connected and what made the control function like a precision instrument.

The Kommandantur formed the entrance to the camp proper. It was a massive stone building, about 40 yards wide and 30 yards in depth. The entrance gate opened into a passage that led under the building into the interior of the camp. A wall about 4 yards high, joined onto the Kommandantur building on the right and left, enclosed the whole inner section of the camp. Within this, at a distance of about 5 yards from it, ran a second concentric wall. The hollow space between these two walls was the pipe, already mentioned. Within it, at intervals of every 200 yards, were little two-storied sentry boxes, equipped with movable machine guns and searchlights. The sentry boxes were built on the principle of railroad switchboxes. They had windows on all four sides, from which the corresponding section of the camp could be overlooked. Guards were kept there day and night, and in case of suspicion they could, by pressing a button, transform night into day. Within the pipe there was the notorious barbed-wire barrier charged with high-tension current. Many a time one could see a prisoner who had tried to break through the wires get caught on them and die.

The rear of the Kommandantur building, with the main tower from which the assembly was blown, jutted out 5 yards into the assembly square. This square was so large that the twenty thousand-odd men who three times a day marched into it for roll call were almost lost in it. Scattered about the assembly square were signs about 3 by 4 yards in size, mounted on high posts so that they were visible from a distance, and announcing in big black letters on a white ground:

> There is a road to freedom.
> Its milestones are:
> Obedience, industry, honesty,
> Order, cleanliness, sobriety,
> Truthfulness, spirit of sacrifice and
> Love for the Fatherland!

Back of the assembly square, arranged in a rough semicircle, was a regular city of barracks, built by the camp prisoners, which had grown steadily since 1933—the seventy wooden barracks in which the prisoners were housed formed only a small part of it. From the assembly square a long wide road led to the workshops within the camp, the so-called Industriehof, which was situated in the left-hand division of the camp, about 200 yards from the Revier. The Industriehof consisted of a number of subdivisions, such as carpenter shops, locksmith shop, smithy, sawmill, etc. Some twenty blockfuehrers superintended here. They were a hand-picked group of brutes and were known in camp as "the terror regiment." Since the Industriehof was considered one of the showplaces for outside visitors, it swarmed perpetually not only with the appointed overseers but with all kinds of uniformed killers. It goes without saying that all work here had to be performed at the double, even carrying loads or pushing wheelbarrows. Only seldom was there a milder regime, for the blockfuehrers never left us alone for any length of time, and when the foremen caught sight of them even at a distance, they feared for their own security and began to beat, bluster and rage. It was as if a tornado had suddenly come up, and many lives were blown away.

Opposite the entrance gate, farther in the interior of the camp and facing on the assembly square, was the Wirtschaftsabteilung, or domestic division, of the camp. This too comprised many subdivisions such as kitchens, canteens, baths, office, laundry, tool room, clothing room, provision room and even its own waterworks and drainage system. The most important subdivision of the Wirtschaftsabteilung was the kitchen, which had to provide meals for some 20,000 prisoners. Of the six hundred-odd prisoners who worked here, several hundred were employed in peeling vegetables in the kitchen. These prisoners were so old and infirm that they were useless for any other work. They were housed in special blocks in the vicinity of the kitchen and worked, in several shifts, all through the twenty-four hours.

Since no one was allowed to show himself outside at night, the night shift, which went on duty shortly after midnight, was escorted to work by a large group of blockfuehrers, and the searchlights on the watchtowers were focused on the procession until it disappeared through the doors of the kitchen.

Often, when I was ordered to work in the Wirtschaftsabteilung, I could see this kitchen squad just coming off duty and marching back. The men's aspect was pitiable. They seemed not like human beings but like rundown machines. Their eyes were vacant; there was no expression in their faces, not even an expression of fear. Perhaps the only sensation of which they were still capable was the feeling of hunger. In their meaningless lives there was only one temptation: to cram a piece of potato or turnip into their mouths as they worked, or even to hide a whole potato in their coats. The kitchen squad were required to keep watch on each other, but thefts occurred almost daily. And if anyone was caught in the act, his hours were numbered.

Another group of useless prisoners was employed in the clothing room, mending socks and underwear. (The Polish blocks, however, seldom received whole socks or patched underwear, so the underwear fell to pieces on our bodies. Our drawers had no buttons and were always slipping down. So we soon hit upon an idea. If we ever got a piece of underwear that boasted a button, we pulled off the button before turning the article in, and sewed it on the clean drawers. Thus a button wandered from one pair of drawers to another and became another of the objects we exchanged for bread.) The menders, of course, had a much better time than the kitchen squad. Their hands did not chap from immersion in cold water or grow numb from holding the frozen vegetables. But by far the most fortunate of all the prisoners in the Wirtschaftsabteilung were the tailors and shoemakers. Since their work required special skill, and their number was none too great, they were comparatively well treated, and even strong and healthy lads who possessed these skills were ordered to this peaceful labor. Only the Jews were excluded.

By far the most dangerous place to work was the Gaertnerei, with its countless hothouses and beds of flowers and vegetables. It comprised an area of about 20 acres facing on the street, next to the Industriehof, along the inner wall. It was under the direction of a blockfuehrer named Krause, who came from West Prussia. He had been a farm hand on a big estate, and his principal job had been sticking pigs; on the strength of this he had been assigned to his post in the concentration camp. For in the Gaertnerei there was a sizable hog-breeding farm; the hogs were fed on kitchen scraps. (The pork, of course, was reserved for the SS staff of the camp and the SS settlement in Oranienburg.)

By a curious freak of nature, Krause, from his long association with hogs, had acquired a hoglike appearance. His under jaw protruded and was pointed like a snout; his rosy complexion was like that of a young pigling; his eyes were slits. There were rolls of fat on his neck, and the whole of him was plump and well-nourished like an acorn-fed swine. But the most hoglike thing about him was his voice, which sounded like the grunting of a whole chorus of swine. Although we always performed our work in quickstep, when we heard Krause's grunting we broke into a regular run, even though we knew that we would spill on our clothes the liquid manure we were carrying and would stink like a sewer the rest of the day.

But in spite of all our haste we never worked fast enough for this guttersnipe. So, in order to speed up our work, he introduced an innovation which had originated in the brain of his assistant and which he dubbed "the rotating labor squad." We had to form a circle, which stretched from the manure pit or manure shed to the places where we had to dump the contents of our barrows. The circle had to keep rotating; in this way a human conveyor belt was formed. The belt must never be broken; if it did, the man responsible was punished, usually by being thrown into the manure pit.

Often enough Krause did not need such pretexts in order to punish us. Even when the circle rotated faultlessly, he was not satisfied. "The swine are strolling instead of working. They'll have to be cured of laziness. No eats today," he shouted as he approached. And when he reached us he seized the nearest man, threw him to the ground and beat him with his cudgel until the blood began to flow. Then he stuck his cudgel between his teeth, as he probably used to do with his knife in his pig-sticking days. Into his washed-out gray eyes came the look of perverse bloodthirstiness we so dreaded, and he reached for a second victim. While our rotating labor squad circled past him with automatic regularity, shoveled up manure and loaded it again, he beat several of our comrades to death. And after work, when, beaten, stinking and hungry, we carried our dead and injured to the barrack, one of us had a slip which must be presented to the room senior and which read: "The pack of swine will have their food withdrawn today."

Every prisoner who was ordered to work in the Gaertnerei looked upon himself as a candidate for death. Often when a man working in one of the other sections found himself beside a prisoner who was disfigured beyond recognition, the first question was: "Were you in the Gaertnerei?" so unmistakable was the mark left on the men.

In size, the Bunker was the smallest section of the camp, but for all that it dominated the whole scene. To the SS it was the pearl in their crown, the symbol of their power, the place from which the new world order was proclaimed with the greatest éclat. The mere thought of the Bunker filled every camp prisoner with unutterable horror, and every one of them would rather be dead than find himself within its doors.

The Bunker was a massive brick structure surrounded by a wall 3½ yards high. The building consisted of various cells, each fitted out according to the purpose for which it was designed. There were regular cells for the so-called prominent prisoners, who were kept there in solitary confinement until they either grew amenable or died. There were the sweat boxes that were so small a man could just stand upright in them but could not turn around. In some of them there was pitch-black night; in others, only half darkness.

A prisoner beginning a Bunker sentence had to bring his bread ration for two days with him. The first three days he had to subsist on bread and water. Not until the fourth day was he brought some soup or coffee. A Bunker prisoner got no blanket and it was not advisable for him to sleep. For, day and night, he had to be prepared to see his cell door repeatedly opened without notice. Then he had to give an account of himself; that is, rattle off his number, block, offense and punishment and, if he was a Jew, he had to state that first of all. The report had to be made briskly and in the proper order. The resultant loss of sleep, combined with the tortures that took place in the special torture chambers, brought the prisoners into the desired frame of mind for questioning; for the chief purpose of the Bunker and its orgies was to extort confessions and information.

The mildest punishment that awaited a prisoner in the Bunker was called "across the horse." The victim of this was laid across a horse and received twenty-five to thirty blows with a stick, the SS men taking turns so that their strength would be fresh; sometimes the blows were administered with a rawhide whip. A victim might be subjected to this punishment for several days in succession. Few survived that.

Another favorite punishment was "hanging" or "tying to the post." The victim was bound with cords, hoisted up on a kind of gallows and left to hang in the air for several hours. A man might be hung up by the hands, feet, arms, back or stomach. The manner and duration of the hanging determined which limbs would be injured and which dislocated.

A prisoner who was sentenced to Bunker punishment more than twice was assigned to the punishment squad, where, in the literal sense of the words, he was worked to death. This process in many cases took only a few weeks, for the punishment squad had to perform the heaviest labor under the most horrible conditions. But since the Bunker was always crowded to capacity, the punishment squad was never at a loss for replacements.

Although the prisoners in the Bunker knew that they would be still more cruelly beaten if they cried out under the tortures, the Bunker often rang with screams. In that winter of 1939–1940, whenever I was employed chopping ice or shoveling snow in the Bunker yard, I thought that the screams, which seemed not only to re-echo from the walls but to permeate the very air, would drive me out of my mind. The comrades of Block 37, which stood nearest to the Bunker, told us that they were often wakened at night by the despairing human sounds that came from it.

Opposite the main entrance to the concentration camp, separated from it only by a street about 6 yards wide, was a section which was destined to become one of the most important Gestapo centers of the Reich. Within this area of about 2000 yards long by 1000 yards wide were to be trained the various Gestapo reserves which were intended for service in eastern Germany and in the occupied territories in the East. Among the buildings planned for this area were barracks which would house several SS regiments, with the corresponding domestic services, a huge canteen, a clubhouse with its own theater, administrative buildings and living quarters for the permanent service and administrative personnel.

The two short sides of the Gestapo district formed right angles with the highroad which cut through the town of Oranienburg and thence led to the east. The two long sides ran parallel to the highroad on one side and to the camp on the other side, but the rectangle thus formed extended beyond the camp and far into the town of Oranienburg. Where city and Gestapo settlement met, a big square was to be laid out to serve as the approach to the Gestapo area.

When I went to work in the Gestapo area for the first time, the main administration building was almost finished. It was a stone structure several stories high, with a façade about 100 yards wide. Millions of building stones were lying around on the site; they were piled in heaps about 15 yards high: fine-quality baked bricks, pressed bricks and broken bricks, all mixed together. Our work consisted in sorting the different kinds of bricks into separate heaps. For this purpose, of course, we had to climb up the mountains of bricks, Then we formed a chain, reaching from the top to the bottom. The bricks were lifted up by the worker at the top and passed from man to man until they arrived at the bottom; and when the last worker had accumulated six or seven he dumped them on the appropriate pile.

To keep one's balance on the loosely heaped bricks, which kept giving way, required a skill that we did not possess. Since we were weak as well as unskilled, the labor on the shifting, sliding bricks was attended with constant danger of death. On the days when the foremen drove us particularly hard, there were always a few who lost their balance and fell headfirst to the bottom, where they were left either dead or seriously injured. Anyone who survived such a fall was usually a cripple for life.

Often, when we were ordered to work at the building site and there were no stones to sort, we were made to shift the already sorted stones from one place to another for no other purpose than to make us perform this back-breaking task. Sometimes when the big trucks arrived with the bricks that were baked in the Klinker works, we had to form a chain, unload the bricks from the truck and dump them on a pile of mixed bricks just in order to sort them out again later. Sometimes, for the sake of variety, they ordered us to transport the fixtures for the drainage system, or used us for other haulage jobs. Everything that had to be transported and would have required dumping trucks, cranes and pulleys, we hauled.

The task of removing and disposing of the excavated soil was almost exclusively the work of the punishment squad. But we were employed on it a few times in the early spring. The excavated soil was carried off in hods by prisoners. Although we worked at top speed, the removal took much more time than the excavation itself. Finally the camp authorities were forced to add a fleet of dumping trucks, which carried off the excavated earth as fast as it was dug out.

Among the Gestapo's spring plans for Sachsenhausen was the transfer to the occupied territories of about one thousand prisoners who were to form the nucleus of projected concentration camps there. They were to furnish not only room seniors but seniors in every division of the new camps and to instruct the foremen in concentration-camp techniques. For this office the camp authorities chose about four hundred of the notorious Danzig criminals. (Among them was our Rolly. The remaining six hundred men were selected from the hardened criminals.)

At morning roll call the day after the group was sent off, all the Polish blocks were ordered to stay in barracks. Our excited imaginations at once began to look for explanations. Surely the deportation of the Polish contingent was imminent. Anton had made it quite clear that it had only been postponed. We spent the morning in suspense and uncertainty until about ten o'clock, when a horde of blockfuehrers appeared and ordered us to march to the assembly place double quick. We had only one reason for doubt left: the blockfuehrers had not ordered us to put on our working clothes, and we clung to the hope that they would not send us on the long journey without them.

On the assembly place we were met by a cutting wind that seemed to blow from all points of the compass at once. The square was quite empty, and with all this unaccustomed free space around us and being unable to move freely ourselves, we felt somehow still more forlorn and lost. Soon the square began to swarm with blockfuehrers, but they paid no attention to us, only marched briskly up and down to keep warm. We noticed that their eyes kept turning to the gate of the Kommandantur.

The solution of the riddle came very soon. A group of five SS officers and five civilians appeared at the gate. The blockfuehrers ran toward them and the group came up to us. I was completely bewildered: I was prepared for blockfuehrers, the Kommandant, SS, Gestapo—but not for civilians. And suddenly a thrill went through me. Were we all going to be released?

But my illusion instantly melted away. When the group reached us, we were ordered to space out so as to make a path between the rows. Then the commission went down our ranks. "Head up," "Head down," "About face," they ordered and studied our faces, our profiles, the backs of our heads. Only then did we notice that the civilians had cameras with them.

About seventy of us, who had passed the inspection, were ordered to stand aside, questioned individually and then photographed, singly and in groups, in all kinds of grotesque attitudes. At the end a group photograph of all of us was taken. We were aware, of course, that these pictures would be used for some shameless propaganda purpose, but that did not trouble us much. The main thing was that our fear of being deported had not been realized.

The next day work was resumed, and the Polish blocks were required to furnish two squads of 100 men each. We had to carry bricks from the building site of the Gestapo settlement to the Gaertnerei and the Isolation District. The trip from the camp to the building site and back took about three quarters of an hour. The load we carried weighed about 40 pounds. It took us all day to carry about 10,000 bricks to the camp—with a wagon, 20 men could have done the same job in half the time.

We had to stand in two rows of 100 men each in front of the heap of bricks, from which a chain of other prisoners passed the bricks down to us. The last in the chain threw the bricks into our hands, which we had to hold pressed together in front of our bodies, and he purposely threw them with so much force at the stomach or abdomen that many men shrieked with pain, and those who were hit particularly hard collapsed.

When we caught the bricks we had to stand with our burden until the last man in the row of 100 got his brick and the whole squad could be led, under guard, down the street that connected the settlement with the camp. So those in the squad who were loaded first were in an especially deplorable situation. Had they allowed us to wear gloves for the work, to protect our chapped, frozen hands—but the camp authorities forbade us to wear gloves, as the sharp stones would ruin them.

In the Gaertnerei section men were working feverishly to set up new greenhouses. In the Isolation District too, the foundations of new buildings were being laid and other puzzling preparations were under way. All the barracks, even the storehouses, were evacuated; only our blocks and a barrack of German Jews were left.

Of course, we immediately suspected that a move on the grand scale was being planned. All kinds of rumors went around camp, including a persistent one that 100,000 Jews from the occupied territories were to be shipped in. That gave us another occasion for gloomy speculations. If the Isolation District was being evacuated to make room, why were we left there? And why had the Gestapo given up the plan of transferring us to Poland? Perhaps they had reflected that they could clear out our barracks faster by simply killing us off.

In the meantime new shiploads of prisoners actually were arriving, including a contingent of Czech students. But they were not taken to the Isolation District, and we kept on speculating for whom all this space was being prepared.

On April 1, two thousand men were marched to work in the Klinker. We were among them. Our first task was to unload the ships that were waiting in the Oranienburg Canal with a cargo of bricks and rubble destined for the harbor bed. Some of us worked in the hold of the ship, which was seven yards deep, and had to shovel up the contents onto several temporary platforms. From the side of the ship a sloping plank led down directly to the bed of the harbor, and across the plank, parallel with the ground, ran neck-breaking wooden platforms. There the rest of us stood and shoveled the rubble and bricks in stages to the bottom.

The comrades on the uppermost platform in the hold of the ship, who shoveled their loads overboard, could not see what was going on beyond the sloping plank. So the loads of rubble and stone that they tossed up often landed on our heads and knocked us to the bottom. Since all ships had to be unloaded and sail back on the day of their arrival, we worked feverishly, and no one could stop to attend to his injured neighbors. Guards kept watch in the harbor as well as in the hold of the ship and were inclined to interpret every unauthorized movement as an attempt to jump overboard and escape by swimming.

When the whistle summoned us to roll call, we threw down our shovels with relief. This first day went far beyond our strength, and we knew that still worse was before us. How would it be when the weather grew warm and thirst was added to all our other hardships?

Our legs would scarcely carry us. Almost crawling, we reached the assembly place. The counting-off roll call had to wait until all two thousand men had arrived. The Oberfuehrer, who had charge of the Klinker, took a notion to while away the time with jokes. First he eyed our group in silence; then he shook his head as if he were concerned about our condition and at last he ordered all those who felt too weak for marching to step forward. About twenty-five men accepted the invitation. For a moment I too felt tempted to report myself, but something in his glance kept me back.

The Oberfuehrer watched silently as one invalid after another detached himself from the labor squad to step aside. When no more came forward, he took his stand in front of the miserable group and ordered "March!" There it was again, the usual trap, in which we had let ourselves be caught once more. The group of weak and injured men moved forward with dragging step.

"March, I said," shouted the Oberfuehrer, and began raining blows on them with his truncheon. His comrades joined in. About half of those who were struck fell like mown grain. The rest summoned up their last strength and began to run, to escape more blows. With a few long strides the blockfuehrers overtook them.

"The cheats are wonderful at leg work; they run like weasels," and they beat the men unmercifully for the attempted "swindle." After the counting off, the prostrate victims were gathered up and shoved into a truck that was driving back to camp with a load of rubbish. The next morning ten of them were dead.

The second day in the Klinker the ships brought cement instead of rubble and bricks, and it had to be carried into the interior of the main workshop. To my astonishment I discovered that this structure was nothing but a huge hall. The walls, which had formerly partitioned it, had been torn out, and the room scaffolding strengthened with lengthwise and crosswise beams. All signs indicated that preparations were being made there to build objects of huge dimensions.

The cement was packed in sacks that weighed fifty kilograms. At first the order went that two men were to transport each sack on a barrow. But when we began the unloading, the foremen took our barrows away and each of us had to shoulder one sack alone. Our backs were not equal to this burden and we collapsed under it. The sacks fell from our shoulders and many burst; the valuable contents were spilled. That was sabotage, and those whom this misfortune befell never rose again.

At the evening counting off the Oberfuehrer tried to repeat his joke of the day before. But this time we were forewarned, and no one reported himself as too weak. That was the cue he had been waiting for. "If you're really so fit, we needn't coddle you so much tomorrow; we can really take you in hand," he said, after he had waited awhile in vain. And we knew that this was no idle talk. Dread of the coming day clutched our hearts and made us suffer mental torture even before the physical began.

The next morning, April 3, as we marched to roll call on the assembly place, we saw at once that about three times as many workers as usual had reported for Klinker work. Probably an unusually large number of ships had arrived. As on the two previous days we took our places on the outer side of the formation. When the counting off began and 4500 men had been counted, it developed that there were not enough guards for the rest. The outermost part of the flank, where I and my comrades were, was therefore detached and ordered back to barracks, where we were to hold ourselves ready for work inside the camp.

Anton went off immediately to look for a suitable substitute, and in a few minutes he had arranged everything. We were assigned to the brick carrying: the familiar hardships began. But everything in life is relative. When we thought of what our comrades in the Klinker had to go through, the brick carrying struck us as play.

We had just started on our second trip to the Gestapo settlement, when I suddenly heard my name called. At first it seemed to me that I had only imagined it. But my comrades had heard it too, for a whispering began around me. "There it is," "Release," "Free," I heard them whisper. Then I also took it seriously. At the same moment a comrade from the indoor squad and a runner stopped in front of me; the runner had a slip in his hand. "Quick, to the Political Division," he cried.

My pulses began to hammer wildly. It was true, then. This was the longed-for moment.

"Quick, to the Political Division," repeated the runner impatiently and urged me to follow him.

Then inexpressible horror went through me. "To the Political Division," he had said! What an optimistic fool I was, to be sure. Releases were never handled from the Political Division—how could I have forgotten that! To be summoned to the Political Division meant no good. Probably they would cross-examine me, torture me.

"What can they want to learn from me?" I wondered, as I followed the runner, and sought in my mind any possible cause. Suddenly I had it! Gucia's library. Probably they had searched our apartment and found all the contraband. Gucia in her passion for books had collected in a special section all the works that the Nazis had burned.

How was I to explain this subversive collection? As my feet mechanically moved forward, my mind was working. Suddenly I had the answer: it was so simple, after all. Gucia had done nothing illegal. We, as foreigners, had not been obliged to get rid of the books forbidden to Germans, and besides, Gucia, as a prospective journalist, had an understandable professional interest in the political contents of those works.

We had reached the gate of the Kommandantur. The runner presented the slip with the summons from the Political Division, and we were allowed to pass. In front of the Political Division stood about 150 prisoners, all summoned here for some kind of hearing. Their faces reflected the panic that reigned within them. And as I took my place among them, my calm threatened to desert me. But I began to give myself good advice: "Whatever they ask you, think before you answer, speak slowly, and don't let yourself be rattled. Yes, and above all, don't forget the prescribed report. 'The prisoner, Jew, No. 9335, Block 38, Wing A, reports himself present,' " I began to recite to myself, over and over. The automatic repetition of the words calmed me.

Then I heard my name and number called. I gave myself a last shake, dragged at my feet, which only with difficulty left the ground. At the entrance to the barrack of the Political Division a blockfuehrer stood and waited for me. I ran forward.

"The prisoner, Jew, No. 9335, Block 38, Wing A, reports himself present." But the blockfuehrer paid no attention to my report. He turned around and went inside. I stood there uncertainly. What was I supposed to do? Then the blockfuehrer turned around.

"Come with me," he said and went down a corridor into a room. I followed. "Wait here till you are called," and he closed the door. I waited. What was I waiting for? I strained my ears. But all was still, uncannily still for this place of horrors.

Then the door opened. The same blockfuehrer ordered me out into the corridor, pointed to the opposite door, on which was written "Political Director."

"Go in there," he ordered.

I went up to the door. My heart seemed to have stopped. Mechanically I opened the door. "The report," went through my head; "make a correct report." I stepped over the threshold, opened my mouth. But a hallucination rose before me and took my voice away. There in the middle of the room stood Gucia, my daughter. I blinked my eyes. Dear God, what tricks my imagination was playing! Now of all times, when I needed all my presence of mind.

I must pull myself together. This was the office of the Political Director. I must make my report: The prisoner, Jew . . . I knew exactly how it went. But I could not bring it out. My eyes hung spellbound on the apparition, which suddenly came toward me and began to speak.

"Good morning, Papa," said the voice. "I have come to bring you good news."

This was no illusion. This was my daughter in flesh and blood. I did not believe my eyes or ears. I had been prepared, first for release, then for cross-examination and blows. But to see my daughter in Sachsenhausen! That I had never even let myself dream.

How had she ever gotten here? How could she ever pass all the guards? How could she be so calm and controlled? She was actually smiling. It was unbelievable!

Then I realized for the first time that the Political Director was standing at the desk, and that in spite of all my good resolutions I had forgotten to report, and that was a capital offense. Now he would jump at me and go to work with his truncheon. And Gucia would have to look on.

But nothing of the sort happened. "Come nearer," said the Political Director, and his voice sounded calm and even human. All this was beyond my powers of comprehension. I moved my feet forward; I opened my mouth again to say something. But my voice still refused to come. Then Gucia came up to me and held out her hand. How gladly I would have taken it and pressed it! But my arm was paralyzed.

Gucia did not allow herself to be upset. She took my head in both hands, kissed me on both cheeks and said in a calm and cheerful voice: "You know, of course, Papa, that we are planning to sail for Shanghai on April 11. I have to settle some formalities first, and for that I need your power of attorney. So, to save time, I applied for permission to come and get your signature personally."

Gucia paused. I understood that now it was my turn to say something. But I could not bring out a word. For months I had longed to see my daughter, had dreamed of this moment. And now that she was standing before me, I could not even say one miserable word of joy. It seemed so unbearable that Gucia should see me in this dreadful condition, like a skeleton, with beaten and swollen face, with close-shaven head, with several days' stubble of beard and the grotesque uniform. Must she not shrink from me, be revolted by me?

But Gucia gave no sign of shock or surprise. "Look, Papa," she continued as calmly as before, and took some documents from the desk of the Political Director. "Here is the confirmation from the Lloyd Triestino Line of our reservations on the ship, and here is the receipt for our dollar deposit for Shanghai. I brought them to show you that everything I wrote you has a solid basis. And here is the power of attorney that you must sign, so that I can represent you at the Finanzamt and get a tax clearance certificate as the last necessary step for your release. When you have signed it, your signature will be certified here at once, and I can finish everything in the afternoon."

She gave me the papers to read. "Is it all clear to you? And do you agree to the power of attorney?"

Of course everything was clear. And of course I agreed to everything that Gucia was doing. But with the best will in the world I could not say so.

But Gucia would not give up trying to get me to speak. She opened her handbag, took out a big bar of chocolate. "Here is a little surprise for you. You like chocolate, don't you? And what's more I've brought you greetings from all your friends. They are looking forward to seeing you soon."

It was too much for me. I would have liked to cry out for joy, for anguish, and tears of helplessness came into my eyes because I could not cry out what was within me. But tears were dangerous. What if they made Gucia weep too? This was no place for outbursts of feeling.

But Gucia's control was not to be shaken. She took out of her pocket a big man's handkerchief, handed it to me. "Here, Papa," she said, as if it were a quite ordinary thing. "And now sign the power of attorney."

I took the handkerchief from Gucia's hand, but I could not wipe my eyes. I felt the drops from my nose run over my lips and drip on my uniform. But it did not matter. The Political Director was watching the whole proceeding calmly, and now he handed me his own fountain pen. "Here, Papa," said Gucia, and pointed to the place where I must sign.

I hesitated a moment. Until then I had carefully avoided showing my hands: at least Gucia should not see how swollen and inflamed they were. But Gucia took no notice at all of my bloody hands, only showed me matter-of-factly where I had to sign. I was very glad, but at the same time I was bewildered. Here was I, a grown man, always energetic and strong-willed, and in this situation I had failed completely. And here was my daughter, young, sensitive, inexperienced—and completely in command of the situation. She had not blinked an eyelash when she saw me in this unexpected condition; she had shed no tears, while my tears flowed uncontrollably. Her voice sounded firm and calm. There was a smile on her lips. Was she not shocked by what she had seen and experienced? What was this girl made of?

Gucia's patience seemed limitless. She had not yet given up the effort to get a few words out of me. "I have brought you a warm pullover," she said, "and the Political Director says you may take it with you." I looked at the Political Director incredulously. He nodded.

"You may take it," he said, "and put the chocolate away carefully, so you won't lose it."

I was overcome. How could all this be possible? What wires had Gucia pulled to accomplish this? How could it be that one of Hitler's elite butchers, with the death's head on his uniform, suddenly spoke so calmly and humanly?

Then Gucia saw that it was no use trying to get me to speak. "Well, Papa, now you know the most important thing, and you can depend on me. Keep well, and think how soon our old wish will come true. We always wanted to go to China. If you have something important on your mind, tell me quickly. Otherwise, good-bye."

"You may go," said the Political Director.

Then it came home to me that I must have frightened Gucia dreadfully. Surely she thought I had lost my power of speech. I must not leave her in that fear. I must say something, never mind what, at least a word. I took a deep breath, once and again. It was a great effort, but finally I got it out: "Good-bye and greet everyone for me."

A few minutes later I rejoined the group outside, and we waited for a runner to take us back to barracks. And now for the first time I realized fully what an unprecedented thing had happened. I, a prisoner from the Isolation District, an outcast from humanity, a man condemned to death, had just spoken with my daughter. Such a thing had never happened since concentration camps had existed.

All at once I felt helpless and miserable. What a pity that I had not made better use of my opportunity to talk with Gucia; now it was too late. But little by little the cool air revived me. It suddenly dawned on me that my release was actually imminent. I drew a deep breath. The anticipation of freedom filled me with a piercing happiness that almost made me cry.

What would my comrades say when I told them what had happened? Would they believe me at all? I felt for the bar of chocolate, the handkerchief and the pullover, which I had hidden in my coat. Here were the proofs. Who would dare to doubt after this?

And what a sensation my story would create. I began to think how I could use my experience for the greatest benefit of my comrades. Here was a Heaven-sent opportunity to raise their spirits, to give them new hope. If Gucia had succeeded in getting permission to see me, there must be some sort of relaxation in the regime. It meant that our future was not so black, that all of us might be released. I would believe it with all my heart, so that I could make my comrades believe it.

While my thoughts were taken up with my comrades, my eyes were fixed on the entrance to the Political Division. Gucia would have to come out that way; perhaps I would see her again. After a while she did come out, accompanied by a guard. Both went down the street past us and disappeared into a neighboring barrack. My heart beat a tattoo. I hoped that Gucia would look in my direction and that I could make a sign to her. But Gucia's eyes were fixed firmly on the ground, and I understood that she was doing so in order not to create any sensation.

An excited whisper went through the rows of waiting prisoners. I stole a glance around me. All eyes were turned toward Gucia. The prisoners who were at work on the pavement and had to stop to let Gucia and the guard pass resumed their work. But in typical concentration-camp fashion their eyes followed Gucia. It was so unprecedented to see a civilian in the camp and a woman at that! I had to hold on to myself to keep from whispering proudly: "Look, that's my daughter; I've just talked with her."

After a while Gucia and the guard returned. I saw plainly that she held a Polish passport in her hand, and I immediately began to put two and two together. Probably she needed it to get my exit visa. My eyes followed Gucia until she went around the corner and out of my sight, and for a long time my companions and I kept our gaze fixed on the spot where this unhoped-for apparition from a free world had disappeared.

It was about two hours before all the waiting men had been questioned and dismissed, and I was glad of it. It gave me a chance to regain my equilibrium. I had time to think and to decide exactly what and how I was to tell my comrades.

When I entered my barrack it was almost time for the noon roll call. Max met me at the door. He saw at once by my expression that something out of the ordinary had happened. "You look so excited, man; what's the matter with you?"

Instead of answering, I pulled out of my pocket the chocolate, handkerchief and pullover and held them under his nose.

Max screwed up his eyes to see better. *"Donnerwetter,* man, where did you get these, what kind of things are they?"

I was enjoying the situation. "They are very good things, and if you knew where and how I got them, you would open your eyes," I said mysteriously.

Max gasped, his face went red and the veins stood out on his temples, a sure sign that he was seething inside. "Don't make a song and dance about it," he screamed at me in a cracking voice. "Speak up and tell me what happened."

I would have liked to keep him in suspense, but his expression warned me that he wasn't a good person to fool with at the moment. "I have talked with my daughter in the Political Director's office." I said, as calmly as I could, "and she brought me all these things."

"What!" shouted Max, as if a tarantula had bitten him. "You talked with your daughter! That's absolutely impossible."

Max's shouting had attracted the indoor squad and a babel of voices assailed me.

"I never heard of such a thing."

"Just look what he's got."

"Incredible!"

"You must tell us all about it at once."

Suddenly I had become the center of attention. Everyone wanted to take me aside and question me. But I refused to speak until all the comrades were there. And Max seemed suddenly so impressed with my importance that he dared not use threats to make me speak.

A few minutes later Anton came back from some errand and was immediately informed of what had happened. He did not believe his ears and came to hear the news from me in person. When I had confirmed the story, he made me hand over the sweater.

"This'll be sent to the clothing room right away. Jews aren't allowed to wear warm clothes here."

"But the Political Director gave me permission," I protested.

"Can you give it to me in writing?" yelled Anton. "The sweater will be handed over; the moths have to eat too, don't they?"

I gritted my teeth, and said nothing more.

By now it was time to go out to roll call. When we came back, the food was distributed in haste, so that there would be time to hear some of my story before work began. At that meal I got so much to eat that I could not dispose of it all. Even from Wing B the food distributor came and brought me a sandwich such as I had never seen all the time I had been imprisoned. Pieces of bread were thrust at me from all sides.

When I began my story at last, there was dead silence. As I described my experience, from the moment the runner summoned me to the moment when Gucia vanished from my sight, I could feel that every man was holding his breath. Of course, I put both poetry and truth into my story. I had determined to forge my experience into new courage and spirit for the others. So I told them I had gathered from Gucia's words that the Berlin Jewish Community had undertaken very important steps on our behalf and that releases would begin again in the near future.

I saw the fire of hope begin to flicker again in the dull eyes around me. My comrades listened to my words as quietly as children hearing some marvelous tale, and they could not hear enough. When the recess was over and we had to go back to work, they embraced me and would have liked to give me an ovation, so happy and hopeful had my story made them. Even on Max it had made a great impression; he shook my hand and promised to let me have more to eat during the next few days and to see that I was not sent to the Klinker, since I was still very weak and needed to recover more before my release. But this gesture of friendship lasted only thirty-six hours.

My story spread like wildfire. Terrific excitement prevailed not only in the other two Polish blocks but in the whole camp. Everyone waited feverishly for evening, when they could hear more. I had become a sensation.

In the evening my comrades from the Klinker came back in a pitiable condition and with an unusually large number of seriously injured. But when they learned what had happened while they were gone, even their eyes lighted up. They took new courage and were full of confidence that at least those who could survive the Klinker would see freedom again.

After evening roll call, emissaries from the other blocks arrived. I had to repeat my story. And so it went on for days and weeks. My comrades could never get enough of it. And I told the story untiringly, over and over. In this way I kept up their failing spirits until my release.

Max gave me the "friendly advice" to hand over my chocolate bar to him, so that he in turn could put it at the disposal of Anton and the assistant. "That will get you a good mark with Anton and it will be sure to make things easier for you," he explained.

This advice did not please me at all. Not that I so much minded parting with the chocolate itself, but I minded parting with it simply and solely because it was a thing that Gucia had brought me, and I had already lost the pullover.

But I realized, of course, that such sentimental considerations were a luxury. "Do as you like with it," I said to Max, as I gave him the chocolate, and I tried to look indifferent. Perhaps I really would buy some peace with it. It soon appeared, however, that Anton and the assistant had only gotten a nibble at the chocolate; the principal beneficiary was Max himself. No sooner was the chocolate consumed than Max's sudden friendship for me vanished. Two days after the great event I had to go back to work in the Klinker.

My chances of coming uninjured out of the camp had diminished once more. What steps could I take to lessen the dangers of the Klinker? During the march to work, I weighed the situation. There was only one chance of safety: that I could manage always to work in the same squad and familiarize myself with the conditions, instead of constantly facing new problems. And I decided to look about me and see which squad was the best from my point of view.

The first day I was assigned to a mixed squad of Jews and non-Jews, who had to heap up clay and carry it to the harbor bed. The loads were very heavy, and running back and forth in quick time was beyond my strength; I knew that I could not stick it out there.

During the first days of this work period, before the numbers of the prisoners in each squad were noted down, a prisoner could change from one squad to another, with a little slyness and caution. So I joined a different squad each day, to see what went on there. But I only went from the frying pan into the fire. There was only one squad in the Klinker where the work was actually pleasant; that was the wood-gathering and wood-sorting squad, but Polish Jews could not aspire to it.

The work itself would perhaps have been bearable everywhere, if the foremen had been more human. But the foremen in the Klinker was even more ruthless slave drivers than those in the camp itself. Three of them in particular were dangerous criminals, before whom not only the prisoners but the other foremen shuddered. All three were among the oldest inmates, and all three had nicknames, handed down from one prisoner generation to another.

The first was named Piefke. He was the superintendent of the construction office, a skilled technician and a real glutton for work. Even Anton used to say of him: "He's so full of strength he's like to bust." Piefke was of middle height, but thickset and sturdy. He could work for hours without stopping to catch his breath; but when he did suddenly stop, a shiver went through all who saw him coming. Piefke set a standard that no one could come up to. So at every inspection several prisoners were picked out and punished for slowness and laziness. He made them go through the whole regimen of exercise—falling down, rolling, running up or rolling down sand hills, and if he was in good spirits, he ended by transferring one or two of them to the punishment squad. This was Piefke's way of refreshing himself in the intervals of work, and it brought him the distinction of being the best-hated of all the prisoners.

The second criminal in the gang was called Schmidt. The shoveling, dredging and hauling-car squads were under his supervision. In addition, he meddled with all the other squads. He had three nicknames: Hauling-car Czar, Ivan the Terrible and the Beast.

Ivan the Terrible was a great expert in his field. We might have admired him for his efficiency, if we had not feared him so. The Beast was mad about speed and he did not care how many victims it cost to set and keep the pace. Since it was his habit to steal up on the workers unnoticed, no one dared to slacken speed even for a moment. When we suddenly saw him in front of us, our hands and feet went like motors. As a result, the Beast's squad was known as the speediest in the whole camp, but also as the one with the greatest turnover in human lives.

The third in the gang was named Cuckoo, because of his shrill, monotonous voice. He supervised the roller squad and was also an expert in his field. Whoever made a mistake could expect no mercy from him, but sometimes even good work brought disaster. We were all convinced that Cuckoo was not quite normal. Often, without any reason, he went into a frenzy; then he would begin to run up and down beside the roller squad and belabor our heads, hands and backs with the truncheon that was never out of his hand. The strange thing was that he attacked us when we were working best. We frequently made up our minds, when we saw the wild glimmer in Cuckoo's eye, to pull slowly—that actually seemed to soothe him. But if the supervising SS appeared at such a moment, and they usually did, they gave us the clubbing we had escaped from Cuckoo.

Nevertheless I decided, once I had worked in the roller squad, to stake everything on staying there. True, the roller squad was notoriously one of the hardest in camp. The roller was the heaviest of its kind, about five feet in diameter and over six feet long: to pull it required an incredible exertion of strength. But at least one did not have to run back and forth, which I was no longer nimble enough to do. Moreover, in the roller squad one could be perfectly sure of not being transferred to another squad, not even when many ships arrived and additional workers were needed. For the roller squad consisted of only thirty men, and the workers must form an ensemble, to pull in time, so to speak. Starting the roller, in particular, required the closest cooperation. Cuckoo knew that perfectly and held on to his men.

The roller work was of two kinds. Usually we had to pull it over the bed of the harbor, in order to pack it down firmly. To either end of the roller was hooked a hemp rope of an arm's thickness. At intervals of every two yards were fastened wooden rods, to each of which two men yoked themselves, and pulled. Often, however, the roller had to operate on sloping ground, such as the sides of the harbor. Then two piston devices that worked on cogwheels were set up on the edge of the harbor, and we had to wind or unwind wire ropes, according to whether the roller was to go up or down.

I came under the protection, as it were, of a comrade in the roller squad who had ingratiated himself with Cuckoo, and only by constant bribing with my daily cigarette—a ration which we had been receiving since the first of April—and sometimes with my bread ration, could I stay there till my release. "Hey, you, I can't use such a crock here. I need muscles," Cuckoo had said when he first saw me; and if my comrade, who happened to hear it, had not given him to understand that I was the source of the extra cigarettes, he would have thrown me out. Of course, once Cuckoo realized how much I wanted to stay in his squad, he tried to exploit me more and more. During the last few days I gave up all my bread to him and lived entirely on soup. One day he served me an ultimatum to bring him three cigarettes the next day or—get out.

It soon became clear to all the prisoners who worked in the Klinker that the military importance of the Oranienburg zone was steadily growing. In April a rumor arose that the three thousand Klinker workers were in the future to be housed on the site. As if to confirm this, machine-gun turrets were set up around the area. Later it occurred to me why Hitler had placed the concentration camp where it was: it diverted public attention from the war-industry center that had grown up in Oranienburg since 1933, as well as from the SS and military settlement.

The days in the Klinker that followed seemed worse than everything I had gone through before. But it was as if a protecting power watched over me: blows which would once have felled me I endured and still lived. The ninth of April came: that was my birthday. And I had somehow taken it into my head that I would be released that day. It was the last day I could catch the boat which left Trieste on April 11.

But I waited in vain for the runner. Nevertheless, my hope would not die. Gucia had hinted that my departure might be postponed for a month, in case she did not succeed in arranging the formalities in time, and I had a glowing faith in her words. We would take the next boat, then.

It was only when we returned from the Klinker that evening and learned that Germany had occupied Norway and Denmark that my confidence sank. Wouldn't this tilt the balance of Italian neutrality toward Germany? But if Italy declared war on the Allies, the sea route to China would be cut off.

As always after events of political importance, the claws of the blockfuehrers made themselves felt in our blocks. The next morning they appeared in large numbers at roll call and gave us a history lesson. "The English," so they said, "at the instigation of the Jewish-plutocratic International, intended to occupy unsuspecting Norway and Denmark, as a springboard for an attack on Germany. But they have missed out. German military genius caught them napping." Then, as if in school, they examined us to see if we had grasped the lesson.

"Why did England intend to attack Norway and Denmark?"
"Who had put this perfidious idea into their heads?"
"How did German military genius react?"

We were called out individually and questioned, and if the answer came too slowly or with evident reluctance, the pupil was beaten up.

In the Klinker during the next two days the same thing went on. The curve of the dead and injured rose incredibly. I got through the first day without incident. But the second day my equilibrium was shattered. It was April 11, the day on which the ship that was to have taken me to freedom left Europe. The spectre of a blockaded Suez Canal rose before my eyes.

Shortly before the end of work a terrific weakness came over me. I was shoveling clay with a big shovel; with every heave the shovel seemed to grow heavier. Suddenly it fell from my hand; I stooped to pick it up. But a foreman, who had come up unnoticed, snatched it from me. I saw him raise it and felt that he was aiming for my head. A prisoner was never allowed to defend himself when he was beaten, but when I saw the shovel whizzing down upon me, panic seized me. I was afraid it would split my skull, and in terror I clapped both hands to my head. The blow struck my hands, which were already badly swollen and full of wounds. It was so heavy that it literally stunned me. In the first moment I felt no pain. Then I felt the blood trickling down both wrists into my sleeves, and shuddered. I wanted to move my hands and could not—it was as if the blow had broken all ten fingers.

"Better the fingers than the skull," I was telling myself as calmly as possible, when I noticed that the foreman was catching his breath in order to deliver another blow. I had a few seconds to prepare. I pressed my hands tightly against my head and my arms against my temples. I noticed that the comrades around me were going on with their shoveling without winking an eyelash. Only one had straightened up and thrown down his shovel; he looked as if he meant to spring on the foreman from behind. I grew hot with fright. He was my cousin: the brave boy, if only he would do nothing mad.

Until a few months before, my cousin and I had been unaware of each other's existence. He came from Lodz and had been arrested there at the outbreak of the war, as he had played a very active role in the Zionist organization "Poale Zion." After several weeks' detention he had been sent with other colleagues to Sachsenhausen and lodged in Wing B of my block. There we heard with astonishment that we had the same name, investigated the matter and found out that we were cousins. Since then we had become great friends.

The young man's control could never be shaken. He bore his fate calmly, without complaint. It was only when we met young women with children on the way back from the Klinker that his face darkened. He would set his teeth, and his voice would sound strange as he said: "The children will drive me mad." For he had left a wife and two small children in Lodz.

I saw the same hate flare up in his eyes now. I wanted to call out, to warn him, but I knew that if I did I might draw the foreman's attention to him. However, the foreman had stopped for breath a moment too long. The "cease work," signal sounded before he had raised his arm for another blow, and fear and danger were over.

It was only then that I felt the pain in my hands. When our soup was distributed after the evening roll call, I could hardly hold my spoon. But in my heart another pain was burning. I dreaded the mockery of the malicious. What would they say to it that just on this particular day I had been so bloodily maltreated? But they acted as if they did not notice that my hands were a bloody mess. No one let fall a mocking remark.

But in the evening, when I came back from the toilet, I saw several men clustered together singing. As I passed, one of them stood up, looked at me challengingly and sang to a familiar tune:

> The ship for Shanghai leaves this minute,
> And Szalet—Szalet is not in it.

The blood rushed to my head. This mental cruelty hit me harder than the blow of the foreman's spade. For a fraction of a second I felt as if I would faint, then a great rage filled me. I gripped the singer by the throat, and I don't know what would have happened if the comrades had not separated us.

But the incident soon spread around. The majority of the comrades were indignant. Shortly before we went to sleep my cousin stole in to find out how I was getting on after the disaster in the Klinker; we could not talk much but his sympathy did me good.

A few days later, when we came back from the Klinker, Anton and the other room seniors of the Polish blocks met us at the gate. They ordered us to take our places on the far left of the assembly square where our comrades were already collected. In stolen whispers our comrades explained this unprecedented order. Early in the morning our barracks had been evacuated and the comrades left behind had to move into new ones near the Industriehof. A little later, loads of prisoners began to stream into the camp. They were all Poles, most of them farmers, and there were even large landowners among them. That was why the Isolation District had been evacuated and additional barracks set up there.

During the next few days the shipments of prisoners kept coming, until in all about six thousand Poles had been brought in. The Isolation District had been surrounded by a high wall, and extra guards had been posted outside it. We had had enough experience in concentration-camp methods to fear the worst; we knew that it was not for nothing that the Poles had been lodged in the immediate vicinity of the Bunker. Their hermetic seclusion meant that they were condemned.

We tried by every possible means to get news of them. It was said that a terrible regime prevailed among them, worse than in the punishment squad, that the Bunker was full of them, that there was a huge number of dead. But we could not learn any more. Once when I stayed behind in camp I volunteered for the squad that carried food to the Isolation District, hoping to learn something that way. But the District was sealed off: we had to put down the kettles on the threshold, as if there were lepers within, and when we had gone, the isolated victims took the kettles in. We never learned what secrets were hidden behind the wall. But we had no doubt the place was a slaughter chamber.

From the day of our transfer to the new barracks, we were promoted, so to speak, to a condition of semi-isolation. We took part in the roll calls on the big assembly place, but we had to stand, or rather lie, in the remotest corner of it. When the blockfuehrers came to roll call, they shouted from a distance: "Jew pack, lie down!" But this intended torment proved a boon. When we came in tired and beaten from the Klinker, it was an actual refreshment to be able to stretch out. During the march back we looked forward to it, and when the blockfuehrers did not give the order to lie down, we were bitterly disappointed.

Max realized that the lying down was a welcome relaxation and wanted to make us pay for it. He complained to Anton that we were dirtying the whole barrack with our clay-smeared boots and put through a rule that we must take off our shoes on entering. Now, when we went to the toilet, we literally had to wade in excrement and urine. And since we were not allowed to go to the washroom in the evening, we had to lie down in our filthy condition and befoul our straw sacks. Finally, Anton changed this order to a rule that everyone must brush his boots before entering the barrack.

With that, new troubles began. There were only five brushes for the whole barrack, and of course a furious struggle for them ensued. For whoever was not ready in time and could not enter the barrack got no evening meal. In this way we never had any peace. What the blockfuehrers did not do to us, Anton did, and if Anton missed an opportunity to harass us, Max took on the job.

Since we had been working in the Klinker, the three Polish blocks had been permitted to visit each other Saturday afternoons and Sundays. But on the following Sunday, Anton withdrew his permission. "Better rest up," he said with pretended solicitude. He and his assistant went off to see their friends right after the evening roll call, and he sent a prisoner to our block at intervals for a professional singer or dancer to entertain his gang. In this way he proved to his colleagues what an important person he was.

One day Anton got news that he had been divorced from his wife at her request. Thereupon he fell into a transport of fury and swore never to rest until he had "twisted the neck of that faithless bitch." In the meantime he took out his rage on us and suddenly decided to beat us on the naked body, as was done in the Bunker.

Anton's clique tried to imitate him. Max outdid the others, and I was his chosen prey. To him my unquenchable faith in release was like a red rag to a bull. And he wanted to do his part to destroy my hopes, because he was eaten up with envy.

In the meantime the Pessach holiday was approaching and its symbolical significance of liberation from slavery intensified my longing for freedom. I was growing impatient, for I had had no news from Gucia since her visit to the camp. But on the very first day of Pessach, an ordinary weekday, as we came back from the Klinker, a comrade of the indoor squad handed me a card. Of course, the indoor squad had already read the message, and before I had a chance to read it myself, they told me that Gucia had not been able to finish all the formalities before the departure of the ship and that we would certainly sail from Genoa on May 10.

From that day on Max persecuted me still more. My life was not safe, and when we marched off for the Klinker in the mornings I sighed with relief. By this time I was already working in the roller squad, and with my newly strengthened hope the work was not so hard for me. I was counting the days; I would have liked to count the hours. And my longing to make the time fly quicker led me to hit on a primitive way of reckoning time.

I had observed that during the morning's work the guards in the Klinker were changed twice and that between each change two hauling-car trains traveled back and forth. Since we began to work at about eight and stopped at twelve, it followed that the guards were changed every two hours and that a hauling-car train took an hour for the round trip. From then on I counted the trains to calculate what time it was. When the fourth morning train was at work, I knew that it would soon be twelve: half the day was almost over. When the fifth train was at work in the afternoon, it would soon be five and time to march back. This primitive time reckoning was soon adopted by the whole Klinker and made it easier for everyone to get through the hours.

Shortly after Pessach, another attempt at escape was made in the Klinker. The fugitive's disappearance was first noticed after the noon recess. Instantly all hell broke loose in the area. Salvos were fired into the air, which meant that we must instantly fall flat on our faces and lie that way until another signal came. Without knowing what had happened, we lay for half an hour, until whistles sounded and we had to run to the assembly place. The blockfuehrers counted us repeatedly, and after several hours of standing we were marched back to camp under a double guard.

Inside, blockfuehrers were running up and down. It was unusually long before the roll call began, and when it was over, we were not allowed to disperse. We waited, full of fear, we did not know for what. Suddenly a covered stretcher was brought and placed in the middle of the square. A microphone was set up. Several minutes later the Kommandant came out and went to the microphone. His speech was full of hate and blood-lust: the next man who tried to escape would be hanged, then shot and cut to pieces. The Kommandant announced, as a final threat, that next time all the members of a squad from which a prisoner escaped would be put into the punishment squad.

When he had finished his speech, he ordered the covering removed from the stretcher. "This is what will happen to all who try to escape," and he ordered us to file past what lay on the stretcher. The procession lasted about two hours. But what we saw remained fixed in our memories forever. On the stretcher lay no human form but a bloody mass of flesh in which neither face nor limbs were recognizable.

In his new unpredictable mood Anton hit upon the idea that we should learn marching songs. He appointed Professor D'Arguto as director, and arranged a repertory for us. The first practice for the two wings was held in our dormitory. Anton had put first on the program, not a march, but his favorite song, *"Guter Mond Du gehst so stille,"* which was also a favorite song of all back-street musicians. First we had to practice the words, and when we had learned them by heart, we at once began to sing the first verse, for most of us had heard the tune played by barrel-organs and remembered it vaguely.

Anton had brought a stool from the day room, squatted on it with his legs apart and listened with a satisfied expression. At first all went well. But when we began the second verse, Anton suddenly sprang up from his stool with a clatter and thundered: "Stop! Enough of this graveyard music. The creature's got no artistic sense, and he doesn't know anything about directing. And that thing calls itself a music professor." In vain the professor tried to explain to him that the song had a melancholy tune and must be sung slowly.

"Shut your mouth," Anton shouted. "I'm no music professor, but I understand my favorite song better than you do." Then he demonstrated the tempo and, to make matters worse, proceeded to direct the chorus himself.

It was a tragi-comic situation: Anton's voice, which sounded like a cracked pot, his ridiculous gesticulations, Professor D'Arguto's anguished expression, our shattered spirits and the trite melody, which with Anton's quickened tempo was still more unendurable. But we set our teeth and started all over again. This time Anton's artistic sense was satisfied.

Although it was almost May, the weather was still cool. During our work in the Klinker we had to take off our coats, but at morning roll calls we were still chilly. So it suited us very well that the distribution of summer uniforms did not begin till May 1, and that our turn came last.

The new uniforms were blue and white striped cotton coats and pants: we called them pajamas. In contrast to our winter outfits, which were a hodge-podge of patched police, military and prison uniforms, the summer pajamas had an actually uniform appearance. Anton & Co. made up their minds to pick out the newest and best-fitting garments and tried on several uniforms until they found the ones that looked best. As if that were not enough, they later ordered everyone who seemed to have a better-looking uniform to take it off and hand it over. Whoever refused was beaten into consent.

These scenes were in the highest degree humiliating. We could more readily understand it when Anton & Co. took extra food and other provileges. But in this place, where death stalked us constantly, to fight over a better-fitting coat was sheer insanity.

When we lined up in front of the barracks in our new outfits, the indoor squad, which always stood in the first row, looked so spick and span that the blockfuehrers noticed it as soon as they came in sight. "These parasites! In the Berlin East End they wore nothing but stinking rags and here they look like shop-window dummies!" Then they fell upon the "dressed-up dudes" and slugged them until breathless. But we felt no satisfaction, only a deep sense of shame.

It was the sixth of May, almost the last day that I could be released to catch the boat on May 10. When we got up in the morning I felt meaningful glances following my every step. But I pretended not to notice, quietly got ready, pocketed my toothbrush, which I had taken a notion to keep as a memento, and silently took my place in front of the barrack. Soon we would march to the assembly place, and perhaps that would be a step on the road to freedom.

A cool but glorious morning received us on the assembly place. Above us hung a shining azure curtain, flecked here and there with small dense white clouds. Clouds! How I loved them! As a boy I had spent innumerable hours lying on my back with my eyes fixed on the sky, following the clouds as they wandered, flocked together and dispersed again, as the sun edged them with silver and the wind whipped them about.

From the Gestapo settlement came the crowing of a cock, which we had heard every morning since we had taken part in the general roll call. And the coziness and peaceful home life that it conjured up filled me with deep melancholy. A yellow butterfly had wandered over to us. It fluttered to and fro in front of our ranks, giving itself up to the joy of motion and, giddy with its winged freedom, fluttered away again. It was the first butterfly that I had seen that year.

At the gate the Kommandant stood with his staff and reviewed our march. Since the last attempt at escape the guards had been strengthened; even the Lagerfuehrer accompanied us to the bridge that morning on his horse. All signs indicated that a black day was ahead.

I marched on the outer flank in perfect step. But blows struck me from all sides. At the place where the road to the Klinker branched off, a large building site had been marked out, where millions of bricks were piled up. Apparently stone structures were to be erected on the site. A group of masons from the first squad, which had marched out ahead of us, was already at work.

In the canal a long line of ships was waiting to be unloaded, and I considered myself lucky to be in the roller squad. Would Cuckoo let me stay there? Yesterday he had issued me an ultimatum—to get him more cigarettes or be fired. I had not been able to get them, and I had only one day before Cuckoo's deadline. He gave me a meaningful look which said: "Tomorrow is the day, and God help you if you have no cigarettes."

In the rest of the Klinker, as we had feared, the devil was loose all day. The blockfuehrers had arranged a race for the workers, and since the porters particularly could not keep up the mad pace, there were numerous victims, not only among us but among all the other workers. When we entered the barracks in the evening, most of the comrades were so exhausted that they dropped on their straw sacks without eating. Measured by the number of victims, that was the worst day since we had been sent to the Klinker.

The next morning it appeared that the number of dead had risen during the night. When we got up we found saveral men dead or dying. They were perishing from sheer weakness. Medical help, a little rest and nourishing food could have saved them, and we begged Anton to do something. But Anton brusquely ordered us to "put the whole bunch of stiffs in the washroom. I don't want to see any carcasses here when I come back," and went off to the office with his report book.

So we had to carry the dying into the washroom and lay them among those already dead. We trembled before the reproach and accusation in their glazing eyes. The washroom was always so full in the morning that we were constantly stepping on each other's feet, and in spite of all our efforts, we ended by trampling the dead and dying on the floor. Anton had more than once staged such a desecration of the dead, and we had almost resigned ourselves to it. But to tread on the dying, to think that perhaps we were giving them the final blow, was a new kind of torture.

We had scarcely assembled in front of the barrack when Anton informed us that, according to the latest edict of the office, all foreign prisoners must wear the initials of their countries of origin on their uniforms. Thus the targets would be marked more plainly. Anton added: "And I can tell you that anybody that's got anything on him when you're searched at the Klinker is practically on his way to the pearly gates."

On leaving the barrack, I had again pocketed my toothbrush. "Perhaps rescue will come today," I had said to myself, and now I was afraid that I would be caught. As the indoor squad came by, I passed my toothbrush to one of the comrades with whom I was on good terms, and asked him to put it in its place later. Max noticed it. With a bound he was at my side, knocked me down and trampled on my abdomen until I fainted.

When I came to, I was dripping with water. My faint had delayed the march to the assembly place and the comrades had poured a bucket of water over me to restore me to consciousness: this had actually refreshed me. Two comrades from the indoor squad seized me under the arms and marched me off, and when we reached the assembly place I could stand on my own feet again.

I felt very uncomfortable in the wet uniform, but I had to suppress any sign of discomfort so as not to draw the blockfuehrers' attention. Unexpectedly it had become warm overnight. The clouds which had covered the sky all the previous day had vanished, and a bright sky and radiant sun smiled down upon us. No breeze stirred. Nature seemed calm and content. But around us on the assembly place the blockfuehrers were plotting misery and death.

It seemed to me that the square was unusually crowded that morning. Surely new shipments of prisoners had been brought in the night before. How many? Would they ever see freedom again? For how many of them was the sun shining today for the last time?

In these reflections I had forgotten my own hopes. Suddenly, through the veil of my thoughts, I heard my name called. Or had I merely imagined it? A whispering began around me.

"This is it."

"Free."

"And he'll just make the boat."

I still had not taken it in when I heard Anton shout my name. Then for the first time I realized what had happened. I stared speechless at the runner, who was standing by Anton, as if he had suddenly sprung up out of the ground.

"Give me your handkerchief," I heard my neighbor say. Mechanically I pulled it out.

"Hey, get going," shouted Anton.

"Go on, man, run," someone whispered behind me.

That broke the spell. A flood of happiness rushed through me. Strength flowed into my limbs. I ran toward Anton. I felt young and strong. It was as if I were not running on my feet but being carried along. I had a few short moments, to take leave of my comrades with a long look and to give Max a farewell glance of contempt.

The runner ordered me to follow and turned on his heel. We had to run along the edge of the assembly place, so as not to disturb the roll call, which had just begun. Here and there a blockfuehrer would turn toward us in amazement.

"What's up?" he would ask the runner.

"Release in the Jewish Polish block."

"Wh-a-at!"

We had reached the office. The runner told me to wait and went inside. In a few minutes he came back and we ran to the clothing room. Again I had to stop in front of the door. From old habit I looked straight in front of me, taking in everything, fixing everything in my memory.

Not far from me was the big gate. Small loads of prisoners were being brought in. The same gate that closed behind them so pitilessly would soon open for me. Soon I would be free, born again. I would breathe the glorious May air, feel the sun, see trees, go home and be free, be free.

I waited—and memory overcame me. Before my eyes unrolled the experiences of all the days since my imprisonment began. I saw the comrades who had come here with me and were here no more. I saw their cruel deaths. Our executioners passed in review. I saw every corner of the camp, heard the screams from the Bunker, felt again my own anguish and fear. Where would I have been if hope and faith had not stood by me through those days of horror?

I must have been standing in front of the clothing room for an hour, and nothing had happened. I grew uneasy. There, at last the door was opening, and the prisoner barber, who always shaved the released before they changed their clothes, was calling me in. But after the shave, he sent me out again. And once more the uncertainty began. Blockfuehrers kept passing me. "What are you waiting for?" they asked. And when they heard "Release," they went inside, puzzled, to check my statement. "The Yid's in luck," I heard them say. "But we'll get them all back again."

Time seemed to be standing still. How long would they keep me on the rack? At last I was summoned inside again. A blockfuehrer sent a prisoner to the storeroom to bring my bundle of clothes, while he himself sat down on a table and began to question me.

"Where is your wife?"

"My wife is dead."

"Have you children?"

"Yes, a daughter."

"Is she pretty?"

Why did he ask me that? It would be better to say no. But perhaps he had seen Gucia, when she was here, and the question was a trap to punish me for lying. But I was spared the decision. For just at that moment the prisoner who had been sent for my clothes came back, carrying my overcoat over his arm.

"The other things cannot be found," he reported.

When I had been brought to the camp I had been wearing a very warm and almost new sport suit and shoes with double soles, which I thought would do me good service in winter. They had evidently taken the fancy of one of the blockfuehrers.

"Well then, we'll have to keep the Yid here," said the blockfuehrer.

I knew that could not be. But my nerves threatened to snap. I could feel the blood drain from my face.

"Ha, ha, ha," laughed the blockfuehrer. "The Yid's afraid we won't let him go home. You don't like it much here? Ha, ha, ha!"

He paused to see what impression his words had made. But I remained expressionless. "Don't let me lose control of my nerves before this beast," I said to myself. And I clenched my teeth so hard that my jaws ached.

Then he began again. "Without a suit, of course you can't leave; we'll see if we can find a substitute," and he sent me out again.

Inside me something screamed: "Let me go out of here naked and barefooted, only let me go." But I was reassured. It was out of the question that they would not release me when Gestapo Headquarters had ordered the release; they were only trying to torture me awhile longer. But I would endure that too.

After about an hour, they called me back. The prisoner had brought me underwear, shirt, suit and shoes, whose rightful owner must have been a head taller than I: the sleeves of the jacket came down to my finger tips; I stepped on the trouser legs; my feet slipped around in the shoes. I must have looked very funny, for the blockfuehrer almost burst himself laughing. But I was overjoyed. I rolled up the sleeves and trouser legs. Luckily I had my own overcoat: that would hide the flapping suit. But my overcoat had become too big for me. I had to make a hole in the belt, two handbreadths beyond the original eyelet, to pull it tight. Suddenly I realized how hollow my cough had sounded lately. Tuberculosis? I asked myself.

My thoughts were interrupted. A blockfuehrer came and led me through the interior of the camp to the first gate. There he left me standing. In front of me was the Kommandantur. That was the most dangerous spot in camp. As long as I was in camp I was still a prisoner, subject to the camp rules. My civilian clothes only made me more conspicuous. I must be on the alert now as never before. Blockfuehrers went past me into the Kommandantur and asked me all kinds of questions, as if they were trying to set a trap. My answers had never been more concise, my bearing never more correct.

After about fifteen minutes an SS officer came out of the Kommandantur and walked up to me, his eyes boring into mine. "All released concentration-camp prisoners are under an obligation of silence," he said. "Whoever spreads, or causes to be spread, reports about proceedings in camp renders himself guilty of treason. The arm of the Gestapo is long and strong. Borders and seas will not protect you from our vengeance. We bring informers back—to disappear forever. And until we get them, we hold on to their relatives who are left behind. Understand?"

I understood, all right. "Jawohl," I answered.

Then a blockfuehrer came and ordered me to follow him. We went up to the gate. It was about eleven o'clock on May 7, the 236th day of my imprisonment, that I walked through the gate. My mind was full of awe at the miracle.

The blockfuehrer took me to the safe, where my money was counted out. Then we went to the Kanzlei, the last release authority. My release certificate was handed to me, then a printed formula was laid in front of me.

"Sign that," snapped the SS man, "and mind you impress it on your memory."

I signed where the SS man's finger pointed; then I read. I had, it seemed, throughout my imprisonment been treated in accordance with international law and had no claims or complaints whatever against the German government.

Then an SS man was called. He received a pass for the guards, and I was handed over to be conducted to the camp boundary.

As we left the room, the SS man, according to custom, took out his pistol and looked to see if it was loaded. Did he think that I would run away from him? For a moment I had to smile. Or was he afraid that I would attack him? Or did he have orders to shoot me in the back?—what was it they said: "Shot for disobedience"? I scarcely dared to breathe. My feet were heavy and walking was an effort.

"Hurry," cried the SS man. "Pick up your feet."

I pulled myself together and we marched off. We went past the Political Division to the main guard. Before me, a few steps away, was the last gate. A few steps more and the nightmare would be gone forever.

The SS man's pass was examined by the two guards: we were allowed to pass. We walked through the gate. The last hurdle was taken. In front of us stretched the camp road, which led to Oranienburg and into freedom.

How different the asphalt felt under civilian shoes. I would have liked to turn and look back at the camp. But turning was forbidden. Behind me walked the SS man with a loaded revolver, and near me ran the gray wall, topped with high-tension wire.

Every fifty yards we passed a guard. "Heil Hitler," said the SS man, each time.

"Heil Hitler," answered the guard.

We passed a group of prisoners at work. They went on working, without looking up. But I could feel their eyes on my back. Suddenly my joy was gone. How could I be happy over my release with all those pictures in my memory? How could I ever again be joyful, ever forget the glazing eyes of the dead, ever stop hearing the moans and screams from the Bunker—ever forget that while I talked, ate, slept, walked about in freedom, thousands upon thousands were being tortured to death?

"Now you can go on alone," I heard the SS man say, and I saw him turn back. I did not answer. I went on a few yards. Then for the first time, I stopped and looked back. I could still see the camp wall: gray, high, a dividing line between life and death. It was a wonderful warm May morning and I was wearing a warm overcoat. But I began to shiver. Suddenly I could not bear the sight any longer; I turned quickly. Before me lay the road to freedom and before me was a mission.

I quickened my steps. There, where the roads crossed, someone was standing. I stopped dead. I did not trust my eyes. Yes, there was Gucia. We both began to run and, meeting halfway, seized each other's hands. For a few moments we laughed and wept at the same time. Then Gucia resolutely wiped her tears away and slipped her arm through mine. With firm step we went on down the road.

"What a glorious day," said Gucia. "I think I saw the first swallow today."

"The lilacs must be out already," I said, "and do you know, Gucia, I think you are right, the single lilacs smell sweeter than the double ones."

I had orders to report without delay to Gestapo Headquarters in Berlin, and then to the Alien Police, where I had to apply for an exit visa. When I stood before the door of the Alien Police official who handled Polish affairs, Gucia looked at me, then her eyes went to the left side of the door; I followed her glance. A sign announced: "Releases of Polish Jews will no longer take place. All inquiry useless." So that was the reason for the sudden cessation of releases.

I knocked on the door. Someone called, "Come in"; I entered, alone. At a desk piled with documents sat a man.

"What do you want?" he said, without looking up.

I handed him my release certificate.

"Wha-a-at?" The man read the paper several times, threw it down in front of him and began to beat on the desk with his fists.

"That is impossible! There have been no releases for months. Where did you come from? Who released you? How did you get out?"

I pointed to the release certificate. "The camp authorities of Sachsenhausen released me," I said.

"Silence!" he screamed. "That is impossible. I will not register the release until I get a teletype confirmation from Gestapo Headquarters."

"But without your registration I can't get an exit visa, and my ship leaves Genoa in three days, and I still have to apply for an Italian transit visa, and the time is—"

"That makes no difference. I want to see the thing in black and white before I'll believe you. Get out of here."

I hesitated.

"Do you want to be thrown out?"

I left. What else could I have done? Outside stood Gucia, her face white. She had heard the shouting and understood everything. We discussed what we should do. Should we go back to Gestapo Headquarters, or should Gucia go into the official's office and try to talk with him? Every hour counted.

Then Gucia had an inspiration. A leading Polizeirat in the Alien Police had gained a reputation among the Poles for being very sympathetic, although he could not accomplish anything for them. Gucia had never before talked to him. Now she asked to see him. The Polizeirat telephoned to Gestapo Headquarters, and within half an hour the confirmation of my release arrived by teletype and the still-fuming official of the Alien Police had to register it.

Thirty hours later we left Berlin by plane. Each of us had an overnight bag. Everything else was lost. On the morning of May 10 we arrived in Genoa, while Hitler's troops were marching into Holland and Belgium. We had just time enough to board the ship *Conte Verde,* the last ship that sailed for the Far East. Exactly a month later, just after we reached Shanghai, Italy declared war on the Allies, and the route to the Orient was cut off.